T0087864

Che, My Brother

Che, My Brother

Juan Martin Guevara
Armelle Vincent

Translated by Andrew Brown

polity

First published in French as *Mon frère, le Che*, © Éditions Calmann-Lévy, 2016

This English edition © Polity Press, 2017

Polity Press
65 Bridge Street
Cambridge CB2 1UR, UK

Polity Press
350 Main Street
Malden, MA 02148, USA

ISBN-13: 978-1-5095-1775-6

A catalogue record for this book is available from the British Library.

Library of Congress Cataloging-in-Publication Data

Names: Guevara, Juan Martin, author. | Vincent, Armelle, author.
Title: Che, my brother / Juan Martin Guevara, Armelle Vincent.
Other titles: Mon frere le Che. English
Description: English edition. | Cambridge ; Malden, MA : Polity, 2017. |
  Includes bibliographical references and index. | Original French title
  from Amazon view of online title page.
Identifiers: LCCN 2016041405 (print) | LCCN 2017000120 (ebook) | ISBN
  9781509517756 (hardback) | ISBN 9781509517770 (Mobi) | ISBN 9781509517787
  (ebook)
Subjects: LCSH: Guevara, Che, 1928-1967. | Guerrillas--Latin
  America--Biography. | Cuba--History--1959-1990. | Latin
  America--History--1948-1980. | Guevara, Che, 1928-1967. | BISAC: POLITICAL
  SCIENCE / Political Freedom & Security / Terrorism.
Classification: LCC F2849.22.G85 G7613 2017 (print) | LCC F2849.22.G85
  (ebook) | DDC 980.03092 [B] --dc23
LC record available at https://lccn.loc.gov/2016041405

Typeset in 9.75 on 15pt Meridien by
Servis Filmsetting Ltd, Stockport, Cheshire
Printed and bound in Great Britain by Clays Ltd, St Ives PLC

For further information on Polity, visit our website:
politybooks.com

Contents

Acknowledgements

To all the companions who, faithful to the spirit of Che, have had the courage to persevere in the struggle for 'the creation of a new society, rich and fair'.

To my fortunate encounter with Armelle that made it possible for me to write this book dedicated to young people, and to the certainty that the world has other Che(s) waiting for the right moment to rise up.

Juan Martin Guevara

1

La Quebrada del Yuro

I waited forty-seven years before going to see the spot where my brother Ernesto Guevara was murdered. Everyone knows he was killed by a coward's rifle on 9 October 1967 in a shabby classroom of the village school in La Higuera, an isolated hamlet in South Bolivia. He had been captured the day before at the bottom of the Quebrada del Yuro, a bare ravine where he had entrenched himself after realizing that his sparse band of guerrillas, weakened by hunger and thirst, was surrounded by the army. They say he died with dignity and that his last words were 'Póngase sereno y apunte bien. Va a matar a un hombre' ('Calm down and take good aim. You're going to kill a man'). Mario Terán Salazar, the unfortunate soldier appointed to do the dirty work, was shaking. True, Che had for eleven months been public enemy number 1 of the Bolivian army, perhaps even of the entire American continent, but he was a legendary opponent, a mythical figure covered in glory, known for his sense of justice and fairness and also for his immense bravery. What if this Che, gazing unblinkingly at him with his big deep eyes without seeming to judge him, really was the friend and defender of the humble rather than the blood-stained revolutionary portrayed by his superiors? What if his disciples, said to be loyal to a fault, would one day decide to track him down and avenge Che's death?

Mario Terán Salazar had needed to get drunk before he could find the courage to pull the trigger. When he saw Che sitting calmly, waiting for the inevitable, he rushed out of the classroom, bathed in sweat. His superiors forced him to return.

My brother died standing. They wanted him to die sitting down, to humiliate him. He protested – and he won this last battle. Among his many qualities, or talents, he could be very persuasive.

I bought a new pair of sneakers to get down to Quebrada del Yuro. It's a deep gorge, falling away abruptly behind La Higuera. It was very difficult, very painful for me to be here. Painful, but necessary. This pilgrimage was a project I'd been carrying around with me for years. It had been almost impossible to come here any earlier. In the first years following Che's death, I was too young, not quite prepared psychologically. Then Argentina turned fascist and repressive and I languished for nearly nine years in the jails of the military junta that seized power in March 1976. I learned to lie low: in the political climate of my country, it was for many years dangerous to be associated with Che Guevara.

Only my brother Roberto came to the area in October 1967, sent from Buenos Aires by the family to try and identify Ernesto's body once the news of his death had been announced. He returned deeply shocked and bewildered: by the time he arrived in Bolivia, the remains of our brother had vanished. The Bolivian soldiers led Roberto a merry chase, sending him from one city to another, changing their story every time.

My father and my sisters Celia and Ana Maria never had the strength to make the journey. My mother had succumbed to cancer two years earlier. If she had not already been in the grave, Ernesto's assassination would have finished her off. She adored him.

I drove here from Buenos Aires with some friends. A journey of 2,600 kilometres. In 1967, we did not know where Ernesto was. He had left Cuba in the greatest secrecy. Only a few people, including Fidel Castro, knew that he was fighting for the liberation of the Bolivian people. My family was lost in conjectures, imagining him to be on the other side of the world, in Africa maybe. In reality, he was only thirty hours away from Buenos Aires, where we lived. We would learn years later[1] that he had travelled via the Belgian Congo where, with a dozen or so black Cubans, he had gone to support the Simba rebels.

On the crest of the ravine, I'm approached by a guide. He doesn't know who I am and I don't want to reveal my identity. He demands that I give him some money to show me where Che was captured – the first sign that my brother's death has been turned into a business venture. I am outraged. Che represents the complete opposite of sordid profit. The friend who has accompanied me here is furious; he can't stop himself from telling the guide who I am. How dare this guide try to get money out of Che's brother just when he is coming to pay homage for the first time at the site of his fatal defeat? The guide steps back with reverence and stares at me wide-eyed. It's as if he has just seen an apparition. He apologizes profusely. I'm not listening. I'm used to it. Being the brother of Che has never been a trivial matter. When people learn who I am, they're dumbstruck. Christ can't have any brothers or sisters. And Che is a bit like Christ. In La Higuera and Vallegrande, where his body was taken on 9 October to be displayed to the public before disappearing, he became San Ernesto de la Higuera. The locals pray before his image. I generally respect religious beliefs, but this one really bothers me. In the family, since my paternal grandmother Ana Lynch-Ortiz, we haven't believed in God. My mother never took us to church. Ernesto was a man. We need to pull him down off his pedestal, give life to this bronze statue so we can perpetuate his message. Che would have hated being turned into an idol.

I begin the descent down to the fateful place with a heavy heart. I am struck by the bareness of the ravine. I expected to find dense vegetation. In fact, except for a few dry, thick shrubs, nature is almost like a desert here. I now find it easier to see how Ernesto could have ended up caught like a rat in a trap. It was practically impossible to stay out of sight of the army, which had encircled the Quebrada the day before.

I reach the place where he was wounded by a gunshot in his left thigh and another in his right forearm. I start with amazement. In front of the puny tree against which he had leaned on 8 October, the dry ground is covered by a star, cast in concrete. It marks the exact place where he was sitting when he was discovered. A profound anguish takes hold of me. I'm overwhelmed by doubts. I feel his presence. I pity him. I wonder what he was doing there, alone. Why wasn't I with him? Of course I should have been with him. I was always a militant, too. He was not only my brother, but my comrade in struggle, my model. I was only twenty-three, but that is no excuse: in the Sierra Maestra in Cuba – the mountain range where the armed struggle started during which

Fidel Castro appointed Che *Comandante*, and where he distinguished himself – some of the fighters were only fifteen! I didn't know he was in Bolivia, but I should have known! I should have stayed with him in Cuba in February 1959, and ignored my father's veto.

I sit down, or rather I slump down onto the place where he had sat. I can still see his handsome face, his hypnotic, inquisitive gaze, his mischievous smile. I can hear his infectious laughter, his voice, his indefinable inflection: with the years he spent in Mexico and then in Cuba, his Spanish had become a mixture of three accents. Did he feel alone, vanquished?

Some of the questions I ask myself have a practical side to them. Others are purely sentimental. Che was not alone, but supported by six fighters who were arrested with him. Could I have helped him escape? That day, five other companions, including Guido 'Inti' Peredo, did after all manage to escape the ambush.[2] Why didn't he? I reconstruct the chain of events that led to the death of my brother. Was Che betrayed? If so, by whom? There are several hypotheses, but as that's all they are, I prefer not to dwell on them. Ernesto was fighting under the name Ramón Benítez. They say he chose the name Ramón in honour of the short story 'Meeting' by Julio Cortázar, which recounted the adventures of a group of revolutionaries in the Sierra Maestra. His presence was shrouded in mystery. On the basis of information provided by the CIA – which had brazenly set up an HQ in the presidential palace of René Barrientos in La Paz – the Bolivian government suspected that Ernesto Guevara was commanding the Ñancahuazú army, without having any proof of this.

Until, that is, the Argentinian Ciro Bustos, arrested in the scrub after being authorized by Che to abandon the insurgency, provided them with an identikit portrait of Che, under the threat of spending the rest of his days in prison.

As I climb back up the ravine, I feel devastated, emptied. An unpleasant surprise is waiting for me in La Higuera. As I enter the hamlet to go and pay homage in the school where Ernesto was killed, a woman breaks away from a group of Japanese tourists and pounces on me. She has just learned from another Japanese woman, a journalist, that Che's brother is here. She cries, and mumbles: 'Che's brother, Che's brother'. She asks me most politely to pose for a photo with her. I have no choice but to agree and comfort her. This Japanese woman apparently considers me to be a reincarnation of Che. I am both disturbed and touched. Almost fifty years after his death, my brother is more than ever present in the collective memory. I'm certainly not Ernesto, but I can, and must, be a conduit for his ideas and his ideals. His five children barely knew him. My sister Celia and my brother Roberto categorically refuse to talk. My sister Ana Maria died of cancer, like my mother. I am seventy-two years old. I can't waste any time.

The school where Ernesto spent his last night has undergone a few transformations. The wall that separated the two class-rooms has been knocked down. The walls are covered with pictures and posters depicting Che's last hours. The chair he occupied when Mario Terán Salazar came to kill him is still there. I imagine my brother sitting there, waiting for his death. It's very difficult.

On the village square stands a large white bust sculpted by a Cuban artist, based on the famous photo by Alberto Korda, *Guerrillero heroico*. This bust, behind which a white cross looms, also has a turbulent history. It was put up in early 1987 and quickly removed by a commando from the Bolivian army, to be replaced by a plaque in memory of the soldiers who were victims of guerrilla warfare. It resumed its place twenty years later, accompanied by a four-metre-high sculpture standing at the entrance to the hamlet. For years, the people of La Higuera and Vallegrande were terrorized. No one dared speak of Che: so as to eradicate all traces of the passage of this 'subversive',[3] the Bolivian government had banned all mention of his name. In response to the imposed silence, legends inevitably began to be forged. At the time of his capture, the peasants of the Aymara community who inhabit the area had no awareness of the importance of this prisoner. They never saw any strangers, and barely spoke any Spanish. After Che's death, hordes of journalists descended on their village. Until 9 October 1967, no one had ever heard of La Higuera. On 10 October, thirty-six planes lined up on the improvised runway in Vallegrande, sixty kilometres away. The natives started to realize that a significant event had occurred, that this prisoner was not just any prisoner.

Ernesto's body was taken to Vallegrande on a stretcher mounted onto the landing gear of a helicopter. The Bolivian military decided to display it in the laundry at the bottom of the garden of the small local hospital, for seventeen hours. They wanted to make an example of him; to show that the whole crew of 'subversives' like this Ernesto 'Che' Guevara would be annihilated. Che was dead, dead, dead! This pathetic end was to serve as a lesson to the people. They should never stray into such a lamentable adventure, one that was inevitably doomed to failure.

His half-naked body was placed on a cement slab. He was barefoot, his eyes open – even though it was said that a priest had closed them in La Higuera . . . Some have compared the image of my tortured brother to the painting known as *The Lamentation of Christ* by the Italian Renaissance painter Andrea Mantegna. The resemblance is uncanny, but it means nothing. Some witnesses said that Che's eyes followed them while they wandered around his body. Others say that the doctor – a secret admirer – responsible for washing his body wanted to embalm it, but didn't have enough time and so took his heart to keep it in a jar. The same doctor, it is claimed, took two death masks, the first in wax and the second in plaster. One nurse was surprised by the peaceful expression on Ernesto's face, which contrasted strangely with the other guerrillas who were killed: their faces were marked by suffering and anguish. I don't believe these idiotic stories. They all tend towards the same goal: to turn Che into a myth. It is this myth that I intend to fight, by giving back to my brother his human face.

After 9 October, fifteen soldiers remained stationed in La Higuera for a year. They told the farmers that they were there to protect them from Che's accomplices who would inevitably come to kill them in vengeance for his death. For it was these same peasants, wasn't it, who had betrayed Che.

In this way, a cult was born, amid whispers and fears.

The shameful trade that has developed around Che horrifies me. Ernesto would have disowned these absurd legends that verge on mysticism. In La Higuera and Vallegrande, a whole tourist business is dedicated to Che. There are guided tours along the 'Che route'. People try to sell you anything and everything. It's disgusting. When I came out of the school, I saw the objects on display, the T-shirts, the flags. I found it all unspeakably vile. Ernesto was fighting for the liberation of the American continent, and now there are people exploiting his image just to make money. People pray to Santito Che, calling on him to perform miracles, for their cows or whatever! Che wanted to give, not take. He believed in man as master of his destiny and not as subject to some kind of higher force that indulges him (or not) with various things. He believed in struggle. He was a humanist.

I went to La Higuera twice, and I will definitely not be going back. It is no longer a hamlet of four wretched houses, but an open-air shop where they are forever trying to squeeze money out of you. All this has nothing to do with my brother. Nothing.

Ernesto's body mysteriously disappeared on the morning of 11 October 1967. A nun on duty at the hospital later told a German Franciscan, Brother Anastasio, that she had heard the rustling of a procession in the corridors of the hospital at around 1 a.m. that night. Rumours of all kinds of course started circulating.

The truth came out twenty years later.

Havana, January 1959

The phone rang late one morning in our house on calle Aráoz in Buenos Aires. My mother jumped. Could it be him? She leapt up, pushing away the table on which a game of solitaire was spread out. For two years, she had been living in a state of deep depression and almost permanent anxiety, finding some solace in this card game that she played while smoking unfiltered dark cigarettes. She was forever worrying herself sick over my elder brother Ernesto. He was fighting at the head of the 8th column 'Ciro Redondo' of the Ejercito Rebelde[1] of the young revolutionary leader Fidel Castro and his 26th of July Movement, with the goal of overthrowing the Cuban dictator Fulgencio Batista and his policies of savagery and terror. Many times, the international press had announced the death of the 'Argentinian doctor Ernesto "Che" Guevara', plunging our family into dismay and uncertainty. But these were just rumours put about by an oppressive regime to confuse the Cuban people and dissuade them from giving any assistance to the revolutionaries. One by one these dismal stories turned out to be false, to our immense relief.

News from Ernesto was scarce. We knew that he was fighting

somewhere in Cuba, that the revolutionary army had won some decisive battles, that it had the support of the population and was moving towards the capital. We lived 6,500 kilometres from the island: to us it seemed like light years away. We clung to every bit of information from the theatre of operations that was then based in the Sierra Maestra, the inhospitable mountains on the south-east of the island where the vegetation is impenetrable and temperatures can dip sharply in winter.

Each of the announced deaths of Ernesto became increasingly doubtful, less and less credible. Yet we lived on a knife-edge, in a permanent state of alert. Without saying so, my parents blamed themselves for not having managed to convince this reckless and untameable son to stay put, even though they had never tried to hold him back. They raised us in complete freedom, encouraging all our activities: travel, discovery, adventure, politics and even rebellion. But this? This revolution in a foreign land where every day he risked losing his life? It was so terribly hard for them to understand it and endure it. This beloved son they had pampered, at whose bedside they had spent so many agonizing hours trying to ease the spectacular asthma attacks that sapped him of all strength and prevented him from breathing, was now risking his life for ideals. And he still hadn't hit thirty! Yet they were forced to admit that this too was something he had learned from them. This was how they had brought us up; but now it had all got out of hand. Ernesto took their lessons to an extreme and gave them a whole new direction.

I was fifteen. I could see that my parents were suffering from his absence, but I could not really appreciate the danger. I admired my brother, the great trail-blazer, alone and almost penniless, who at the age of twenty-one headed off on a

4,500-kilometre-long motorbike jaunt and then, a year later, set off again on his bike with his friend Alberto 'Mial' Granado for several months. Then he left on an even longer expedition, at the end of which he met a gang of Cuban revolutionaries with whom he set off to remake the world, at gunpoint, on a remote and exotic island. None of my friends can boast of having such a brother.

My mother grabbed the receiver and answered the phone: 'Hello?'

'*Hola vieja*,[2] it's your son, Ernestito.'

My mother was never very demonstrative. But she could not hold back a cry. In six long years she had heard Ernesto's voice only once, when he briefly called her from his camp in the Sierra Maestra. Since his final departure from Buenos Aires on 8 July 1953, each of us – my father Ernesto Guevara Lynch, my mother Celia de la Serna, my brother Roberto, my sisters Celia and Ana Maria and I – had exchanged regular letters with him, at least until his immersion in clandestine activities. Family communication was always carried out in writing rather than by phone.

My mother beamed. 'It's Ernestito!' she yelled. She suddenly seemed so happy. The news was excellent. Ernesto told her of the victory won by the Ejercito Rebelde, its triumphal entry into Havana and the retreat of Fulgencio Batista. But he hadn't phoned us in Buenos Aires to talk about his exploits, he explained. It wasn't the *Comandante* who was phoning, but the son and brother. He wanted to hear his mother's voice, he had missed it so much. The *vieja* and he loved and respected each other so deeply and intensely. She was the person who had mainly shaped Ernesto. She was into politics and protest before he was. She passed on her love of reading to him, and taught him French, which she spoke fluently. Ernesto was said to be her favourite. This favouritism dated back to the disease that had consumed his childhood: the chronic asthma which prevented him from attending school in the normal way and forced my mother to home school him until he was nine.

I never suffered from their close relationship: as the youngest – I was fifteen years younger than Ernesto and eleven years younger than Roberto – I myself enjoyed a privileged place in the family. Besides, the day after Ernesto's phone call, when the world learned of the victory of Fidel Castro, my mother made this statement to the journalist Angelina Muñoz from the magazine *La Mujer*: 'Of my five children, Ernestito is the most famous, but they are all wonderful', before adding: 'I don't know who I will find in Havana. The last six years have been a vital, intense time for my son. He must have changed. I'm a little intimidated. I never wanted to hamper his freedom. If my husband and I had done so, we wouldn't have the relationship that we have today, a comradely relationship. My son has never had to confront his family, we've always tried to understand and share his anxieties.'

On the evening of the providential phone call, we all gathered at home, euphoric and confused. We asked ourselves the same question: would we recognize Ernesto? Who was this bearded man with an unruly shock of hair held in place by a beret, this *Comandante* appearing on the front pages of newspapers across the world? What did he have to do with our Ernesto?

In Buenos Aires, people were celebrating in the streets; they had just learned of their heroic compatriot's victory. All the newspapers announced the triumph of the Cuban revolution. Friends and relatives who had always been the most resistant to Ernesto's ideas were celebrating too. The Guevara and de la

Serna clans had apparently just given birth to a great man and they were bursting with pride. At least for now. Some would later have all the time in the world to try and distance themselves from him when things turned sour in Argentina.

Two days after the phone call, on 6 January 1959, my father, my mother, my sister Celia and I left calle Aráoz for the Ezeiza International Airport. We were off to Cuba. Unfortunately, Roberto and Ana Maria could not come with us. Roberto had work commitments, I forget exactly what; Ana Maria had just had a baby. I was strutting about in the three-piece suit my parents had bought me for the occasion – my very first suit. I would finally be seeing my big brother again, the joker who had introduced me to the adventure stories of Emilio Salgari and Jules Verne. It hardly mattered to me that he had become *El Comandante* or *El Che*. Of course, I felt a vague sense of pride – after all, his mug was plastered all over the papers – but it was all still rather distant as far as I was concerned.

We were elated. Fidel Castro had quietly decided to bring us to Havana to celebrate the victory without telling Ernesto. My brother would have rejected the idea; he didn't want to waste the money of the new revolutionary Cuban state. Over the two years they had fought side by side, Ernesto and Fidel had been bound by a strong, manly friendship that the Cuban intellectual Alfredo Guevara would sum up later in an interview with the Spanish daily *El País*: 'Fidel encountered far too many mirrors in his life; Che was not a mirror, he was a cultivated man and had his own values. He spoke to Fidel on equal terms, he *was* an equal, perhaps the only one among us. He knew that Fidel was the leader and Fidel listened to Che and respected him; there was a perfect complicity between them.'[3]

Fidel knew how attached his friend was to his family. Ernesto had risked his life to free a country that was not his. So Fidel felt it would be unfair if he was the only one left out of the party. He instructed his other *Comandante*, Camilo Cienfuegos, to tell us we should go the airport with our luggage. We needed to take a Cubana Airlines plane chartered for the repatriation of Cuban political exiles not only from Argentina, but from Chile, Ecuador and Mexico. This charter flight promised to be an interesting occasion . . .

The first exiles turned up at Ezeiza as heavily laden as mules. One of them in particular was carrying a hundred or so books, bursting out of several bags. Appalled, my father complained to the pilot about the excess weight. We had to fly over the Andes to land first in Santiago, where other exiles were waiting, and then Guayaquil and finally Mexico. The pilot reassured my father and we took off in a very festive atmosphere.

In Guayaquil, the plane began to describe large circles instead of starting its descent to the airport. This manoeuvre lasted almost an hour. The landing gear was refusing to operate. Things got really tense. Then the machinery finally unjammed, thank goodness, and we eventually landed. To think we might have crashed before seeing Ernesto again!

The journey took forever. At each airport, we were mobbed by reporters who wanted to interview Che's parents. And we thought that our presence in the exiles' plane had been kept secret! My father gracefully submitted to their requests: his gadabout son had apparently become an international hero!

Coming into Havana, we were again worried that we might crash because the landing gear was still playing up in spite of the repairs carried out in Guayaquil. Finally, the plane touched down gently on the runway of the José Martí airport in Havana.

We were exhausted, but overjoyed at the idea of seeing Ernesto again.

When he disembarked, my father knelt down and kissed the Cuban soil.

Bearded armed guerrillas were waiting for us on the tarmac to escort us through the crowd to Ernesto. For security reasons, he had stayed inside the terminal. That morning, Camilo had suggested he should go to the airport 'where there was a surprise in store for him'. He didn't have time to get angry, to argue that he absolutely refused any special treatment for himself and his family. After all, Fidel had not yet arrived in Havana. The victory was still fresh. All Ernesto needed to do now was look forward to seeing his family again.

When my mother caught sight of Ernesto, she rushed towards him and her feet got tangled in the forest of television cables littering the ground. She gave him a long hug; it was a moment of extraordinary intensity. My mother sobbed in Ernesto's arms, as he tenderly embraced her. My father, Celia and I observed the scene. We were deeply moved. For six years my mother had dreamt of this moment. So many times she had thought her son was dead!

For my father, things were different. He loved his oldest son too, but they had a difficult relationship. Our whole family was a bit cracked, but when it came to being crazy, my father was miles ahead of the rest of us. Let's just say that his continual eccentricities always managed to exasperate his relatives. In addition, though he would later come to accept Ernesto's ideas, at this time, in January 1959, he shared neither his son's political opinions nor his unfailing rectitude. He had other ambitions for Ernesto. He planned to use this trip to Havana to sort Ernesto out and convince him to return to Buenos Aires so he could pursue his medical career as an allergy specialist. We would soon see that Ernesto had other plans. My father didn't seem to understand that, for his son, this revolution was much more than an adventure that would now make way for more serious things. Ernesto told him on the very first day: 'My medical career, well, let me tell you I gave it up a good time ago. Now I'm a fighter working towards consolidating the government. What will become of me? Who knows? I don't even know which land I'll leave my bones in.' With his usual sense of humour, he added: 'Never mind, *viejo*, your name is Ernesto Guevara too, so you can still hang my medical degree on the wall of your architect's office and set about killing off patients to your heart's content.' It should be noted that my father called himself an architect and even practised the profession, but had never actually graduated . . .

My brother now looked nothing like the doctor he had been when he said goodbye on 8 July 1953 in the Retiro station in Buenos Aires, where he became 'Che'.[4] He was transformed, and looked older but quite splendid. Before, he had talked so quickly, gabbling his words that seemed to be running to keep up with his galloping thoughts; now, he was more poised. My father noticed with surprise that he now seemed to mull things over; he thought before speaking. He had left Buenos Aires clean-shaven; he now had a beard, with wispy sparse hair, but a beard all the same. He had liked wearing his hair short so as not to have to comb it; now he had an unruly mane. He had lost weight. Until then, his appetite had varied considerably; depending on his asthma attacks, he had either stuffed himself or picked at his food. He now always wore the olive-green uniform, the broad elastic belt in khaki, and the black beret with the red star showing he was a *Comandante*. He had more self-assurance, presence, charisma and authority, if such a thing is possible: Ernesto had always had a strong character, a natural ease of manner, the soul of a leader. As a kid he had already been the gang leader, without ever having to impose himself, just because he inspired confidence. At his side, even the older boys felt protected. His friendship was steadfast, his loyalty unwavering.

I noticed the respect he seemed to inspire in his men. It was my brother standing in front of me, smiling with affection as he tickled me just like in the old days; but he was a transfigured man. I was eager to discover this new brother, who had distinguished himself so bravely in battle and, with 3,000 comrades in arms, had overcome a sophisticated army of 50,000 men backed by the world's greatest power, the United States. But what mattered most to me was rediscovering the complicity of our childhood.

We travelled by jeep to the Hilton Hotel where we were to stay for a while, we didn't yet know how long. The atmosphere in the streets of Havana was that of a country finally liberated after a long subjection. In every district, music blared out on all sides, and people danced as they celebrated the victory of the young revolutionaries to whom they owed the restoration of their freedom. There was a deafening hubbub. Guerrillas from the Sierra Maestra, barely literate, who had never left their villages or their mountains and had never had an opportunity to gaze at a city, admired the luxury of the capital, the skyscrapers, the cars, the hotels.

At the Hilton, the scene was surreal, and completely exotic to a young Argentinian like me. A tall black man and a dwarf in livery were standing before the doors: guards from another world. The American actor Errol Flynn was pacing up and down in the lobby: the arrival of Che's column in Havana had caught him while he was on vacation. The luxurious lobby was a baroque mix of guerrillas sprawled on sofas and tourists bewildered at finding themselves so suddenly transformed into improbable witnesses of an ongoing revolution. All these groups seemed stunned: they'd hardly had time to digest the turn of events. As we observed the scene, equally stunned, *Comandante* Camilo Cienfuegos arrived with his troop. The rumpled guerrillas rose to their feet as one man. Camilo was handsome and imposing with his luxuriant beard, his long hair, his beige cowboy hat and his Thompson submachine gun slung across his shoulders. He burst out into a great roar of laughter. He too had become a legend. Ernesto went over to him and embraced him before introducing him to us. They were firm friends. The Hilton employees were dumbstruck. Everything had happened so fast! It was an incredible spectacle, and I savoured every second. The tables were piled high with firearms, leaving no room for a plate or even a cup. The soldiers were ragged and unkempt. They had just emerged from two years of hiding. Their uniforms, dirty and discoloured by time, the sun and the weather, had been chucked down on the ground with their amulets; their boots were shredded and full of holes. I was astounded to see that young men my age were already officers in the revolutionary army. But the most surprising thing of all was Ernesto. My family had always been marginal, unconventional, totally rebellious in the face of authority. So it was staggering to see that my brother, the very same man who had avoided Argentinian military service on the grounds of his asthma, was now a *Comandante*.

We were put up in a suite on the sixteenth floor of the Hilton. My mother went out onto the balcony and took in the scene:

the Vedado district, the Rampa, the Malecón, the Castillo del Morro, the sea. She was overwhelmed by happiness. She had set herself a goal: she would make the most of her son, meet this Fidel she had heard so much about in Ernesto's letters and the newspapers, and learn all she could about the revolution and its political, philosophical, economic and practical objectives. My father's aims were more mundane. Among other things, he wanted to do some networking. It might just conceivably be of use to him later on.

Our trip had been gruelling. We all went to bed amid a riotous din of celebration from the street. We were thrilled and still amazed to be sleeping under the same sky as Ernesto.

When he came to have lunch with us the following day, he was surprised to find my father in the middle of a photo session with an uncle and a cousin of Fidel, Gonzalo Castro and Ana Argiz. Their pride in the recent fame of their respective relations had brought them together. Ernesto was irritated. He would have preferred his father to behave more discreetly, more in tune with the solemnity of the circumstances. But you might as well have asked a starlet to become invisible at the Cannes festival! My father was a flamboyant man and these providential events had given him a perfect opportunity to tread the boards. As a result, Ernesto's annoyance – and mine – would grow over the next few days as my father made one faux pas after another. He would in fact commit a series of unforgivable blunders, and be obliged to make a hasty departure.

One of my brother's finest qualities was his probity, his innate and unshakable sense of fairness and justice. This unfailing rectitude was inherited from our mother, who was forever coming up against my father's whimsicality and his tendency to 'take his chances'. He was in his element at the Hilton. Luxury suited him, and indeed enchanted him, especially as it was a long time since he had enjoyed it first-hand. Moreover, even at the homes of our affluent relations, we had never experienced this kind of modern comfort that seemed typically American. Our bathroom had a huge bathtub and jacuzzi. The refrigerator had an ice dispenser! For a teenager like me who had never travelled and came from a dilapidated house, such opulence was alien and disturbing. Even for my mother, who had been raised among silks and satins, it was shocking and intolerable in the context of the revolution. Two days after our arrival, she demanded that we be transferred to a less luxurious hotel. We found ourselves in the Comodoro, by the beach, in a suite with an unbelievably huge round bed which the Mexican actress María Félix had slept in. Our window overlooked a jetty with yachts moored along it. The hotel roof had a heliport. Ernesto landed there several times to make surprise visits. The Comodoro was hardly any less luxurious than the Hilton, but it was the only hotel available. So we would have to adapt!

Fidel Castro came over from Santiago de Cuba to Havana two days after us. He was feted as a hero. He made a speech and took up residence on the twenty-third floor of the Hilton. Ernesto was seeing a young woman called Aleida March, a Cuban revolutionary he had met in the Sierra Maestra who had had to go underground to avoid arrest and torture. But Ernesto was living in a monastic room in the fortress San Carlos de la Cabaña,[5] where members of the fallen regime were already being put on trial – a task with which Fidel had entrusted him. Indeed, Ernesto would be severely criticized for this, because of the many death sentences he handed down. He explained in an interview: 'My position is a difficult one. I bear the full responsibility for the sentences I pass. In these circumstances, I cannot have any contact with the accused. I do not know any of the prisoners in La Cabaña. I limit myself to exercising the functions of head of the supreme court and coldly analysing the facts. I start with the assumption that revolutionary justice is true justice.' Aleida later recounted in her autobiography that the trials, which Che never attended except sometimes when they went to appeal, were very difficult and unpleasant for him, especially when the families of the accused begged him to show clemency.

Ernesto has been accused of cruelty. Nothing is more false. In the Cuban scrub, he treated enemy captives humanely. When they were wounded, he went back to being a doctor and treated them. In the Bolivian scrub, he set them free. The prisoners in La Cabaña were not choirboys: they were the worst torturers in the Cuban dictatorship. They were men who had intimidated, threatened, killed and tortured ordinary people. Ernesto told us that the trials had been decided on by the revolutionary leaders to avoid the rough justice of the street, which was even uglier. The people are generally inclined to lynch the agents of a tyrant who has forced them to endure horrors.

Ernesto categorically forbade me to enter La Cabaña. But I did actually attend one trial. On my third day in Havana, I headed to the basketball stadium on the road to Boyeros. It was there that the first trial took place, the only one that was held in public, involving a sadist known for his cruelty, Sosa Blanco. My memory of it is quite awful. On the basketball court where he was tried, there was the sickening atmosphere of a football match. The public was overexcited and kept screaming: 'Murderer!' Even if the accused was guilty of inhumanity, the spectacle could not have been any more painful. Ernesto had warned me that these trials would never give any satisfaction to anyone. He was right. I decided there and then I would never try to get into La Cabaña.

Ernesto sometimes came to the Comodoro for a change of scene. We would wait until his entourage had left the room; then we could forget all about the revolution and talk about Argentina and the good old days. Ernesto asked countless questions about the family, inquiring after everyone, and especially Roberto and Ana Maria, who had stayed at home. I longed to be alone with him. When the opportunity arose, I began by removing his beret and telling him: 'You may be a *Comandante* for others, but not for me!' So he started provoking me and teasing me. It was his way of taking his mind off things and relaxing. He also seemed to need those intimate moments that allowed him to forget his responsibilities and simply become a brother again. There were things that belonged to us alone and that he couldn't share with the people around him. And after all, he had missed us for six years.

One day when we were alone in his office, he decided he wanted to box. He took off the sling he wore to support his dislocated shoulder and gave me a punch. I hit back with a blow to his elbow. He pretended to be in agony and bent over double. As I went over to help him up, he landed another blow that sent me reeling. I was furious and swore at him. He laughed out loud. He asked me to sit down and said: 'Let that be a lesson to you, *hermanito*.[6] Never drop your vigilance in the presence of the enemy.'

The rest of the time, he would nag me to go on to higher education. 'You need to learn', he kept saying. I was the only sibling who completely refused to go to university. Ernesto was a doctor, Roberto a lawyer and Celia and Ana Maria architects. I wanted to start work as soon as possible and become a wage-earner. One day when he was going on and on at me, I shut him up once and for all, saying: 'If I'm not mistaken, you have a medical degree, right? And what use has that been to you? What surgery have you hung your degree certificate in?'

'But there's more to studying than that!' he retorted. 'It's a necessary discipline.' My argument was more a piece of self-defence than anything else. I didn't want to study, and that was that. My mother was too tired to push me and my father too busy leading his own life outside the home. On the other hand, I read voraciously. This allowed us to have interesting conversations. Ernesto was an extremely bright and cultivated person. He was a disciple of Marx, Engels and Freud, but also of Jack London and Jorge Luis Borges, of Baudelaire, León Felipe,[7] Cervantes and Victor Hugo. He had an extensive knowledge of the works of Merleau-Ponty and Jean-Paul Sartre. When Sartre, with Simone de Beauvoir, was introduced to him in Havana after our departure, he was very surprised to discover that, behind the guerrilla, Ernesto was an intelligent, scholarly man. Ernesto consumed on average a book a day, taking advantage of every free moment to delve into some volume or other. He had a special fondness for *Don Quixote*, which he read six times, and Karl Marx's *Capital*, which he considered to be a work of monumental significance in the development of mankind. He knew Pablo Neruda's *Canto General* by heart, and got into the habit of reciting it during offensives. Ever since childhood, he had taken refuge in both poetry and prose when things got difficult. Poetry – and also *mate*, the bitter drink typical of Argentina, related to tea; it is drunk with a *bombilla*, a kind of metal straw pierced with tiny holes. And then he wrote divinely. While he is never considered as an author, he left an oeuvre of 3,000 pages comprising journals, essays, letters, speeches and war manuals. So much so that the Cuban writer Julio Llanes dedicated a book to 'Che the writer'.[8]

So that he could get around Havana and its surroundings more easily, my father asked Ernesto for a car and a driver, reckoning that he could pull strings to obtain benefits in kind. He hadn't reckoned with his new son, whose nature jibbed more than ever against the simplest privileges, including and especially for his family! Ernesto insisted on being paid a soldier's meagre salary: 125 dollars a month. He refused to be paid any more than his men, even if other 'dignitaries' of the regime earned 700 dollars per month. He also grew angry when a milkman dropped off an abnormally large ration of milk at his door. This integrity completely took my father aback. He found it misplaced and ridiculous, given the sacrifices Ernesto had made for the revolution. For the same reason, he thought it was quite acceptable for Che's parents to enjoy a few privileges. After all, they had 'lent' their beloved son, the apple of their eye, to Cuba, and had suffered deeply as a result. While my father regularly had words with Ernesto, constantly asking him to explain his decisions and his ideological choices, he was extremely fond of him. This son continued to disconcert him. Father couldn't understand why Ernesto picked up such low wages. All these scruples annoyed him. As did the fact that Ernesto refused to give autographs, insisting 'I'm not a movie star.'

Out of respect for our parents, and so we could travel around the island, Ernesto nevertheless agreed to put a vehicle at our disposal, on one condition: my father would pay for the petrol. But as usual, Ernesto *padre* was leading a hand-to-mouth exist-ence. He was stony broke. So he tried to argue back. 'Things are a bit tight, son', he said. To which Ernesto replied: 'Things are tight for the Cubans too! You can manage, *coño*!'[9]

My father pretended to acquiesce. But behind Ernesto's back, he manoeuvred to get his own way, insinuating that Che had agreed. When Ernesto found out, he was furious. He lectured our father. But nothing would stop him! He always did as he pleased. I never knew what was going through his head: it was impossible to understand our father. You might as well plunge blindly into a maze.

Ever since our arrival, my father had decidedly shown a lack of discernment or discipline, or both. He seemed not to have grasped what had happened to his son and the extent to which this revolution had turned him into a man of even more punctilious honesty than in his youth. Ernesto now considered that the most trivial of his acts was a way of sending out messages. If Che wanted to set an example of the 'new man' he wanted to create to build a society based on equality, his conduct must be beyond reproach. And so, by extension, must ours. Who was this new man, according to Ernesto? 'A young communist whose duty is to be essentially human, so human that he draws close to humanity at its best, who wants to purify himself through work, through study, through the exercise of permanent solidarity with the people and all the peoples of the world; who develops his sensitivity so as to feel anguished whenever a man is murdered anywhere in the world, and who exults whenever a new flag of freedom is raised somewhere else', he declared in a speech in October 1962.

My father seemed not to understand. Maybe he was hiding his head in the sand to avoid the obstacles Ernesto put in his way to keep him on the right path of the revolution and be a good example to others. At the invitation of my father, three Argentinian union leaders had flown with us from Buenos Aires, which seemed strange, even inappropriate – but as I said earlier, we had long since abandoned any attempt to understand my father's motivations. I just imagined he hoped to do business with the help of the union men. Why? I don't know. My father always went about things firing on all cylinders, but failed miserably in all his undertakings, despite his immense intelligence. He was a dreamer and an artist, certainly not a businessman, despite his many attempts to become one.

I became suspicious when, one morning, he told me about his appointment with the managing director of Bacardi, the spirits company. He asked me to go with him. He didn't say anything to Ernesto, of course. We went to the Bacardi headquarters, an imposing Art Deco building in the Avenida de Belgica in Havana's old town. We were received by José 'Pepin' Bosch in his magnificent, spacious office. They served me a daiquiri in a glass at the bottom of which there was a pearl floating. I couldn't believe my eyes! My father calmly discussed matters with Bosch. He was perfectly at ease. Like my mother, he was born into a patrician family of the Argentinian upper bourgeoisie. I made little attempt to follow their conversation, busy as I was gazing around in amazement at the luxury that surrounded me. Upon leaving, my father mentioned the possibility of doing business with Bacardi in Argentina.

The next day it was the managing director of the Pedroso Bank that we went to see. Imagine how revolutionary *he* was! When Ernesto learned of this, he flew into a rage. 'You just can't do that!' he tried to explain to my father. 'I've just carried out a revolution, *che*! You can't go around compromising yourself with all the managing directors on the island. You're going to make me lose all credibility. If you absolutely have to meet some dignitaries, go and see the president! I'll fix an appointment for you.' That's how we met Manuel Urrutia.

I was on edge too. My father was thoughtless, made mistake after mistake, and didn't seem to gauge how serious things actually were. Cuba was about to undergo repeated assaults from the world's greatest power. The fact that my father was in dialogue with the president of the biggest bank was unacceptable. Although I was not a *Comandante*, I suggested he leave. He'd definitely become too much of a burden. I guess Ernesto made the same suggestion. Anyway, we put him on a plane to Buenos Aires. He later said that business had forced him to return to Argentina. What business? We didn't know, and frankly, we didn't care. We'd all learned to stop paying the least attention. My father's authority hadn't survived the (extremely ambiguous) separation of my parents. At the time, in fact, they no longer lived together.

We could breathe again once our father had left, released from his endless faux pas that set our nerves on edge. Ernesto was overwhelmed by work. He laboured tirelessly, sixteen hours a day, giving himself body and soul to the revolution, convinced that it wouldn't be long before the United States demonstrated their discontent. He had very little time to devote to us. His partner Aleida March didn't get to see much of him in private either. But she continued to be his assistant, as in the days of the Sierra Maestra, and they were thus able to steal a few moments together. In spite of everything, he still managed to free himself occasionally and paid us unexpected visits at the Comodoro, sometimes in a jeep, sometimes in a helicopter. My mother and sister Celia lived for these surprise visits, and every day hoped another one was imminent, but meanwhile they kept very busy: they went sightseeing and studied all they could. It was from our mother that Ernesto had inherited his curiosity and keen intellect. He appreciated her advice most of all. She was one of the few people who told him the unadorned truth. In the position he now occupied, he had more need than ever of her outspokenness. As for Celia, out of us all, she was the one who was most like Ernesto. They had the same integrity of character, the same superior intelligence, and they read the same books.

One day Ernesto made time to take us to Santa Clara. We wanted to see the site of the decisive victory of the Ciro Redondo Column.[10] It was in Santa Clara, in fact, that a few weeks earlier Ernesto had had the idea of derailing the armoured train carrying arms and munitions for the regime. This act of sabotage hastened the taking of the city and the fall of Fulgencio Batista. In addition, it was in Santa Clara that the March family lived, and Ernesto wanted to introduce us to them: Aleida was about to become his wife and the mother of their four children: Aleida, Camilo, Celia and Ernesto. My brother already had a daughter, Hilda Beatriz, from his first marriage to the Peruvian Hilda Gadea. So we spent a few hours with Aleida's parents, who were charming peasants, simple and hardworking. Unfortunately for us, Aleida and Ernesto were summoned back to Havana for an urgent matter, and had to leave. My parents, Celia, her husband Luis and I continued on our way to Escambray.

Back in Havana, I explored the city, often guided by Harry 'Pombo' Villegas or Leonardo 'Urbano' Tamayo, two guerrillas of the Sierra Maestra who later accompanied Ernesto on the Bolivian Ñancahuazú campaign. Pombo and Urbano had fought at his side, so I took advantage and asked them lots of questions. All their information was completely new to me, and so exciting. They described my brother's exploits, his heroism, his fraternity, his deep humanity. Yet this exceptional man whose bravery and achievements were being related to me was still just my brother. And in spite of all those stories, I still didn't grasp Che's importance. I was just a teenager. Two and a half years later, when we went to join him for the last time in Punta del Este, Uruguay, for the Economic and Social Inter-American Conference, I finally began to see the place he would occupy in history. Today, I regret not having been able to assess the scope of the events that I was living through. For me, it was mainly one intoxicating whirlwind. I also regretted not having got to know Fidel on that particular stay. But a few months later, he paid us an unforgettable visit in Buenos Aires.

On 9 February, two days before our departure, a decree of the prime minister Fidel Castro declared Ernesto to be a 'Cuban-born citizen with all due rights and obligations'. My mother was filled with pride. She was convinced that the Cuban revolution was good and just. She saw in Che the fruit of what she had sown. As for Ernesto, he saw my mother as the architect who had allowed him to climb to the top of the building. He was grateful to her for being a woman who had managed to move on from her role as mother, the role of 'I look after you, I gave you life', and take up the role of comrade. As always, they found themselves on common ground.

When they separated, they were closer than ever. It was a real wrench for my mother to leave, but she had other obligations in Argentina: my brother Roberto and my sister Ana Maria had become parents and she took her role as a grandmother very seriously. As for me, I wanted to stay in Cuba with my brother and participate in the revolution. From Buenos Aires, my father forbade me to do so. Before leaving, he had again asked Ernesto to return home and resume his medical career. In vain. Cuba had already taken his eldest son. He wasn't prepared to surrender his youngest son too! However eccentric and carefree my father might have been, he wanted to keep hold of his children. I was deeply disappointed and angry. My mother would surely have let me stay. *She* would have understood. And Ernesto? I didn't know. I hadn't asked him. My father's decision was irrevocable and no one seemed to oppose it. After all, I was only fifteen.

If I had stayed, I too would have fought at Ñancahuazú. With my help, Ernesto might have survived. I don't think I've ever forgiven my father for forbidding me to stay.

3

An eccentric couple, always short of money

Before I launch into the history of my family, I would like to clarify one essential point. In the subject under discussion – basically my brother Ernesto – the essential elements are not only the ordinary traits that characterized our family and its influence on Ernesto, but the phenomena and situations he observed and judged: these were more important than the minutiae of our existence. I try to be strict with my memory. Some episodes come back to me more like sensations than actual memories. However, there are also moments that remain etched in my memory as sharply as photos.

My parents Ernesto Guevara Lynch and Celia de la Serna y Llosa married in a private ceremony at the home of my aunt Edelmira de la Serna de Moore on 10 December 1927. The marriage had been arranged in haste: they had met only a few months earlier at the home of a mutual friend. The de la Serna family didn't attend the wedding, as they disapproved of the union: my father was a *tanguero* without a degree and probably without future, a night owl who, at nightfall, headed off, carrying a weapon, to dance tango in the disreputable suburbs of Barracas, a neighbourhood on the outskirts of Buenos Aires. Our national entrechat was, at that time, the exclusive domain of the working classes and immigrants. It wasn't danced in the wealthier parts of town. 'Decent folk' believed that this erotic pas de deux, which mimicked the motions of love so closely, was completely depraved. For a man like my father, this was exactly where the attraction of tango lay. He was a seasoned seducer. He was apparently so irresistible that he seduced my mother when she had barely emerged from the Sacred Heart, a boarding house run by French nuns. At that time, young men were supposed to pick up their sex education with prostitutes in brothels, not with girls of good family like Celia de la Serna.

My mother, who came from an old wealthy family of the Argentinian upper bourgeoisie, was not, however, the self-effacing and submissive young girl that the nuns had tried to shape. She had a strong character, difficult, rebellious and independent, and she was highly intelligent. She devoured books in both Spanish and French. She wouldn't take orders from anyone. As an early feminist, she was one of the first Argentinian women to cut their hair in 'tomboy' style, to wear trousers, to smoke and drive. I don't know if it's true, but my father often related that when he had first known her, she was so devout that she put crushed glass into her shoes to make herself suffer. When I got to know my mother – I mean, when I became aware of her personality – she'd become impossible to live with!

As the black sheep of his own family, an outsider, a dreamer, the young Ernesto Guevara Lynch was always going to seem attractive to my mother. She was twenty, had a rough-hewn face with high cheekbones, a long nose, dark, very penetrating eyes, set widely apart, dark hair, and a slender figure. She was not a classic beauty but she stood out. She had presence, and sex appeal. You noticed her.

At the time of their wedding, my father was a partner in a shipbuilding company, El Astillero Río de la Plata. The company was in trouble. A friend suggested that my father buy land in Misiones to grow *yerba mate*. Misiones is a subtropical province, a remote wilderness on the Argentinian border, a sort of narrow stretch of lava or mud hemmed in between Brazil and Paraguay, and the Paraná and Uruguay rivers where Roland Joffé shot his film *The Mission*. It was conquered by the Spanish Jesuits in the seventeenth century and is inhabited by Guarani Indians. Murders and robberies are common. The territory operates more or less outside the law. To defend himself, a man must be able to wield an axe or a revolver. Misiones is also subject to dramatic climatic upheavals and swallowed up by a thick, lush vegetation wherein countless dangers lurk. Here, every insect – they have exotic names such as the *jején*, *ura* or *mbarigüi* – stings, bites or transmits malaria. The *mbarigüi* is so tiny that it is barely visible and can get through any mosquito netting. Snakes abound.

However, it was a tempting proposal for a man like my father, who was prepared to take a risk. And my mother was the ideal woman to follow him willingly on this crazy expedition. They seemed made for each other. Celia de la Serna was fearless. She would even court danger when the opportunity arose. If she was prepared to embrace this harsh lifestyle – even though she was pregnant – this wasn't just because she wanted to blindly follow her husband: she was drawn to adventure. And then she was thrilled to get away from her family, who had raised her in something of a nunnery atmosphere.

Che's various biographers have written that my parents came from the aristocracy, from the Argentinian oligarchy, and were thoroughly bourgeois. This always makes me smile. The oligar-chy has two components: power and money. My parents had neither. Conversely, they had an amazing ability to break free from the established order, to refuse to do what was expected of them. While they were indeed both from wealthy and notable families, they were a couple of eccentrics who had no money and were always trying to get hold of some. They were far from being conservative in their outlook: instead, theirs was a bohemian, liberal existence, forever on the move, financially precarious – a completely different life from that of *their* parents. Still, their whimsical side did originate from their respective families.

My paternal grandparents Roberto Guevara Castro and Ana Lynch Ortiz were the children of Argentinians who had fled the autocracy and the fiscal policies of the *caudillo* Juan Manuel de Rosas[1] – who recruited men into his army by force – to seek their fortune in California. To achieve this, my great-grandfather Francisco Lynch, the son of an Irish immigrant, undertook a long and dangerous journey from Uruguay to Chile through the Strait of Magellan, to Peru, Ecuador and finally San Francisco, where he spent thirty years and where my grandmother was born and raised until she was twelve. The family of my great-grandfather Juan Antonio Guevara, which came from the province of Mendoza which it helped to estab-lish and develop, also went into exile for political reasons: his family members had dared to challenge Juan Manuel de Rosas and were forced to live under the threat of retaliation. When this threat became too intense, Juan Antonio and his brothers decided to emigrate. They crossed the Andes, settling first in Chile before continuing on to California, attracted by the Gold Rush. Francisco Lynch made his fortune in the 'Golden State'; Juan Antonio failed miserably. Neither he nor his brothers ever managed to discover any gold. The years of exile in the area of Sacramento, the capital, produced nothing.

The fall of Juan Manuel de Rosas in 1852 finally allowed the two families to return to Argentina where my paternal grandparents met. They produced eleven children, whom they raised in Portela, an *estancia* or ranch in the province of Buenos Aires.

Roberto Guevara Castro was a renowned geographer and engineer in charge of the territorial divisions of Argentina and Chile, on the one hand, and Argentina and Paraguay, on the other. It was also his job to establish a land registry for the province of Mendoza, a task which took fifteen years. He would leave for months at a time, with his men and mules. I never considered him to be a true adventurer, in so far as he had vast resources at his disposal. But he rather liked carrying out his job in difficult conditions – with weapons at his side, of course. On his visits to Portela, he would talk about his many expeditions. These anecdotes were told to us later on, by our uncles and aunts, because my grandfather died in 1918, long before we were born. One of these stories particularly gripped my imagination: one day one of his mules decided she was tired and would go no further. Laden with essential tools, she threw herself down a cliff, which put my grandfather in a serious quandary. This was how I learned that mules are the only animals that commit suicide.

While my grandfather was traipsing about the mountains marking out borders and facing all kinds of dangers, including repeated attacks from Indians, my grandmother was raising her large tribe by herself. She was a high-spirited, fundamentally independent woman. And she was an atheist! In a deeply Catholic country like Argentina, this reflected an extremely liberated mind. Later, her children would all become religious, under pressure or out of ambition, except my father, who mocked social conventions all his life long.

Ernesto adored my paternal grandmother and went to Portela at the first opportunity. It was he who, when she fell ill, remained at her bedside until the end. And it was also due to her death that he decided to abandon his engineering studies and take up medicine. My grandmother returned his love a hundredfold: he was her favourite, just as he was the favourite of my mother and my aunt Beatriz. Beatriz was my father's sister. What a character! Always with her little hat. In Portela, she would sleep with a gun at the foot of her bed. When a mosquito annoyed her, she fired a shot that echoed throughout the Pampas. So my grandfather made a hole in the net for the barrel of the gun to fit through. This made the net quite useless. Beatriz never married. She worshipped Ernesto. After the victory of the Cuban revolution, she made a point of finding, reading and cutting out every little article written about him; in this way, she built up a valuable store of documents. From time to time she would suddenly turn up at our home, waving newspaper clippings and exclaiming indignantly: 'I have no idea why they all accuse Ernestito of being communist. He's so nice, so nice and so kind!' For her, communists were people you didn't want to have anything to do with – evil and cruel. So how could her beloved nephew possibly be a communist? And yet Ernesto regularly sent her letters which he deliberately signed 'Your communist nephew', 'Your proletarian nephew', or 'Stalin II', so as to enrage her. But he loved her dearly. He wanted her to understand him, as he felt very close to her. He liked provoking people so as to get a rise out of them. He found it amusing. Ernesto was a troublemaker, born to rouse controversy.

My mother had been orphaned at the age of fifteen. The family of her mother, Edelmira Llosa, had been powerful. Among other things, the Llosas built the first subway in Buenos Aires in 1908. Her father's family had done almost as well. Juan Martin de la Serna came from an old family of the colonial era, very influential on the national stage. Our great-grandfather Martin José de la Serna took part in the revolution against Juan Manuel de Rosas (the one my paternal grandparents had fled from). Arrested and imprisoned for his subversive activities, he managed to escape to join General Juan de Lavalle in Montevideo, and campaigned with him until Rosas was defeated in Caseros in 1852. He then founded the city of Barracas del Sur (now Avellaneda), of which he became mayor. While the Serna family was part of the upper bourgeoisie, they did not share the ideas and the values of their peers. They were a family of intellectuals bound to the land, anticlerical freethinkers, even if they did send some of their children to religious schools.

My grandfather Juan Martin de la Serna was a lawyer, diplomat and professor in the faculty of law at the University of Buenos Aires. His pupils included several future leaders of the Radical Party, in which he himself became a very active member. From what I have heard, he was a highly intelligent and cultivated man, fluent in both French and German. He was also a pioneer of Argentinian aviation. He seemed to succeed in everything he did, and yet he jumped into the sea from the deck of a ship in 1908. There has long been doubt as to the causes of his suicide. They said he had syphilis. My mother was two years old.

Thirteen years later, her mother died in turn, after a long illness. The seven Serna-Llosa children inherited a vast fortune. They lived in a beautiful *estancia*, 100 kilometres south of Buenos Aires, called Manantiales. When not living in her Convent of the Sacred Heart, my mother was raised by her big sisters, Sara and Carmen. If the atmosphere in Manantiales was strict and disciplined, politics was often discussed. Three Serna-Llosa children stood out in particular: my aunt Carmen, my uncle Jorge and my mother.

As a teenager, Carmen read the Mexican poet Amado Nervo and fell madly in love with him. She started writing him letters to which, against all odds, he replied. A regular correspondence arose between this mature man and this innocent young girl. In fact, when she learned that he was dying in Montevideo, she rushed to his bedside and stayed there until his death. She was eighteen. A few years later, she married the poet, journalist and art critic Cayetano 'Policho' Córdova Iturburú. They both became card-carrying members of the Argentinian Communist Party, in which they remained active until Policho was expelled fourteen years later.

Left-wing militancy never stopped Carmen taking care over her appearance. When she was arrested and thrown in jail by henchmen of Perón, who ruled the country with an iron hand, she was more bothered by the hideous uniform worn by the prisoners than by the incarceration itself. One day she went to an anti-Peronist demonstration, and police fired on the crowd. All the protesters lay down on the tarmac to avoid the bullets, except for her. My aunt remained standing to avoid damaging her beautiful dress! The Iturburú couple would have a huge influence on Ernesto.

My uncle Jorge de la Serna was a lunatic. Of my father and Jorge, we never knew who was the most cracked. The Serna family got into the habit of calling my father 'el loco Guevara' ('crazy Guevara'). But Jorge was almost as barmy. After years of marriage in which he produced several children, he fell deeply in love with a young employee for whom he left my aunt. Beside herself with rage, my aunt pulled strings and managed to have him declared insane. And Jorge found himself locked up in an asylum! He spent several weeks there before he could demonstrate that he was sane. One day, as my father was calling him a *viejo loco*[2] during one of their many altercations, Jorge pulled a paper out of his pocket and, waving it furiously under my father's nose, said: 'Me, an old fool? I may have been interned, but they let me out! I've even got the certificate that proves I'm not crazy! You may be outside, but you really are barking mad!'

Jorge was an agricultural engineer. He was also an adventurer with a highly pronounced taste for risk. An outstanding swimmer, he was in the habit of throwing himself into the coldest and choppiest waters, often as naked as the day he was born apart from the white cap he wore so he could be seen, as he hated to go unnoticed. In Mar del Plata, he purposely plunged into the ocean when the flag was red, the currents treacherous and the waves huge. He struck out to sea, and was able to swim for four or five hours. A crowd inevitably formed on the beach. And he totally ruined our day as we were scared he would drown. One day, exasperated by his whims, and deciding it was time to bring them to a halt, the lifeguards decided to call the police. Jorge was stopped. Of course, he was back at it the very next day. He enjoyed extreme sports long before they were called that. He took off in his old crate and, once he was aloft, cut the engine. He also went gliding. He had a very nimble mind and an enterprising spirit; he had never studied, but wrote some decent poetry – he dedicated several poems to the araucaria, an Andean conifer. At first he actively campaigned for an ultra-nationalist party, then became a communist. He also had an excellent knowledge of mechanics, and travelled around the country on a motorcycle. He then married a well-to-do young woman but finally left her for the employee mentioned above; he tired of her, too. Divorce cleaned him out: he lost his land and his fortune. He was ruined, and began working for the Ministry of Culture. That's when he surfaced in our lives and Ernesto became his friend. Up until his divorce, in fact, we had seen little of Jorge. My mother had moved away from her family; she felt that she had been wronged in the matter of her inheritance, because of her marriage to 'el loco Guevara'. My grandparents' fortune should have been divided between their seven heirs. But some of my uncles and aunts had manoeuvred to deprive my mother of her share. So my parents hadn't been able to live tranquilly on their incomes as they had initially envisaged. The law at the time forbade a young girl to marry before twenty-one without the consent of her family and authorized the latter to disinherit her in case of disobedience. And my mother had married in haste.

So my parents left for Misiones after buying a two-hundred-hectare plantation of *yerba mate*. They settled in Puerto Caraguatay, a nondescript little place, extremely isolated, located 2,700 kilometres (one week's sailing) from Buenos Aires. Puerto Caraguatay was nothing like a port. It was an impenetrable jungle with a pier. Nothing more. No roads led there. You reached it via the Rio Paraná. And while there is a track leading to it nowadays, it remains impassable on rainy days.

My father immediately began building a chalet on stilts carved from tree trunks. He had no degree but many talents. From the chalet windows there was a view over the Paraná River, 600 metres wide at this point. My mother, like her brother and later

Ernesto, was an excellent swimmer and swam in it regularly despite the dangerous currents and my father's protests.

For the birth of their first-born, something which could not possibly be envisaged in the inhospitable jungle of Puerto Caraguatay, my parents rented an apartment in Rosario, the capital of the province of Santa Fe. This is where Ernesto was born on 14 June 1928. They went back to Misiones a few weeks after the birth. They were happy. My mother was twenty-one, my father twenty-eight. They had quickly become very fond of their log home, their lives as pioneers. They regularly went out riding in the surrounding country. Despite the difficulties and the total lack of comfort, it was an exciting life, so very far from the Convent of the Sacred Heart for my mother, and from San Isidro, the affluent suburb south of Buenos Aires, where my father had lived . . .

Ernesto spent the first two years of his life in this wild land. My father liked to stress that he had been deeply affected by it. My older brother was precocious and easily absorbed everything. When they needed to stock up, my parents had to travel by boat to a village populated by *mensús* (short for *mensualero*, a man who works for a monthly salary), the martyred people of seasonal farmers descended from the Guaranis, natives who had been given the task of protecting the Jesuit missions for two centuries. A hundred years after the departure of the missionaries, the *mensús* had still failed to break their chains. They were employed in *yerba mate* plantations and lived in a state of semi-slavery and extreme poverty. Their oppression at the hands of the landowners was total and cruel. They were paid in kind: they were provided with slums and vile food in exchange for their labour. They got into debt to buy the alcohol they consumed in their rare moments of leisure. If they attempted to escape, they were caught by the landowners who beat them to death, as an example to others. This iniquity came as a terrible shock to my mother. She rebelled against such injustice; it was the first of which she had been a direct witness. My father decided meanwhile to pay his *mensús* in pesos and instantly became persona non grata to his peers. He was accused of communism and subversion by the other *yerbateros* who conspired against him. Perhaps that's why the whole Misiones venture suddenly seemed doomed to failure. The family returned to Buenos Aires; my father thought this would just be temporary, and entrusted the running of the plantation to a partner. He intended to return after having restored order to El Astillero Río de la Plata, which was in decline. In reality, the Puerto Caraguatay episode had just come to an end. In San Isidro, where my parents wound up at my grandmother's, Ernesto began to suffer from acute asthma. It was strongly recommended that he avoid the subtropical climate of Misiones which would damage his fragile lungs. This brutal diagnosis would henceforth dictate the way our family lived. Because of this disease, we became nomads.

Ernesto's state deteriorated rapidly in San Isidro. The dampness caused by the proximity of the River Plata aggravated his asthma within a few months. His health became my parents' top priority. So they packed their bags and spent the following months travelling the country in search of a suitable climate. Penniless, they went from one family home to another: my grandmother's *estancia* in Portela, the *estancia* of our cousins Moore de la Serna in Galarza, in gaucho territory, and an aunt's house in Miramar. This was a time when they had no fixed abode.

Since our childhood we had been accustomed to moving, adapting to changing circumstances. We never stayed put, or enjoyed financial stability.

In 1932, Ernesto was four, my sister Celia three. Roberto had just been born. My parents were alarmed by the asthma attacks that seemed to be worsening. They were convinced that the disease afflicting their first-born was the result of a bronchopneumonia he had contracted in Rosario shortly after his birth. Their life was marked by increasingly frequent, increasingly terrifying crises. They consulted the best lung specialists, who prescribed different remedies and remarked that they had rarely seen such a serious case in a child so young. No treatment worked. My parents were in despair. Finally, a renowned doctor advised them to go and live in Córdoba, a mountainous province in the centre of the country, an area they had never visited and where they didn't know anyone. But this didn't matter – they were willing to make any sacrifice to alleviate my brother's suffering! They cast off the ties that had always brought them back to Buenos Aires and immediately departed by train for Córdoba, where they would spend the next fifteen years of their lives. We would never really have roots, or any place of which we could say 'this is our home, our anchor'. But Alta Gracia was the place that came closest to this concept. We would all grow up in this unfamiliar province.

4

As free as the wind

In the 1930s, Alta Gracia was basically a spa town of about 20,000 inhabitants, in the central province of Córdoba, nestled at the foot of the Sierras Chicas mountain range. Its pure, dry climate was considered excellent for curing lung diseases. It was a peaceful place, too quiet for my parents, who thought there was only one good thing about it: it was an opportunity to improve Ernesto's health and make his life easier.

Over the fifteen years my family would live there, they would move some ten or so times. They first moved into the Hotel de la Gruta for a year, then to various villas: Chichita, Nydia (where the museum to Che now stands) and Carlos Pellegrini, then to different chalets: Fuentes, Forte and Ripamont, finally returning to the Nydia villa. We were a travelling clan living in perpetual chaos – well, the rest of my family was: I myself hadn't been born yet. Each Guevara household was inevitably transformed into a shambles. They were cleaned (with buckets full of water) only if we had visitors. Villa Chichita in particular was in a dreadful condition, with cracks running along the ground, walls and roof. With its very high ceilings, and poor insulation, it encouraged the draughts that cheerfully blew through it. The heating didn't work and my parents had no money to fix it. In my father's defence, Alta Gracia wasn't a good place to do business. He still managed to get a hotel construction contract through a friend, drew up the plans, then rapidly squandered the money he had made. I seem to remember that in the aftermath he also masterminded plans for a golf course. Anyway, the good times lasted only a few months.

In the winter, everyone shivered. One day, my mother had the idea of buying a large tablecloth that went right down to the ground and placing a little heater under the table. This allowed us at least to keep our legs and feet warm. The rest of the house was freezing cold. But my mother never complained, she seemed to adapt readily to all situations. Though she had had such pretty dresses in her youth, she now dressed as modestly as possible. She usually wore trousers and a simple blouse, occasionally a skirt or dress. She cut her hair short, which at the time was a big no-no for a woman. When she went past, people would whisper, 'Celia drives a car! Celia wears trousers! Celia doesn't go to Mass!' Alta Gracia was one of those provincial towns where everyone knows everyone else and malicious gossip is rife. My mother, who had seriously considered taking the veil as a young woman, now gobbled up priests for breakfast. We suspected that her anticlericalism was due to her years in boarding school, where the nuns had forced her to kneel on corn kernels to recite the Lord's Prayer 10,000 times over. Be that as it may, she had developed a deep loathing of the church since leaving the convent and discovering the world. Just seeing a religious building made her feel ill. She knew she was the subject of gossip but didn't care. We had a bad reputation. My parents were known as eccentrics – permissive liberals who gave free rein to their children, who in turn were a bunch of kids who hung around with anyone they liked. And the Guevara offspring were indeed as free as the wind. No timetable was imposed. Furthermore, my parents treated their girls the same way as the boys: there was no difference. The only thing they required from their children was respect and study. The family was close-knit. Nobody bothered about what people might say – Ernesto less than anyone.

My mother wasn't in the least a traditional housewife, she cared nothing for hygiene or cooking, and indeed didn't have the slightest idea about them. She admitted without false shame that stewardship of the home was really not her forte, and in those self-critical moments when she scrutinized her flaws, she regretted the fact. But she was an excellent mother to her five children (Ana Maria and I were born respectively in 1934 and 1943). Our studies were her main priority. And she spared no effort in this domain. This was especially true for Ernesto – less for me, later on – and she taught him reading, writing and French. Until the age of nine, my brother repeatedly had to stay at home because of his asthma. My mother gave him the lessons he couldn't follow at school. Thanks to the quality of her teaching, he finally not only caught up with his peers, but overtook them.

The firmness of Celia de la Serna's character was legend-ary. She was neither affectionate nor expansive. It was no easy task to obtain a hug or a compliment from her. As she prized discipline and scholarship above all, she forced us to cultivate ourselves, to learn, to know and to doubt. She was imbued with an unfailing Stoicism, very Judeo-Christian in character, sacrificial. But she also had enormous reserves of compassion, a great capacity for solidarity and understanding. She was differ-ent from my father, and capable of much greater constancy. She would read a 500-page-long book, while he read poetry because it was shorter. Unless he simply browsed through a quarter of a book and then related the whole plot as if he had read it from beginning to end.

In our family, everyone did what he wanted. My parents didn't impose any discipline on us, being convinced that their children should grow up in absolute freedom of thought and action. From a very young age, we had to solve our own problems. My parents never tried to find solutions for us. They encouraged resourcefulness, convinced that we must live our lives ourselves, at our expense if necessary. They kept saying that life would teach us. We didn't have the right to fail, to lose, to abdicate or to complain. If one of us started whimpering, they exclaimed: 'Whiners can go to church!' They were extremely demanding about the efforts we put in. For us, everything was crystal clear. We knew exactly what they expected from us.

It was a house full of lunatics: each and every one of us was cracked, and the head madman who kept sway over us was our father. We bugged each other, we argued, we drove each other to distraction. We never got bored. Instead, what fun we had! My brother Roberto, for example, drew up a law stating: 'Whoever bends over has agreed they are up for it: thus decrees the law.' This meant that if you bent over to pick something up, you'd get a big kick on the behind. Suddenly, no one dared to bend down. If you saw an object on the ground, you immediately thought it was a trap and left it there. One day when a cousin was visiting us, Roberto put a small portable grill down the back of his trousers, with a long shirt to hide the dent caused by the object, and bent over pretending to pick something up. Respectful of the punishment to be inflicted, my cousin almost broke his foot by kicking Roberto on the backside! The game of ripe fruit was also introduced. All our mates in the district had to go through this test in order to be accepted into the Guevara gang. It involved hanging by your arms from the branch of a tree three or four metres above the ground until you had to let go from exhaustion. As usual, Ernesto excelled at this game. He could stay there hanging almost indefinitely. He also liked to walk along the railings of bridges while staring into the void. When Roberto and Ernesto fought, Ernesto usually had the advantage. He was not only older but also fiercer. But Roberto knew how to take advantage of his older brother's weak point. In revenge, he sometimes hid a bucket of ice water in a spot in the garden. At the appropriate time, he poured it out on Ernesto's head. This paralysed him, because of his asthma.

When still very young, Ernesto showed signs of a good strong character. Yet he was shy. My aunt Carmen said he owed his shyness to his superior intelligence. In fact, he grasped things with lightning speed. He rarely needed to have things spelled out to him. He had an iron will, and an unusual boldness and capacity for decision. He inherited the sometimes contradictory qualities of my parents: the contemplative and yet enterprising side of my father; the determination and discipline of my mother. This perfect blend allowed him to realize his dreams and to complete his projects. My parents always insisted that we should finish what we started – even if there was a vast difference between their approaches: my father wasn't in the least bit interested how you reached your goal, while for my mother, it was essential to act in a fair and honest manner. In this regard, I recall two significant anecdotes. When I was at junior school, I myself signed my school reports instead of my parents – I was far from being the best student and I didn't want to hear tedious reprimands. In any case, no one asked me how I was doing – except Ernesto, who insisted that I work harder. One day, my father accidentally got hold of a school report and signed it. The next day, the headmistress summoned me and asked me to explain the difference between the two signatures. I made up some silly story: my father had been ill and his hand had just trembled. She phoned to check. My father went to the school and the headmistress explained her suspicions. He listened attentively, with an expression of gravity on his face that left no doubt about his seriousness. But what did he do? He confirmed my lie, as coolly as you could wish! When he came out, he said: 'You idiot! Couldn't you tell me that you signed your reports? And couldn't you have imitated my signature better?' My mother never found out: she would have been furious. When I was thirteen, I was arrested by the police. My father told me off for getting caught without trying to find out why I had been arrested. My mother asked me what I had done to end up at the police station. This was typical. The only thing that interested my father was the result: how I got there was of little concern. For my mother, the path I had taken was just as important.

Bravery and boldness are other qualities valued by the Guevara family. Again, Ernesto exemplified them. I heard that one morning – he must have been ten or eleven – a ram that had escaped from its enclosure was terrorizing the neighbourhood. Ernesto chased it, caught it by the horns, and fought with it until he had brought it down and overpowered it. He had bloodied knees but didn't seem to notice. He went to school like that, as if nothing had happened. All his friends admired him. They spontaneously placed themselves under his authority. He had no need to give orders or to stick out his chest. He had an innate capacity for leadership. It was sometimes difficult for Roberto to have such a brother. And things would get even more complicated for him over the years. However, Ernesto was not pretentious or boastful. He did things with the greatest simplicity, without ever boasting.

At home there was a continual to-ing and fro-ing of friends from every level of society. Our door was always open. My parents had no class bias. Indeed, they wanted their children to rub shoulders with people from every background. So our friends were the sons of miners, caddies from the golf course, workers, hotel employees and later refugees from the Spanish Civil War. My mother fought to ensure that the school served free meals to needy children (she achieved her purpose). On weekends, she took a whole group out to the mountains in our car, the Catramina, an old, rusty, dented jalopy that my father had bought from a friend. The Catramina had only one seat left. Later, it had only one door – the others had dropped off! Too bad. You could still drive it. Indeed, it would be our first and last car. My father was the kind of man for whom things generally went from bad to worse. He started with a nice car, and then a jalopy, and finally he didn't have any car at all! He was able to live in a palace or a hut.

Che's many biographers have talked primarily about my mother and forgotten my father, as if he had never existed, as if we had never had a father. This is completely wrong! Everyone should know about this amazing character whom everyone loved and thought so funny, charming, bright, colourful, talented and even divine. He was a snake charmer, incredibly intuitive, gifted with an extraordinary capacity for storing away knowledge, and endowed with an astounding grasp of mathematics. The only problem was that he was *our* father. Because, as a father, he was irresponsible, inconsistent, and rarely brought things to fruition while constantly coming up with new ideas and projects that never led anywhere. He was an artist who forced us to live unpredictable lives, an ambitious man who was incapable of persevering, a poet who wrote no poetry but was forever seeking metaphors, a lover of life, walking here, there and everywhere, or driving at breakneck speeds. Both present and absent, he was more a friend than a father. He played with us all but didn't really look after us.

Physically, he was tall, rather handsome and dashing, an excellent dancer, athletic, agile. He attracted women. I also think he had several affairs before my mother finally threw him out. There's a family story about it, which always made us laugh. One day when he was out walking with Ana Maria in Mar del Plata, they met a woman he knew. He started preening himself and flirting with her. Suddenly my sister exclaimed, 'But Papa, you say that to all the women!' My father was crestfallen!

He was gifted with a deep intelligence, exceptional even, but you had to take everything he said with a pinch of salt: you never knew if he was exaggerating or not. He embellished everything, twisted things and facts to suit himself so subtly that you could never accuse him outright of lying. Even though he never finished his studies in architecture or engineering, he built houses and hotels thanks to his connections, and he actually had an amazing number of friends. When people called him an 'architect', he nodded his head in sign of confirmation. When they called him 'doctor', he again went along with it. He said he was a graphologist but had never studied graphology. This didn't stop him being able to fully understand a person's character by examining his or her writing.

His pockets were almost always empty. And when they were full, thanks to some big project that had put him back on his feet, he soon squandered the money he had earned. He took us to the best restaurants or to the cinema. He would ask us, for politeness' sake, what film we wanted to see. But in the end he got his own way: he chose the film, fell asleep in his seat and then had the nerve to talk as if he had seen it and to argue about it with us – when we *had* watched it! This infuriated Ernesto. We would eat the best food for one night and then live hand to mouth for the next few months. If he came home carrying a bouquet of flowers – and this often happened! – we knew that he had spent his last penny. He was equally satisfied with life whether he had any money or not. In his family, he was considered the failure. All his brothers had degrees and careers. And while he liked to be called Guevara-Lynch, like a well-to-do man, he was a wild character who didn't get along with anyone. He was a *déclassé* bourgeois. That doesn't mean he was revolutionary, proletarian or socialist. He was a weather vane. He went where the wind blew, like a feather. He spent years being pro-Yankee and then anti-communist before ending up as an arch-communist in Cuba, playing the role of Che's father, living off the Cuban state and singing the *Internationale*! Well, he was also anti-Peronist, anti-Francoist, pro-republican, and was even active on behalf of an anti-fascist organization in Córdoba. He supported the Spanish exiles who lived in Alta Gracia and formed a large colony. He was impossible to classify. He couldn't care less about anything and always fell on his feet, like a cat. It was crazy, what his children lived through day by day as a result. At home we had everything or nothing.

He joked incessantly, played tricks on people, had a biting

sense of humour. Our friends always said he was the most entertaining and likeable member of the family. He made everyone laugh. He was a keen observer, drew very well and could turn out an amazing caricature in five minutes. He seemed afraid of the new. If he had anything new, he deliberately broke it. He was an atheist but extremely superstitious – while trying to hide the fact. He often wore a waistcoat over his shirt. He would put it on and take it off several times before finally keeping it on, to ward off bad luck. You weren't allowed to make any remarks to him about this: he got angry and said that it stopped him breathing. If he saw a number 13, he waved his arms up and down like a bird to keep the curse at bay. On a staircase, he always avoided the thirteenth step. One day, I pointed out to him that it was silly to jump over this step: whatever he did, the thirteenth step was the one on which he set foot after the twelfth. This put him in such a quandary that he fell silent and refused to speak to me for a month. Similarly, he always left a place the same way he had come in. One day we went to call on a female friend who was out. Her door was locked. We didn't have a key but got in through a window. When we left, he climbed out of the window. It would have been impossible to take the door to leave. He was also a hypochondriac, constantly on the brink of death. He spent his whole life complaining of imaginary diseases. If it wasn't polio, it was something else. Nobody paid any attention. Our friends thought we were harsh and insensitive. They sometimes saw my father rising to his feet, and placing his hand over his heart, saying he was suffering a heart attack. They were astonished that my mother didn't call an ambulance. At the same time, he was capable of running silly risks by going to dance tango in the rough parts of town.

Our house was filled with books. We all took an interest in literature, philosophy and culture. We could run short of everything, everything around us might crumble away or fail to work, the pipes could clog and so on: nobody showed the least alarm. But a shortage of books . . .? Inconceivable! We had French books that had not yet been translated into Spanish. Trotsky's works, for example. My brothers and sisters were all studious. Celia and Ernesto, in particular, were voracious readers. They annotated all the works they read, made them their own. If we then wanted to read one of these books, we were faced with all their notes in the margins. Ernesto was even worse than Celia. You had the sense that he was conversing with the author. He read a lot in French. He used to take a book to the toilet, and stay there forever. So you needed the toilet? Too bad! If you asked him to come out, he'd start to declaim Gustave Flaubert, Alexandre Dumas or Charles Baudelaire, in French, just to rile us even more! Things usually ended in an argument. Endless dialogues which echoed throughout the neighbourhood. At home, we didn't talk, we yelled. Even moderate conversations invariably ended in bawling and squalling. My parents never assumed they were right. On the contrary. Anything could be, and even should be, discussed, argued over. Critical thinking was encouraged. They taught us never to blindly accept a dogma, a particular belief. Everything had to be vigorously debated. Ernesto was the best debater in the family, the most intelligent in terms of thought, analysis and the capacity for provocation. He always developed the deepest, clearest and most precise critiques. From his youngest years he was an incredibly disciplined reader, taking advantage of the times when he was bedridden with asthma to devour literature.

My mother's militancy probably stemmed from her own family. The de la Serna family were also tireless debaters. Protest was in their blood. For example, they denounced General Franco when all the upper bourgeois families in Argentina supported him. But until the two years spent in Misiones, politics was, for my mother, an abstract concept. The injustice inflicted on the *mensús* sparked in her a political awareness drawn from experience and testimony. Given the anti-fascist activism of my father, and the political activities of my mother, our family was definitely engaged and active. But my parents never belonged to any political party, only to individual movements. At home, everyone was free to think more or less what he or she wanted, provided of course we didn't support fascist ideas. Our home was a meeting place for many politically active characters. This hyper-politicized family atmosphere would shape Che.

In 1934, my father was involved in the war between Paraguay and Bolivia. When Bolivia, supported by the United States, attacked its weak neighbour in order to annex it, defenders of Paraguay met regularly at our house. Later, my mother told me that Ernesto, who was five at the time, listened to the conversation with an unusual attention for a child of that age and did not miss a single detail of the debates.

When our uncle 'Policho' Iturburú was sent to Spain to cover the Civil War for the newspaper *Crítica*, my aunt Carmen came to live with us. For security reasons, Policho sent his reports to our house. My family read them before forwarding them to the newspaper, so we were the first to be informed of events. Ernesto had stuck a huge map of Spain onto the wall of his room. He followed the conflict and marked the advance of the Republicans with little flags. He was nine years old. There were other reasons for our taking a close interest in the vicissitudes of the Spanish people: the doctor and Republican activist Juan Gonzalez Aguilar had fled into exile in Alta Gracia, closely followed by Colonel Enrique Jurado, hero of the Battle of Guadalajara. Our families became very close.

Whichever house we lived in, the floors and walls were covered with political tracts. In the 1940s, my mother joined the de Gaulle Committee, a French-Argentinian organization supporting the Resistance; she put a portrait of de Gaulle up on the wall of our living room. She then joined the anti-Peronist organization Monteagudo, attended clandestine meetings and demonstrated in the streets against General Juan Perón, shouting 'Long live freedom, down with Perón!' When one day the police tried to calm her down by grabbing her arm, she started screaming: 'Let go of me, Gestapo!' In 1954, she got drunk to celebrate the French defeat at Dien Bien Phu. She even threw a party at our house in Buenos Aires, placing a copy of *Paris Match* prominently on the coffee table, with its headlines about the humiliation of France. The contrast struck me.

The Alta Gracia years were good years, even if relations between my parents began to deteriorate at the time. They had a love-hate relationship. I think my mother was very much in love in the early years of their marriage. She needed love to marry a dreamer like my father and put up with all his eccentricities! But she gradually tired of his antics. My father, meanwhile, started to fall prey to depression. He said he was suffering from neurasthenia. Alta Gracia was a very provincial town. Not only did nothing ever happen there, but it was also a sanctuary for critically ill patients. For a Porteño[1] night owl like him, this quiet existence was torture. He spent most of his time at the Hotel Sierras, the fashionable meeting place of the local petty bourgeoisie. The establishment had a wonderful pool where we would all go swimming. Ernesto had started swimming and excelled in it, as did my mother and my uncle. The champion of the butterfly stroke, Carlos Espejo Pérez, had befriended him and gave him free lessons. Years later, during the Cuban invasion, Ernesto's talents as a swimmer would be very useful to him in crossing the rivers of the Sierra Maestra.

When it came to practical jokes and brawling, Ernesto and Roberto got along like a house on fire. They were at the head of a gang of Robin Hood types in short trousers. My parents suspected that their activities were not always entirely kosher, but they left them to their own devices, true to their policy of non-intervention. Besides, my brothers did nothing inherently reprehensible. They even had to their credit a respectable feat of arms which remained enshrined in the annals of Alta Gracia. The electricity company (a subsidiary of the Swiss company Erliska) had suddenly increased its tariffs, to a quite scandalous degree. The inhabitants of the province of Córdoba were unaccustomed to submitting to arbitrary measures. However, despite their repeated protests, the price of electricity was not lowered by a penny. My brothers found a solution. They discovered a municipal ordinance stipulating that each electric bulb in a public lamp post was to be replaced by the electric company the same day that it blew. The municipality could also impose a fine of ten dollars per defective bulb on the company. So Ernesto, Roberto and their gang set about breaking all the bulbs! The mayor turned a blind eye to the cause of the damage and the electricity company eventually revised its tariffs. Ernesto drew a lesson from all this: action was sometimes the only effective remedy against injustice.

My parents both looked after Ernesto when he was ill. They took it in turns to be at his bedside, read to him and helped him with his homework. My father spent hours teaching him to play chess. Ernesto soon outclassed him. He quickly became an outstanding player. Thanks to the climate of Alta Gracia, his asthma attacks became less frequent and decreased in intensity. My parents insisted that he lead a normal life, and made him do sports. He played golf and rugby and gave them one hundred per cent. He was unable to do things by halves. Ernesto was so fierce on the rugby field that his friends dubbed him 'Fuser', short for 'Furibundo² Serna' (he used the name Guevara-Serna, having removed the particle as being too bourgeois for his taste). He wasn't the best player but he always had possession of the ball. He owed his other nickname, 'Chancho' (pig), to his flat nose and the fact that he rarely went through the shower after a game. He even went dancing – despite being a poor dancer who had no sense of rhythm – without changing into something clean. The world remembers Ernesto in his impeccable green uniform, wide belt and beret. His dress style has become iconic. We always laughed at this in the family. Ernesto was the shabbiest, most fashion-resistant man ever! Every day he wore the same shirt of threadbare nylon, hanging half out of his trousers, with mismatched shoes picked up in a jumble sale. He had such a sense of mockery that he himself derided his shirt. He was dubbed 'Mr Once Weekly' because he changed his shirt only once a week. When he finally took a shower, he would do it while still wearing his shirt! This way, he felt it was clean. He took the joke so far that he adopted the nickname Chancho, which, far from making him angry, made him laugh. In fact, when he began to write articles for the rugby magazine *Tackle*, he signed them 'Chancho'. My father took offence and got angry. He didn't like his son to treat himself as a figure of fun; he felt personally insulted. With his usual humour, Ernesto brazened it out and instead started to sign 'Chang Cho'.

So he wasn't interested in his physical appearance and didn't seem aware of his sex appeal. Yet girls had flocked around him ever since adolescence, obviously attracted by his charm and personality. The fact is that he was said to be extremely attractive, with large expressive, laughing eyes, a thick black mop of hair, and an easy smile. In addition, he was reckless, athletic, brilliant and cultured. *Todo el paquete!*[3] as the Argentinians say. His friend Alberto Granado (the older brother of Tómas, one of his best friends from Alta Gracia), with whom he would set off on the famous motorbike journey that produced *The Motorcycle Diaries*, told me years later that all his girlfriends, without exception, begged him to introduce them to the handsome Ernesto.

My brother lived his romantic relationships with the same intensity as the rest of his life. I'm always being asked about Ernesto's love life. 'How did he get on with women?' And I always answer: 'I knew he had affairs. Of course, he loved women.' He simply loved some more discreetly than others. 'I'd stop being a man if I didn't love women', he admitted to a reporter one day . . . He was a gentleman. He courted Aleida March with great delicacy and patience. He wrote her beautiful poems, taking his time not to rush her, asking her to fix his shirt collar when he was driving, or comb his hair when his arm was broken, instead of trying to kiss her. Aleida was a young revolutionary, eight years his junior; she regarded him as a mature man.

In her autobiography, she says that his eyes and especially the way he looked at people had immediately charmed her. He had a certain aura, he was a man of courage, full of virility and poetry at once. Ernesto fell in love with her in the Sierra Maestra. In fact, as he would confess to her in a letter sent in 1965 from the Congo, he had had to 'struggle (a little) in an inner combat where the irreproachable revolutionary was having to fight the other guy'. The first present Ernesto gave Aleida was the perfume Fleur de Rocaille by Caron.

Before Aleida, María del Carmen Ferreyra had been the great love of his youth. In 1950, this beautiful girl experienced her first passionate love affair, with Ernesto. Chichina – her nickname – came from a family of the upper bourgeoisie. She led a gilded existence, dividing her time between a country house, the Palacio Ferreyra, and an *estancia*, La Malagueña. The Guevara de la Serna family were notorious outsiders without a penny to their name – but this name was still able to open the doors of high society. Not that the company of the upper bourgeoisie was particularly interesting or flattering to us, except maybe to my father. In any case it certainly wasn't for Ernesto. He had unwillingly fallen deeply in love with a well-to-do girl, an heiress, everything he already hated. The Ferreyras were wealthy and very conservative landowners.

The fact that he had rubbed shoulders with the sons of the proletarians and peasants of Alta Gracia had consolidated my brother's visceral intolerance for injustice. My father used to tell us that, when his eldest son was still just a kid, he couldn't stand any form of unfairness; it made him angry. It was impossible for example to impose on him anything he viewed as arbitrary. He would then fly into a black rage which subsided only when people made up for their mistake and apologized. He defended his positions at any price, with unstoppable arguments. He had realized that one class was oppressing another, and at a very young age he started to rebel against this injustice.

We lived with one foot in each world, sparingly in Alta Gracia and in a sort of discreet opulence during the summers that we spent each year with our more affluent relatives. Ernesto took note of the contrast between their lifestyles and that of some of his friends. He immersed himself in philosophy to find an explanation for inequality. In Portela, he almost exclusively sought the company of the poor and the vagrants. Together they would go off to drink *mate* under the bridges. He always stood out, and did things differently. Not to impress others or get noticed; he was really special, unique. My mother encouraged this difference. She knew she had in him an exceptional child, a gifted student, able to play chess at near professional level and to develop political and philosophical theories that were surprising in one so young. She took care to feed his thirst for knowledge. As for my father, he taught him to dominate his illness by stimulating him physically through sport. Ernesto had become a great athlete. He often accompanied my uncle Jorge in his crazy expeditions, by air and sea or over the mountains. They were both equally daring. Nothing amused Jorge more than to see Ernesto turn up at the home of a family of the upper bourgeoisie dressed like a navvy, putting forward his subversive ideas and observing their reactions.

The fact remains that Fuser-Chancho arrived at the Ferreyras' looking like something the cat had brought in. At the time, he was studying medicine. Chichina's parents, a highly sophisticated couple, did not at first know what to think of this madman. They were fascinated by his great intelligence and vast erudition, but baffled by his self-confidence and his impertinence, his tramp-like clothes and his philosophical mind. The ideas he came out with were, in their view, rubbish. They talked it over together, deciding that he was still young and would have time to change as he grew older. Meanwhile he held forth endlessly, with amazing ease, in their many elegant rooms, surrounded by a gaggle of courtiers. Could this rebellious boy, this subversive hippie, one day become a good match for their daughter?

Twice, Ernesto asked for Chichina's hand in marriage and was rejected by the lovely lady. I have often wondered if she regretted this once he had been transformed into a mythical hero. Politically, I doubt it; she didn't share his ideas at all, and would certainly not have liked to be the wife of a revolutionary. The journalists never left her alone.

5

A unique character

I grew up in the shadow of Ernesto. I could never escape it.
Until 1956, I was just Juan Martin Guevara, 'El Tin', 'Patatin'
or 'Tudito' as he had nicknamed me. From 1957 onwards, I was
the brother of the revolutionary Ernesto Guevara, Fidel Castro's
companion and a fearless warrior. And then a legend. I learned
to live with this. It hasn't always been easy. His absences sad-
dened me, his death devastated me. I always say that he had to
be someone's brother. I detached myself from the almost unreal
image of the public man, the icon. I had to. In Buenos Aires,
his picture is everywhere: it adorns the walls and pavements.
Corrupt politicians claim him as their own, even though he was
the very embodiment of integrity. Ernesto was a fanatic for the
truth, whatever the price. He hated anything superfluous.

Ernesto was fifteen years old when I was born in Córdoba, in
calle Chile. He was already a real breath of fresh air. He came
in, went out, travelled, came back, set off again, lived his life.
When he was at home, he treated me like a son. Contemporary
accounts say that he adored me, he cared for me, took me for
walks, dandled me in his arms, cuddled me. My father said that
Ernesto was greatly devoted to his family, his home; he would

have defended them tooth and nail if necessary, and he was especially fond of me. He sent me letters from all his travels. I don't remember the details, of course. I realized how affectionate he was from the photos, and from rereading his letters: in the most difficult situations, he asked after me, when he did not write to me directly. As soon as I was old enough to understand and talk about things, I took him as my model. He was bold, crazy, mischievous, funny, adventurous. He was also selfless and fiercely loyal. I don't recognize him at all in the image of pain and suffering that we are sometimes shown of him. Just look at the photos! He was always smiling, joking all the time. His laughter was contagious. We often had our meals together at midday. I don't know where the others were: everyone went about their own business. I knew he would come home for lunch and I waited. I wanted to make the most of his presence because I knew it was fleeting. I savoured those moments. If Ernesto became a nomad very early, he remained very attached to us, our mother in particular. He was a ray of sunshine in the house, and too bad if this sounds like a cliché: it's exactly the effect he had. I can't describe it any other way.

He told me funny stories. He was a jokester, a mocker, capable of both great seriousness and of childish antics. He often asked me to make his *mate*. He was excessively punctilious about the preparation of his favourite beverage. I took great pleasure in boiling his water; I was thrilled to be useful to him. If the water had cooled while we were chatting, he tried to send me back to the kitchen to re-heat it. I refused. He then pretended to beat me. We play fought, and ended up in one another's arms.

He was a great brother, more than a brother, indeed: a faithful companion. Yet his relations with us were complex. He didn't play the role of the bossy and overbearing big brother;

instead, he was protective. For him, knowledge and learning were essential and, like my parents, he never tried to impose things on me. He preferred to use his influence to convince me. It was enough for him to say: 'I think it would be good for you to do so and so.' Going out with him was a liberation, a joy. When he took me to the cinema, it was a real treat.

He behaved the same way with the rest of the siblings, though his relations with them were different. Celia and Ana Maria also worshipped him. The two sisters didn't always get on well with each other – they downright hated each other at times – but with Ernesto everything was fine. Celia was – and remains – a very difficult, if not impossible person. She could be funny but seriousness was her natural state. When Ernesto began to study Karl Marx, she did the same. She followed in his path, confident in his judgement. The death of Ernesto devastated her. The pain was intense; it went on for ever. Of all of us, it was she who remained in denial about his death the longest. Even after Roberto came back from Bolivia, she refused to believe it. She clung to the inconsistencies in the story, the doubts. She never went to Quebrada del Yuro; she couldn't bear it. Even now she is barely able to watch a documentary about Che. If she sees a picture of Ernesto lying dead, she buries her face in her hands. She vowed never to speak publicly about it and she has kept to this vow. She accuses me of being too media-friendly and disapproves when I talk about Ernesto. She considers that he belongs to the domain of the family, as something private and sacred. Things are black or white for her. She refuses to see that things might be grey. She continues to behave like a big sister and forgets that I'm seventy-two years old! I haven't been able to tell her about this book.

Until their teens, Roberto and Ernesto were very close. They went around with the same gang. Roberto was not such a crazy, gadabout character as Ernesto. He was sedentary, sensible. A good student, he became a lawyer, married a daughter from a 'good family', Matilde Lezica, with whom he had five children and moved to San Isidro, before separating, remarrying and having two more children. He did everything the normal way. He also liked the odd scrap – he was the kind of guy who gives you a kick under the table and then blames you for touching him. One thing he had in common with Ernesto was an iron will. I remember one day when he was participating in a local marathon with some friends. The route passed our house. After a few kilometres, the others abandoned the race as they came by ours – they couldn't care less about finishing the race as they didn't take it seriously. But Roberto did! He carried on. In worthy Guevara fashion, the idea of retreating was intolerable to him. He finished the marathon exhausted, in such a sorry state that we had to carry him home. He took days to recover.

Of the three sons, Roberto was the one who best lived up to father's expectations. The intimidating shadow of Ernesto, however, hovered over him. Ernesto succeeded in everything, and was missed when he was away; he distinguished himself on the domestic, local, national and international scenes. Ernesto triumphed on every front. This wasn't easy for Roberto, even though he was neither jealous nor envious. He wasn't especially interested in politics. But he eventually did get involved, constrained and forced to do so by events: the death of Ernesto first and foremost, then my detention during the military dictatorship. His activism intensified over the years. So much so that he found himself imprisoned in Mexico in 1981, like Ernesto in 1956, for his role as a leader within the Partido Revolucionario de los Trabajadores (PRT) – I'd been arrested for belonging to the same party six years earlier. At the time of his arrest he was living in exile, having fled abroad to escape the terrible and bloody repression being inflicted upon Argentina. He had continued to engage in political activities from a distance. We must not forget that, from 1957 to 1983, being related to Che spelled danger.

While Celia was always politically active, she plunged head-long into the political arena at the time of the military dictator-ship, ignoring the risks. She married and divorced a few years later, and had no children. During the so-called 'years of lead', which began in 1974 – before the coup of 24 March 1976 – and extended until 1984, Roberto and Celia tried in vain to plead my cause, risking their lives to do so. The henchmen of the dictator-ship didn't hesitate to track down and eliminate 'subversives', wherever they might be.

Ana Maria was the most self-effacing of all of us. After mar-rying Fernando 'Littl'Un' Chaves, a university professor and PRT activist who also experienced political detention, she went to live in the provinces, first in Tucumán and then Jujuy. She was hard-headed, like Celia. She was also persistent: she contin-ued with her architectural studies while expecting her children. There was no question of her curbing her activities just because of her five pregnancies.

Some of us got along better with my mother, others with my father. There were two clans. On my mother's side: Ernesto and me. On my father's: Roberto and Ana Maria. With Celia, it depended on the time and the kind of conflict involved. The two Ernestos often quarrelled. The father reproached the son for his political views and his wanderings. The son reproached the father for his irresponsibility and his inconstancy. One example: in a letter sent to my mother from Bogotá in 1952,

Ernesto wrote: 'Let the *viejo* shake his feathers and head off to Venezuela; life is more expensive there than here, but the pay is better and so it's perfect for someone who looks after his money (!!!) the way he does . . . *Papi* is very intellistupid.' I guess my brother hated to see our mother unhappy. The infidelities of her husband and the precariousness of their situation had finally exhausted her. Their separation, decided on in Alta Gracia, became a reality in Buenos Aires. And yet no uncoupling could have been more ambiguous than this one.

At sixteen, Ernesto enrolled in the Faculty of Córdoba to study engineering and stay close to Chichina. He continued to see his friends Carlos 'Calico' Ferrer and the brothers Tómas and Alberto 'Mial' Granado. To support himself, he worked in the municipal road maintenance department, the Dirección Provincial de Vialidad. Meanwhile, my parents had decided to bring the family back to Buenos Aires. We first moved into my paternal grandmother's and, thanks to some money from a small inheritance my mother had finally obtained after family litigation, we bought a dilapidated house, 2180 calle Aráoz at the corner of calle Mansilla in the Palermo district. Today, Palermo is fashionable and middle class; at that time, this street corner marked a border. Between calle Mansilla and calle Santa Fe, you entered civilization. In the other direction, you were moving into the notorious suburbs, the flea markets and the cotton mills – an area of thugs.

Our house was an old stone building, beautiful but poorly maintained, with two storeys, a small four-room affair with a huge terrace and two large balconies. The ground floor was occupied by a garage, but we no longer had a car. You reached the first floor by a dark staircase, with some steps missing. In the early days, the front door was never locked because nobody knew where the key was. We finally found it, only to lose it again. This kind of practical detail didn't matter to us. How many times did I have to climb up the façade, clinging to the gutter to open the door! Passers-by and neighbours looked at me dumbfounded. My parents weren't bothered in the least. I realized then that, thanks to them, I was never ashamed of anything!

The interior of the house was a joke: a mixture of disorder and decay. The paint was peeling, the ceilings were dripping, floorboards were missing. Nobody ever repaired anything. One morning the water heater broke down. A few days later, the bathroom window was shattered, so that not only did we now wash in cold water but we had to bear the icy wind rushing into the room in winter. Taking a shower became an ordeal. The refrigerator handle came away in a visitor's hand one evening, and wasn't replaced. As a result, anyone who opened the fridge got an electric shock. This annoyance quickly turned into a joke. Visitors were sent to the kitchen to get something out of the fridge. We could hear them screaming. What a laugh! We had very little furniture and what we did have was terrible. The dining table was wobbly. It came with two benches. We regularly bickered about who would get the bench that stood against the wall, so that we could lean back in comfort.

However, as usual, we had a varied library that became rather well-known. Our friends came to use it. They claimed that our books opened their eyes and encouraged them to question the conservative views of their parents. My mother was a teacher: she advised them what to read and then talked with them, about politics, literature, history, philosophy and religion. As a result, she was very popular with the young people who regularly invaded her home. So many people came and went that she often didn't know who was in. 'Aráoz' was the people's house. Though she didn't cook, my mother was always ready to rustle up a salad and put a steak on the barbecue. Still, we often ate eggs and rice ... as we couldn't afford anything else. Our friends liked to repeat that our family was unique. And it was!

We didn't know where my father lived. He had bought a studio in the city centre, at 2014 calle Paraguay; he'd given the key to all our friends so they could go and study there in peace. But he sometimes slept at home. He also sometimes took his siesta there, either in the dining room or in a bunk bed in our room, the boys' room, always on the top bunk; he sometimes fell out of it. He was absent most of the time, and when he was there, I wondered what use he was to us.

My parents fought a lot. And when that happened, it was better to clear off. At this time, I was generally much more worried when they were together. My father was very bad sport. One day he was playing a game of chess in the Portela garden with my mother, and she was about to beat him. The idea of losing was absolutely unbearable to my father. Checkmate loomed. His bad mood was made apparent in exasperated sighs and frowns. Suddenly he jumped up, overturned the table and sent all the pieces on the board flying through the air. My mother flew into a rage. My father was indignant. 'What makes you think that I did it on purpose?' He never hesitated to cheat in order to win.

My grandmother Lynch suffered a brain haemorrhage. As soon as he heard the news, Ernesto left everything in Córdoba to return immediately to Buenos Aires. He did not leave her bedside. He tried to get her to eat and drink, he wiped her forehead with infinite patience. But it was all in vain: she died seventeen days later.

Ernesto moved into our room. It was cramped but led onto a large balcony. It was furnished with bunk beds, a wardrobe, a chest of drawers, two shelves and a table on which books were piled. Being the youngest, I was made to sleep on the shabby old couch in the dining room but I couldn't care less: Ernesto had returned, this time for good! My joy was immense. He enrolled in the faculty of medicine where he met his best friend, Berta Gilda 'Tita' Infante. They became inseparable and immediately began to share their literary, philosophical, political and medical discoveries. When life separated them, they maintained their relationship through a copious, intimate and magnificent correspondence, which lasted until the end. Tita is the author of the best text ever written about Che.[1]

Though he didn't excel in college, Ernesto got good grades. In particular, he was able to take an impressive number of courses. Was he an enthusiastic student? Surely not. One day, Ana Maria and her friend Olga found they were suffering from a condition that looked like eczema. Their legs were suddenly covered with red spots. Concerned, they asked Ernesto for his opinion. He replied, in a burst of laughter: 'What do *I* know? Go to the doctor's!' Olga was afraid of him. Or rather, she was very intimidated. He teased her constantly and she never knew what to say. Ernesto was a master of the clever and sometimes scathing retort. He was very witty and was particularly playful with girls. It amused him. In his presence, women seemed to lose their self-possession.

When he began to specialize in allergies under the aegis of Professor Pisani, a renowned specialist, he decided to use us as guinea pigs. We all refused. With him, you never knew what to expect! Indeed, when a friend finally agreed to help out with the experiments, Ernesto gave him several injections that made him sick. So our apprentice doctor fell back on a rabbit he had installed on the terrace, to father's chagrin. Ernesto didn't care. At that time, our father's opinions no longer interested anyone. He had lost any authority over us. The fact remains that the rabbit managed to escape by jumping from the terrace on to the street. The whole neighbourhood was in turmoil: our neighbours were convinced that Ernesto had injected the creature with a virus that would infect everyone.

Imitating my father, Ernesto divided his time between several homes: my mother's, my grandmother's, my aunt Beatriz's and the studio on calle Paraguay. We rarely knew where he was and nobody asked any questions. He appeared and disappeared. He needed quiet to study and our house was in permanent revolution. When there, he liked to sit on the balcony with a book. When he wasn't in the faculty of medicine or the Natural History Museum with Tita Infante, he occupied his free time in reading, writing, playing chess and trying to earn a few pennies. He was always in a hurry and never seemed to have enough time for anything. To earn money, he would get involved in the most scatter-brained schemes. The first was the manufacture of an insecticide he had concocted in the garage by mixing gammaxene with talc to obtain a cockroach poison that he called Vendaval, and patented. The powder was placed in small green round boxes that he sold in the neighbourhood. Father immediately offered to help by introducing him to friends of his who might invest. Ernesto's reply? 'Do you actually think I'll let myself get eaten alive by your friends?' My father's connections were all people in high places, politicians, captains of industry and landowners. Ernesto was already suspicious of such people. He had to stop manufacturing Vendaval after a few months: not only had his product not had the expected success, but the powder had drifted into everything and the smell was unbearable.

Ernesto's ideas were always fanciful. In that respect, he resembled my father. After the fiasco with Vendaval, he decided to buy a lot of shoes in a clearance sale, sell them and make a bit of money. Back home, he discovered that instead of selling him pairs of shoes, the guy had offloaded a hundred left shoes! He found himself with a whole heap of these shoes – and bravely wore some of them himself!

One of his greatest satisfactions in those days was that he managed to be exempted from military service. 'These shitty lungs have finally been of some use!' he concluded. Wearing a uniform? Not his kind of thing. He hated protocol (a word that, my parents laughingly said, he'd never even heard), he mocked the bourgeois, and continued to pay no attention to his clothes.

I was still a child but I already knew that my older brother was a unique character. I compared him with Roberto, who got along much better with father and behaved more as a worthy bourgeois son. He made less of a splash, frequented the sons and daughters of good families, and played in the San Isidro rugby team. At that time, rugby was a sport for gilded youth. As I've said, Ernesto was also part of this team before he stopped playing, despite the protests of my father. I later followed his example: I hated the elitist atmosphere.

I was hanging out a lot with all kinds of people, thugs and drop-outs. I felt comfortable with them. We played football, bound together by the intoxication that the freedom of the street gave us. I learned all about camaraderie, discretion and

silence – rules of conduct that would be very helpful to me
during my detention. Our worst enemies were the cops. On one
occasion, I ended up at the police station for a petty crime. The
neighbourhood was full of thugs. We knew of their activities
but nobody ever dreamt of reporting them or even commenting
on their misdeeds. In their presence, I had to limit my vocabu-
lary, at least if I wanted to continue to be accepted by my gang.
I was accused of speaking like a grown-up, of being mature for
my age, and expressing myself very well, which all contrasted
with my small size. I owed my maturity to Ernesto. Since childhood, he had advised me on what to read, explained things to
me, talked to me about politics as an equal. I was inevitably
influenced by his erudition. He also taught me reams of saucy
poetry, which I eagerly repeated to the girl friends of my sisters.
They were deeply shocked. I told Ernesto: he burst out laughing. Ernesto had a deep sense of self-criticism. He had no mercy
for himself, never forgave himself, never showed himself any
indulgence. His rigidity and integrity would later give him the
right to be demanding with others. But not everyone wanted to
submit to his discipline. He was both reasonable and inflexible.
For him, time was divided into a little fun and a lot of work.
He never stopped; he was always thinking about the next step,
his future projects. He was a machine! In Cuba, while serving
as minister of industry and working twelve or fourteen hours
a day, he also cut sugarcane as part of the voluntary work programme he had set up.

A major event occurred when I was in high school. Others
may have thought it of only relative importance, but for me,
raised as I had been in a hyper-politicized atheist environment,
it was a disaster. This was the attempt to introduce exemptions
from law 1420 on free, public, secular education – an attempt to

reintroduce religion into schools. I began to militate against this with a group of students. This was my first face-to-face encounter with repression and civil rights. I became one of the founders of the Student Centre. My activism dates back to this time.

My mother supported me. She was the other person who had shaped my personality. If I spent so much time out on the streets, it's because I was as free as a bird and she was tired of raising children. I was seven years old when she suffered a second bout of cancer – she had the first one right after my birth – and had both breasts removed. My father was largely absent during the event. He was suspected of having a new mistress. Ernesto, however, was very much present. My mother had always been his rock. He studied her illness intently and anxiously: he wanted to be able to heal her, to find cures.

With father, his relationship had become really difficult: something of a battle. As soon as they had a chance, they started fighting. My father began to fret about this son with his cut-and-dried opinions. He had now lost all influence over him. Ernesto was impossible to control, and expressed his desire to take a break from his medical studies to go on a trip. He dreamed of adventures. However politicized he was, when our cousin Guillermo Moore de la Serna asked him to join the anti-Peronist movement for which he was campaigning, Ernesto replied, 'No, no, I'm not interested.' He thought he could quench his thirst for distant horizons by getting hired for the summer as a male nurse on a tanker owned by the national oil company YPF. A tanker, just imagine! My parents were not best pleased, but, as their philosophy dictated, they didn't intervene. In Córdoba a few years earlier, when they were about fourteen and eleven respectively, Ernesto and Roberto decided one morning to go and help with the harvest. The vineyards were far away. They took the bus then walked kilometres to reach their destination. My parents were worried about the plan, but they had let the boys go ahead. My brothers returned after a few days, as sick as dogs: they had eaten too many grapes. At the time this fruit was a luxury treat.

The experience on the oil tanker was a bitter disappointment to Ernesto. Instead of seeing the world, he had just gazed at the hold of a ship for several months. Maritime shipping had the effect of convincing him that, from now on, he would confine his roaming to dry land.

6

'The American country with the best food'

I have often been asked how I felt when Ernesto headed off. A better question would be: what did I feel when he came back, as he was forever coming and going? When he reappeared, it was party time. In the family, everyone started yelling: 'Hey, listen, Ernesto's back, Ernesto's home!' We phoned everyone to let them know. Everyone wanted to see him and hear his voice: my parents, my brothers and sisters, my uncles, aunts and cousins.

I was still very young, but I have a very clear memory of the hubbub caused by his departure on 1 December 1950, the first of many that would take him further and further from Argentina. He was twenty-one years old and heading off on a long journey armed with a bicycle and his meagre savings. He had refused any financial help from my parents: he wanted to stay independent.

My uncle Jorge de la Serna had installed a small Micrón engine on Ernesto's bike. Before he started pedalling, he posed for a photo in front of the house, a beret on his head, sunglasses perched on his nose, a spare wheel hooked over his shoulder, and a bundle of things on the pannier. We were all out in the street watching as he disappeared down its tree-lined vista. His goal was to travel through northern Argentina without any specific destination, keeping going for as long as his strength would allow. He hoped to visit San Juan, San Luis, Mendoza, Salta, Jujuy and Tucumán. Some of these provinces were still underdeveloped. If Buenos Aires was a sophisticated city, the north of the country was exotic, and magnificently backward. Today, *el Norte* is very fashionable. At the time, it was another world, neglected and ignored. It reminded the citizens of the capital that Argentina, far from being European, was South American.

Northern landscapes were – and still are – spectacular and disorienting. Green, mountainous Tucumán was considered to be the garden of the republic. The extensive wine valleys of Mendoza went on forever in the shadow of the towering Andes and their snow-capped peaks. Salta was famous for its gigantic cactuses, its crimson rocks, its hills undulating like waves and its white colonial cities. Jujuy was Andean, very similar to Bolivia with its beautiful adobe villages built under the famous Quebrada de Humahuaca, a mountain range striated in seven colours.

Ernesto made a first stop in Alta Gracia, at the home of Tómas Granado. In San Francisco del Chañar, he visited his friend Alberto 'Mial', a biochemist who worked in a leper colony. There Ernesto was confronted by abject poverty for the first time. He was profoundly disturbed.

In a few months, he crossed twelve provinces and covered some 4,500 kilometres. He had some unforgettable adventures. On the way, he made the acquaintance of the Aymara Indian populations, sharing their dwellings and their meagre pittance. He learned to spend freezing nights in the open and to go for days without food. He coped with his asthma alone and proved to the sceptics – and perhaps to himself – that he was able to complete such a substantial trip.

Meanwhile, in Buenos Aires, my parents were moping about: there was little news from Ernesto, and because of his asthma and his taste for risk they imagined that he would get into some real scrapes. He had never been this far by himself. He was left to his own devices in areas where he knew no one. Yet the Tucumán local newspaper, *El Tropico*, published the very first article about him, a paragraph with the headline 'Guevara, un joven raidista cumplirá una extensa gira' ('Guevara, a young globe-trotter, sets off on a big trip'). One way or another, Ernesto had managed to get noticed in Tucumán – though the news did not reach us. At that time, the circulation of local newspapers was limited to the area where they were published.

Ernesto returned safe and sound after three months. It was party time again. He had so many stories to tell! He had changed, perhaps grown darker. We had no idea at the time that the anxiety caused by this first adventure was merely the prelude to a series of future worries for the family. Ernesto would never stop travelling. Far from satiating his thirst for travel, this expedition had given him wings. In his diary he wrote: 'I have just realized that this thing that had been growing in my city-slicker's heart has matured: it's a hatred of civilization, the coarse image of a crowd moving like some crazed woman to the rhythm of this terrible noise; I think it is the complete opposite of peace.'

He had more or less completed his journey pedalling his bike along, as the Micrón engine had finally given up the ghost. He took it to the dealer in Buenos Aires for repair. Amazed at the distance he'd covered, the dealer offered to give him a new engine if he would sing the praises of the Micrón in an advertisement. This was the second time that Ernesto's photo had appeared in a newspaper.

So the family was together again. Well, almost. My father came and went as and when he wanted. Roberto was studying at the faculty of law; Celia was doing a course in architecture; Ana Maria was in high school and I was in junior school. I didn't bother much about schoolwork; already, I'd decided it wasn't my thing. I was an anomaly. I preferred to learn out on the streets, playing football. Ernesto was concerned about my lack of school spirit. He was forever telling me off. 'You have to work, study, learn', he kept telling me.

He had resumed his course at the medical school and often slept at aunt Beatriz's; she kept a jealous eye on him. When he came home, he was usually accompanied by a friend: the two of them would settle down in his room to study. My mother had hired a Bolivian woman as a maid, Sabina Portugal (this wasn't her real name, which was too complicated to pronounce, and like many Indians from the Altiplano, she'd invented a Spanish name for herself). Sabina belonged to the Aymara tribe. She was a typical woman of the Bolivian Altiplano: very austere, very self-effacing, she fulfilled her duties with zeal but in silence. She spoke little Spanish, and her mother tongue was Quechua. Yet Ernesto managed to understand her without any problems. He liked nothing better than to spend long periods of time with her; he was curious about her life, her origins, her people. He asked her lots of questions and she answered with good grace. It was extremely rare for Argentinians of our social class to be so interested in a person's background. She was at first taken aback by this, but Ernesto had soon become the only person she could express herself freely to. They even became accomplices. He could return home at any time, and she would cook his favourite meals for him. Ernesto was neither arrogant nor smug. Although he was highly educated and cultured, he did not pretend to understand the mysteries of the universe any better than this simple maid. Instead, he felt that he had a lot to learn from her. Indeed, Sabina taught him many things. In retrospect, I came to understand her influence on him, as thoughts of revolution started to germinate within him. She was the person who made him decide he wanted to visit Bolivia.

While he worked hard for his exams, Ernesto really had only one idea in mind: to decamp. In a single school year, he polished off an impressive number of subjects. He told us he was heading off on a second trip. This time he planned to leave with his friend Alberto Granado on a journey of eight months. When my father expressed surprise that he was prepared to leave the beautiful Chichina for such a long time, Ernesto said: 'She'll wait for me if she loves me.' Moreover, the first leg of the journey was to be to Miramar, a seaside resort on the Atlantic coast where the Ferreyra family had a residence. There he would say goodbye to her, at least – so he thought – for the time being.

From Miramar, Ernesto and Mial would then cross the country from east to west, heading for Patagonia; they would then cross the Andes to reach Chile, Peru, Ecuador, etc. The route was not finalized. Everything depended on their means of locomotion, La Poderosa II, an old 500cc motorbike. They hoped that it would get them all the way to the United States. My uncle Jorge de la Serna had tinkered with the machinery to try and get it back into good shape. He was an excellent mechanic. Ernesto had also received financial support from my uncle Ernesto 'El Pato' Moore (the husband of Edelmira de la Serna and father of our cousin Guillermo, at whose home my parents had got married) who had delved deep into his savings for the occasion. As I said before, Ernesto was very popular. Adventurous spirits in the family, and there were a few of these, seemed to recognize themselves in him. But history would prove that he was crazier, and more daring, determined and idealistic, than any of them.

Ernesto and Alberto left Córdoba to the sound of their sputtering motorbike one morning in January 1952. We had seen Ernesto off a few days earlier. I was eight. For me, this motorcycle journey sounded fabulous. I wondered how they were going to make it to the United States, that faraway country where our grandmother had been born. It reminded me of the adventures of Mancha and Gato as related by Aimé Tschiffely, that Ernesto had recommended I read. The book tells the story of two horses who leave Buenos Aires for Washington with their owner, the Swiss professor Tschiffely, who has undertaken this crazy journey to prove that Argentinian horses are sturdier than others. In the book, the two animals eclipse the rider: the story is told from their perspective. Gato dies en route but Mancha reaches their destination. Ernesto must also have been thinking about these horses when he decided to push on all the way to the United States.

My parents had begged Mial to look after their son and stop him getting into any danger. As far as they were concerned, this whole new journey was rather pointless. They clung to the idea that Mial could curb their son's follies, if necessary. He was six years older than Ernesto. The irony, of course, was that as the journey unfolded, Ernesto became the master and Mial the disciple. Ernesto had finally become the leader and guide. As for stopping him from doing anything at all, it was simply impossible. When he decided, for example, to swim across the Amazon River, Alberto couldn't hold him back. 'You're stark raving mad. The river is full of piranhas! They'll eat you alive!' he said in an attempt to dissuade him. Ernesto turned a deaf ear, dived in and swam to the other bank. 'I vowed to myself that I was going to do it. I had to respect my promise', he then told the dumbfounded Alberto.

My mother was sad and my father furious. He couldn't understand why Ernesto had decided to abandon his studies, although he had promised to complete them on his return. No doubt my father didn't believe Ernesto's promise because of his own history. Besides, what had he ever done to demand the constancy of his children? He only ever dropped in briefly at home, even though he still behaved like the master of the house while there. My mother and he continued to quarrel and I would run out into the street so I wouldn't have to listen. Their arguments were fierce. My father was living with another woman without acknowledging the fact. My mother suffered from the separation. She would suffer even more when Roberto and my sisters left home in turn. As usual, our finances were at rock bottom. I don't remember much about my father's professional activities at that time. It is clear, however, that he wasn't earning any money, or not enough, or that he was spending it elsewhere. Anyway, my mother was having a very hard time of it. She was soon forced to find work. She, who had such modest tastes, first found a job in the jewellery store in Alvear, one of the finest hotels in Buenos Aires, then in a bookshop that also served as a florist's. She also did translations into English and French. She never complained and tried as usual to see the positive side of things. Still, she was sinking into a deep depression. Her legendary buoyant mood and political commitment had declined. She was worn out. Her double mastectomy, the infidelities of her husband, and the absence of her beloved son were more than she could bear. The only thing that brought her any comfort was Ernesto's letters. They were sporadic; he apologized for this, but he didn't have the money to buy stamps. Sometimes he didn't even have enough to eat.

I'm not going to narrate the journey Ernesto and Granado undertook. My brother kept a diary, published as *The Motorcycle Diaries*, adapted for the screen by Walter Salles and starring Gael García Bernal and Rodrigo de la Serna – a distant cousin – in the lead roles. What I can say, however, is that over the months, we noticed a change in his correspondence. Gradually, as he continued on his journey, he was transformed. The tone became more thoughtful, more serious, less touristy, more engaged in reality and the social problems he was discovering along the way. He talked more and more about politics and embarked on economic analyses.

At the end of the trip, he separated from Mial, who had decided to stay on to work in a leper colony in Venezuela. Ernesto returned to Argentina to finish his studies as promised. He had only one word to say: he left Mial assuring him that he would be back soon. In Caracas, he took a plane chartered by our uncle Marcelo Guevara to transport racehorses. The flight had a stopover scheduled for an indefinite period in Miami. Ernesto found himself stuck there for two weeks, stony broke. We never learned all the details of his forced vacation in Florida. He later said he had spent 'the worst weeks of his life' there. We speculated that the racial segregation had scandalized him. The American civil rights movement was only just emerging.

Among other iniquities, we need to remember that blacks were not allowed to sit in buses. Ernesto must have been deeply shocked.

His return was a new opportunity to celebrate. My mother seemed to regain some of her strength and spirit. Her son's presence was enough to make her happy. Ernesto resumed his classes in the faculty of medicine. He still had fifteen subjects to tackle. It was a lot for one academic year, but he was determined to finish once and for all with his studies. We thought this would be impossible, especially after an interval of eight months. People forgot that Ernesto had learned while still very young to study intermittently. He had developed a method. He read at a furious speed. He worked without seeking to go too deeply into what he learned. He wanted the diploma that would buy his freedom.

One day he telephoned us from my aunt Beatriz's house and announced: 'Call me doctor'. He had won his incredible bet. Proud as a peacock, my father told everybody that even if Ernesto was not the best student in the medical school, he had still broken all records for the speed with which he was graduating.

Ernesto, however, had no intention of practising medicine, at least not at that time, even if Professor Pisani had offered him a position in his laboratory. Any other young practitioner would have been flattered to be offered such a place. Ernesto had other plans. He wanted to leave.

On the evening of 7 July 1953, the house was full of guests. Once again, we were seeing Ernesto off. But this time, he was leaving without any guarantee that he would return. There was nothing to keep him in Buenos Aires any longer. Chichina had refused his second marriage proposal and they had split up. Mial was still in Venezuela. Ernesto's plan was to make his way over to join him, at a relaxed pace.

He left with his friend Calico Ferrer. First stop: the Bolivia which Sabina Portugal had told him so much about. His goal: to become familiar with the Aymara people and the miners whose conditions of life and work were notoriously inhumane. The miners were the only unionized workers in Bolivia. Ernesto wanted to understand, or rather observe, their struggles. But on the evening of 7 July, he wasn't thinking about this. He was enjoying his last few hours with his family. There was music to dance to, with laughter filling the house. Ernesto jigged around without harmony or grace.

My mother had made a suit for him. Now that he was offi-cially a doctor, he would surely need a suit for job interviews. She had made it with all the love she felt for Ernesto. Though she wasn't much of a housewife, she could still sew and was particularly proud of her work. Unfortunately, a few months later, Ernesto wrote from Guayaquil (Ecuador) to announce the sad news: 'I'm sorry to tell you that your work of art, the apple of your eye, died heroically in a jumble sale.' He'd sold the suit as he needed the money and had to shed excess baggage.

The final departure took place on 8 July, on a platform in the Retiro General Belgrano station. He was heading off yet again, and my mother's heart was broken. Now that he no longer had any time limit or obligation, what would he get up to, this vagabond, this rebellious son, so far away from her protection? But she put a brave face on it as she wasn't the kind of mother to make her children feel guilty. The whole family was on the platform. When the train started, Ernesto laughingly uttered a premonitory sentence that would assume its full meaning only later: 'Aquí va un soldado de América' ('Here goes an American soldier'), while my parents ran along the platform like in the films.

Ernesto never returned from this adventure that took him to the Sierra Maestra in Cuba, via Bolivia, Peru, Ecuador, Colombia, Panama, Costa Rica, Nicaragua, Honduras, El Salvador, Guatemala and Mexico. I won't go into any more detail about this trip. For one thing, I wasn't there. For another, his correspondence from that time has been published. But I can talk about the effect his absence had on his relatives.

Ernesto sent us letters, some addressed to the whole family, others to one person. Everything depended on the odd jobs he picked up en route and whether he had enough money to buy stamps.

Whether he wrote to us personally or not, the result was the same. Each letter was an event around which the whole family gathered. Everyone's efforts were required: his handwriting was illegible and sometimes took hours to decipher. One of us, usually my father or my mother, read the letter aloud and stumbled constantly over the words, trying to divine their meaning. Telephone communications were out of the question because of the cost. Also, putting through a long distance call was a challenge in any Latin American country. For this reason, we went for years without hearing Ernesto's voice.

His letters were a clever mix of humour, irony, questions about the family, and discussions of economic, historical and philosophical matters. As he got to know first-hand the countries he was travelling through and the poor people he met in them, his political awareness grew and his outrage at injustice exploded. You could sense the transformation, how his humanistic concerns developed. He saw how the weak were exploited by the powerful: he became a communist.

In Bolivia, he discovered the miserable fate of the miners, the abominable way they were treated, the bloody repression they suffered if they rebelled. In Peru, he saw the indigenous peoples struggling to survive, deprived of the most basic human rights. And so on. Each country was an example of the ruthless domination exercised by the American empire. In this regard, he refused – and I do the same – to call the United States 'America'. America, he said, is the whole continent. All the peoples in the continent are American.

His contempt for the United States and his revolt against its empire continued to grow. He attacked my father who had always defended the homeland of his mother. He wrote harsh, serious-minded postcards to him, in which he cited his 'friends the Yankees'. He treated my mother and my aunt Beatriz slightly more gently, resorting to irony: he accused them of belonging to the class of oppressors, even if it wasn't their fault. However, in a letter dated May 1959 sent to the director of the Cuban magazine *Bohemia*, he said: 'I am not a communist either.'

A few months after his departure he wrote to Beatriz: 'Despite my wanderings, my endemic frivolity, and other defects, I have deep and well-defined convictions.' He added, with the customary humour with which he seasoned even his more serious remarks: 'Stop sending me money, it costs you a fortune, while I only have to bend down to pick up all the banknotes that litter the ground hereabouts, there are so many that I've gone down with lumbago. In fact I only bend down 10 per cent of the time, to maintain public hygiene, because so many pieces of paper fluttering about and lying all over the ground represent a public danger.' In April 1954, he wrote to my mother: 'America will be the scene of my adventures and will play a much more important role for me than I had originally thought. I reckon I have finally understood it, and I feel I am a member of the American people, a people who have different characteristics from any other people on Earth.' It became increasingly clear to us that he wanted to be taken seriously, that his commitment was maturing. At the same time, he continued to wander about without any specific mission. He was seeking an outlet, a cause that would impel him to commit himself fully, to devote his life to it. Meanwhile, he made a decision: to extend his wandering for ten years or so. One of his greatest dreams was to visit Paris: 'It's a biological necessity, an objective I can't possibly abandon, even if I have to swim the Atlantic to get there', he wrote to us in 1955.

With Ernesto's long absence my mother's depression returned. She had stopped working and spent her days in a dressing-gown playing solitaire and chain smoking. It was a dark period. My siblings had left home. Now I was the only one still living with her. I spent more and more time out on the street. At the time, our district, although in the city centre, was almost rural. The milkman sold his products from a horse and cart. My father continued to drop by regularly. Ernesto sent more letters to my mother than to him, so he came to read them at home. I was juggling with several lives. My existence was compartmentalized. I moved from the company of street urchins to that of the great Argentinian families. My father insisted that I go with him when he was making official visits to his powerful friends. Perhaps he imagined that rubbing shoulders with these people would make me want to get an education and have a successful career. We often went, for example, to visit the family of José

Alfredo Martínez de Hoz, later the minister of the economy under Jorge Videla during the military dictatorship. Given the way my father frequented such unsavoury characters, it was not surprising that Ernesto mocked him!

The political situation in Argentina was unstable. Juan Perón was in power for a second term. His wife, the highly popular Evita, died in 1952. The country was deeply divided and rocked by a series of deadly attacks. The misunderstanding between left-wing Peronism and 'orthodox' right-wing Peronism intensified. On 15 April 1953, a terrorist group comprising privileged young students and anti-Peronist professionals placed a bomb on the central Plaza de Mayo, killing seven people and injuring dozens while Perón was giving a speech from the balcony of the Casa Rosada, the presidential palace. His supporters responded by setting fire to the headquarters of the Socialist Party, the Radical Party and the elegant Jockey Club.

In the face of this chaos, the armed forces were growing impatient. Perón had also set the Catholic Church against him by trying to abolish religious education in schools and proposing that divorce be legalized.

My father was a devout anti-Peronist. At that time, I was only ten years old and I was torn between his reactionary, anti-working-class views and the outlook of humbler, more working-class families, including those of my friends in the neighbourhood. I have since moved on. With what I know now, my vision has changed. I consider Peronism (beyond and independently of Perón) as a very important movement, of enormous and complex significance for our country.

The fact remains that, like any Argentinian, my father had internalized the eternal political violence of our country, a violence both verbal and physical. He never went out unless he was armed; he was convinced that we were heading for a military coup. My mother harboured the same fear. Fiercely anti-militarist, she explained that the army had always supported the reactionary right. She had thought a great deal about the role of the armed forces in America: was it defensive or offensive? On 16 June 1955, we obtained an answer that, alas, could not have been any clearer. Having interpreted a statement the Vatican had made about him as an excommunication, Perón called for a supporters' rally on the Plaza de Mayo. When the crowd had gathered, the navy sent several planes flying in low to bomb the square. Three hundred and sixty-four people died and hundreds more were injured. Perón's days seemed numbered. The military had had enough. Perón fled on 16 September and went to Spain via Paraguay.

At the time of these fateful events, Ernesto was in Mexico. He had arrived in September 1954 in the company of a Peruvian woman seven years older than him; he'd met her a year before, in Guatemala. Her name was Hilda Gadea, and she was a woman 'with a platinum heart, to put it mildly', as he had written to tell us. Hilda, a political refugee, was an exceptional person: she was the first woman to head the finances of the Executive Committee of the Alianza Popular Revolucionaria Americana (APRA – American Popular Revolutionary Alliance). Mexico was at that time a safe refuge for exiles driven from their country by political repression.

Ernesto moved into a small apartment with Hilda. He first made his living as a photographer in a news agency. Then he became an allergy specialist in a public hospital. His commitment had hardened after eight months in Guatemala. His letters were now more aggressive, angrier than before. In Costa Rica, he had passed through the territories dominated by the United

Fruit banana company which, more than any other, personified Yankee imperialism. He told us he had 'crossed regions where countries are not true nations, but private ranches – or plantations'. The barbaric methods used by the multinational company to maintain its hegemony in Central America had finally put him off capitalism for good. On 10 December 1953, he wrote to aunt Beatriz: 'I have had an opportunity to go through the land owned by United Fruit, and this has once again convinced me of the vileness of these capitalist octopuses. I have sworn before a portrait of old, tearful Comrade Stalin not to rest until these capitalist octopuses have been annihilated. I will better myself in Guatemala and become a true revolutionary.'

The United Fruit Company was at the time a fierce repressive machine that kept its employees in bondage and governments in subjection with the help of the CIA. Passing through Costa Rica had marked a turning point in Ernesto's life and, by extension, our own. From that moment on, the existence of every Guevara would be influenced by Ernesto's political activities.

When he arrived in Guatemala in January 1954, this small Central American country was a young democracy ruled by the son of a Swiss pharmacist, Jacobo Arbenz Guzmán. Though he was a professional soldier, Arbenz was a socialist. He had participated in the overthrow of the dictator Jorge Ubico, and had first become defence minister before being elected president in 1951. His election was the first election by universal suffrage in the history of Guatemala.

The Arbenz government immediately distinguished itself with a series of progressive reforms. It supported voting rights for all, and labour legislation. It enacted agrarian reform that consisted of seizing uncultivated land for redistribution to peasants. The largest landowner in the country, the United Fruit Company, was very hostile to these reforms. It was not long before the US Secretary of State John Foster Dulles – who was also a shareholder in United Fruit – started making threatening remarks at a conference where several foreign ministers were gathered. 'Communists!' he bellowed, in reference to the Arbenz government. It was the signal to let slip the dogs of war.

United Fruit, the US State Department and the CIA plotted an invasion. Guatemala was isolated, abandoned by its neighbours. As the storm brewed, Ernesto and Hilda were visiting the Mayan ruins of Petén. They became aware of events only on their return to Guatemala City. Initially, Ernesto did not believe in the US invasion. And if there *was* an invasion, he was convinced that the president would resist. But Arbenz's attempt to buy weapons from Western Europe had failed. He had met with a flat refusal and been forced to turn to Czechoslovakia. As the boats bringing Czech-made weapons approached the coast of Guatemala, they were seized by the Americans, who now had an excellent excuse to declare Guatemala 'an ally of the Soviet Union' – whereupon US bombs rained down on the capital. Ernesto's optimism turned into revolt. He immediately went into action out on the streets. He tried to organize resistance in various groups: trade unionists, political parties, etc. He told Hilda he had a 'fool-proof plan': he would 'seize strategic points in the city, take possession of communications, and ambush those trying to enter'.[1] This was the first time he attracted the attention of the US services, who opened a file on him.

In Buenos Aires, my parents were worried. They were following events closely, convinced that Ernesto had taken part in the fighting. The tone of his last letters left no doubt about his desire to do battle with the authorities. On 10 May 1954, he sent us a letter saying, 'I could become very rich in Guatemala, but this would involve going through the laborious process of validating my degree, and opening a clinic to devote myself to allergies . . . To do this would be the most horrible betrayal of the two selves engaged in battle within me, the socialist and the traveller.'

We had no more news from him for several weeks (in his last letter, he had sent me some stamps and encouraged me to eat meat from Argentina: 'Little brother, make the most of being in the American country with the best food'). My parents felt that from now on their eldest son would become a constant concern. My mother not only combed the press looking for the least little report on the situation in Guatemala, but also read up on its literature, its history, in short, everything related to the country. She wanted to know everything, understand everything. What perils was Ernesto running?

Quite real dangers, in fact: enough for the Argentinian attaché d'affaires in Guatemala City, one Nicasio Sánchez Toranzo, to set off in a desperate search for this Ernesto Guevara in the streets of Guatemala City so as to warn him of the danger hanging over him. He had heard the name of this compatriot of his by one of those happy accidents that sometimes save lives. He ran around looking for him everywhere: the trade union headquarters, the bars, the student centres. When he finally found him, he spoke bluntly: 'Leave immediately. They intend to kill you', he told Ernesto. 'Who and why?' asked my brother, who couldn't believe what he was hearing. 'Don't take offence, but you need to be aware that the US embassy is aware of your every move. You're a marked man. All you can do now is save yourself. I've come to warn you.' Ernesto was dumbfounded: 'I didn't know I was so important! But I don't think this is the end of the story. If my plan works . . .'

None of the plans worked. Surrounded and crushed by the

US strike force, Jacobo Arbenz resigned on 27 June and fled to Mexico. Ernesto was terribly disappointed. He hid for a few days before finding refuge in the Argentinian embassy. He was offered repatriation. He chose to go to Mexico.

Discover the world or change it

Ernesto had been in Mexico for ten months. He seemed to like it. 'The country of the backhander has received me with all the indifference of a large animal, neither stroking me nor baring its teeth at me', he had written to aunt Beatriz on his arrival in the country of Pancho Villa. He had established regular contact with Ulyses Petit de Murat, a poet and scriptwriter who was a close friend of my father, and this allowed my parents to occasionally receive indirect news of their son.

Ernesto's letters betrayed a certain discomfort. He seemed torn between two contradictory impulses: to engage in struggle, or to continue wandering. In October 1954, in response to his parents who were begging him to go back to Argentina to resume his medical career, he wrote to my mother (whom he called affectionately 'my mother, my little mother'): 'at bottom (and on the surface), I'm an incorrigible vagabond and I have no desire to see *that* career interrupted by a sedentary discipline. My faith in the ultimate triumph of what I believe in is total; however, I don't yet know if I will be an actor in it, or a mere spectator interested in the action. The note of bitterness some of you seem to have detected in my letters undoubtedly stems from this situation; the truth is that my vagrancy always gets in the way of everything, and I can't bring myself to end it.' This tension obviously raised a moral issue for him, as confirmed by the letter he sent to his friend Tita Infante in November 1954: 'it would be hypocritical to set myself up as an example: the only thing I can boast of is that I have fled from everything that held me back, and now, even as I am about to engage in the fight (especially on the social level), I am quietly continuing with my travels as events dictate, without envisaging bringing the war into Argentina. I have to confess that this is my main headache, as I'm caught in a terrible dilemma between chastity (here) and desire (wandering, especially around Europe) and I see that I'm willing to prostitute myself completely shamelessly whenever the opportunity arises.'

As I've already said, Ernesto had an exemplary capacity for self-criticism. He was able to analyse his smallest faults, weaknesses and acts with amazing lucidity. Seeking an outlet for his ideals, he was eager to locate and do battle with all the imperialist exploiters and torturers in the whole world. Or, for starters, in America. To discover the world or change it, to live his life or sacrifice it, these were the fundamental questions that tormented him. At this time, they might have seemed grandiloquent, perhaps even extravagant. Given what he later accomplished, they make complete sense. Ernesto died for his ideas. It's as simple as that.

This inner conflict, which left him no respite, found a definitive resolution: Ernesto met Raúl Castro, the younger brother of Fidel. He owed this meeting to Hilda Gadea. Ernesto's partner moved with ease in circles of political exiles. Ernesto and she regularly attended meetings and events organized by the political leaders of Peru, Guatemala, Argentina and . . . Cuba. Raúl and Ernesto were, after their first meeting, inseparable.

On 26 July 1953, the Castro brothers attacked the Moncada barracks in Santiago de Cuba.[1] The assault, aimed at destabilizing the dictatorship, ended in dismal failure. The members of the rebel group were summarily executed or arrested by Batista's troops. During his trial, Fidel conducted his own defence. He was a lawyer, and what a lawyer! His fervent and magnificent appeal on behalf of the oppressed Cuban people, entitled *History will absolve me*, lasted three hours. It so moved the whole country that in May 1955, under popular pressure, Batista ended by granting Fidel an amnesty in exchange for the promise – which he obviously had no intention of keeping – that he wouldn't do it again. After his release, Fidel went to Mexico with the goal of eventually returning to Cuba. He reconstituted his rebel group, which he called the 26th of July Movement.

Ernesto met Fidel for the first time on the evening of 7 July 1955 at the home of a girl friend of Hilda's, a certain Maria Antonia. It was the Devil's own luck that these two exceptional men should meet just when they needed each other! They took to each other immediately and spent the whole night talking. Ernesto was totally seduced. As for Fidel, it took only a few hours for him to recognize the value and potential of Ernesto. 'I need this guy', he must have said to himself – and he offered to make him the field doctor of his movement. By dawn, Ernesto had enlisted. No more procrastination or dilemmas. He had at last found his vocation. I believe he accepted the post as doctor *faute de mieux*. His last trip had led him to one conclusion: medicine was not enough to heal the wounds of humanity.

He had no military training, however, since he had been exempted from military service in Argentina. His medical degree would at least be his passport to guerrilla life. Training began a few weeks later under the command of a sixty-three-year-old Cuban colonel, Alberto Bayo. Raised in Spain, Bayo had trained the Republican troops in the Spanish Civil War. To prepare their eighty-two men for guerrilla warfare without attracting attention, Castro and Bayo chose a *hacienda* in the mountainous Chalco area, about thirty kilometres from the Mexican capital. The vast ranch was owned by an old friend of Pancho Villa. Combining theory and practice, the training lasted three months, after which Bayo declared Ernesto to be the most promising pupil in the contingent. He was impressed by his intelligence, discipline, determination, courage, great culture and camaraderie.

In the mountains, Ernesto had become Che; as we said earlier, he was given this name by his companions because of his habit of adding *che* to all his sentences, like the worthy Argentinian he was. The name didn't bother him; on the contrary, he liked to be reminded of his roots. Che and the drink of *mate* were his two 'Argentinisms'. *Che* had another meaning, too: it came from *Mapuche*, which means 'people of the land' and refers to the indigenous peoples of southern Chile and south-west Argentina.

Ernesto had told us nothing of his new activities. But he still regularly wrote to us. I remember in particular a letter received in October 1955, after Perón had gone into exile, because of the way my father reacted to it. Ernesto deplored the events, not because he was a Peronist but because he thought that Perón had at least the advantage that he opposed the Yankee imperialists and was a lesser evil compared to the military. Anyway, my anti-Peronist father stormed over to calle Aráoz waving

Ernesto's letter in the air. 'Just listen to what he writes!' he shouted.

The tone of Ernesto's letters had changed. He still wielded humour and derision and asked for news of everyone. But though he alluded to his plans, he did not openly discuss them. He gave us clues but was hazy about details. He mentioned his 'Cuban friends' and his articles in a medical journal; his 'itinerant house' and the impending birth of his first child, his daughter Hilda Beatriz; his second ascent of the highest peak of Mexico, the volcano Popocatépetl (5,426 metres – 'I have stormed Popo', he wrote to tell us), and his scientific work. My father complained of the enigmatic, riddling nature of his missives. We had to decipher not only his handwriting but the actual meaning of his words! Only much later did we realize that the dangerous climb, from which he had returned with frozen feet and his face inflamed, was actually one of the military training exercises imposed by Colonel Alberto Bayo. You needed to be in excellent physical condition to trudge through Cuba's Sierra Maestra.

On the other hand, he told us that, having one day 'overdone the tequila' and been led into 'a gesture of absurd chivalry', he had asked Hilda to marry him.[2] He also mentioned his forthcoming participation in a medical congress in Venezuela. He was about to become a father and seemed to be taking his job seriously. Perhaps he would finally let his 'itinerant house' put down roots. Preferably in Argentina with his family. My parents, however, remained concerned. No doubt their instincts warned them . . .

We were informed of his detention in the Miguel Schultz prison for immigrants during the summer of 1956. The Cuban cell of the 26th of July Movement had been uncovered by federal leaders in Mexican Security. It was clear to them that the group was preparing to strike in Cuba. In a letter dated April 1956, Ernesto had indeed talked about his growing interest in 'the doctrine of San Carlos' (Karl Marx), 'far more interesting than the study of physiology'. But from this to ending up in jail! For a long time, we had no news; my anxious father had moved heaven and earth to find out what had happened to his son. His cousin, retired admiral Raúl Lynch, was the Argentinian ambassador to Cuba. He could use diplomatic channels to find out. In Mexico, there were Ulyses Petit de Murat and the Argentinian ambassador Fernando Lezica, who was the uncle of my brother Roberto's wife. My father had asked all these people to obtain reliable information. Thus it was that we learned of the existence of Fidel Castro.

Ernesto could finally open up and tell us the truth. In a letter to the family, he spoke of Fidel for the first time: 'Fidel is a young Cuban leader who asked me to join his movement a while ago, a good while ago.' We were informed by third parties that, of all the members of the Cuban group who had been arrested, Ernesto had proved the most insolent. He was the only one who proudly brandished his Marxism-Leninism. He had concluded his letter by saying, 'I will triumph with it [the Cuban revolution] or I will die in the attempt. If, for some reason that I cannot foresee, I am unable to write again, and if later on my luck deserts me, consider these lines as a farewell more sincere than grandiloquent. From now on, I will not consider my death as any kind of frustration.'

Filled with alarm, and knowing just what her son was like, my mother began to devour everything she could read on this Fidel Castro she had never heard of. She wanted to know into whose arms Ernesto had thrown himself. What she read did not reassure her. Quite the contrary. The profound and daily anxieties of my parents now became entrenched. My father tried to involve his acquaintances, asking them to visit Ernesto in prison. Ernesto responded by asking him to immediately stop sending him 'these undesirables'. When Petit de Murat visited him, Ernesto rejected any help from which his Cuban companions could not also benefit. He refused any special treatment. Petit de Murat described his 'magnificent moral attitude'. He seemed very impressed by Ernesto's probity.

The news of the detention of the 'Argentinian doctor' had spread throughout Latin America. Our family and friends were stunned by his 'wild plans'. They made no bones about sharing their reactions with my parents. The phone rang continuously in calle Aráoz. Our relatives advised us to rant and rage, to bang our fists on the table and get Ernesto back on course. Personally, I felt it was such a great story – brilliant, in fact! What an exceptional guy my brother was!

The period that I call 'the pre-Che' period was coming to an end and we were entering the 'post-Che' period, a confrontational time for our family. We would be carrying the burden of Ernesto's commitment, his growing popularity and, above all, his confrontation with the powers that be.

I had just turned thirteen and my political education was already well advanced. My mother and I had many conversions. Our relationship was much more one of friends than that between mother and son. On the other hand, I rarely talked politics with my father because we were hardly ever in agreement. In this field, my guiding lights were my mother and my sister Celia. And Ernesto, of course, but he was far away. His letters continued to arrive regularly.

I still remember the first time he signed 'El Che'. It was a letter to my mother dated 15 July 1956. As she was now convinced that Fidel Castro would again try to mount an invasion of the island with the participation of her son, she sent a letter of reprimand to Ernesto, in which she expressed her incomprehension and her doubts. Cuba was not Ernesto's country. If he wanted to fight injustice, why didn't he fight against our national tyrant instead of going and putting his life in danger thousands of kilometres away? Argentina was then under the rule of Pedro Eugenio Aramburu, the general responsible for the Revolución Libertadora (the Liberating Revolution), in other words, the 1955 coup against Perón. Aramburu was just one more dictator who persecuted the Peronists, imprisoned them or murdered them. His sectarianism had even gone as far as passing a law making Peronist propaganda, the mention of the names of Eva and Juan Perón, and the possession of images, symbols or sculptures and so on depicting them, all illegal. This persecution would provoke a first hardening in the nascent Montoneros movement.

My mother feared for her son. Worried sick, she was trying for the first time to tie him down, despite his being twenty-eight years old. For his part, Ernesto was accustomed to my mother supporting him in everything he did. I guess he was surprised to be so firmly admonished. I here reproduce part of his reply, because this essential letter marked a turning point in our lives:

I am neither Christ nor a philanthropist, *vieja*, I'm even the complete opposite of Christ and philanthropy strikes me as something [illegible], for the causes I believe in, I fight with all the weapons at my disposal and I try to beat my opponent to the ground rather than let myself be crucified. Regarding the hunger strike, you're completely wrong: it has been started twice over; the first time, they released twenty-one of the twenty-four inmates in our group and the second time they announced the release of Fidel Castro, the leader of the Movement, which will take place tomorrow. Thus only two people, including me, will remain in prison. I don't want you to think, as Hilda has insinuated, that the two people in question are being sacrificed, we're simply the ones whose papers aren't in order, which is why we don't have access to the same resources as our comrades. I intend to seek asylum in the nearest country, which will be difficult given the inter-American [*sic*] reputation that I've been saddled with, and wait there until someone calls on my services. As I've said, it's likely I won't be able to write for a longer or shorter period.

What terrifies me most is your lack of understanding and your advice on moderation, selfishness, etc., in other words the most appalling faults that an individual can have. Not only am I not moderate but I never will be, and if one day I realize that the sacred vocation has given way to a feeble flame, all that will be left for me to do is vomit on my own shit. Regarding your request that I indulge in a moderate selfishness, that is to say a vulgar, cowardly individualism, and in the *virtues* of X [a family friend],[3] I must tell you that I have tried to liquidate it within myself; I'm not talking specifically about this type of individualism, unknown and pusillanimous, but the other, bohemian type, indifferent to others and fostered by a sense of self-sufficiency that poisons one's mind; and I'm not talking about my own strength. Since those days I spent in prison and the training I underwent, I have completely identified with my comrades in arms . . . One of your serious mistakes is to believe that moderation or 'moderate egoism' can produce great inventions and masterpieces. Great works need passion, and revolution cannot be achieved without large doses of passion and daring, qualities usually present in groups of human beings.

Another strange thing I've noticed: you keep repeating the name of Aunty God, I hope this doesn't mean that you're returning to the cage of your childhood.[4] I also have to tell you that the series of SOS's you have put out is absolutely worthless. Petit [de Murat] got scared, Lezica slipped away and delivered a sermon to Hilda (against my will) on the obligations of political asylum. Raúl Lynch behaved well, at a distance, and Padilla Nerva said that different ministries are involved. They all wanted to help me on condition that I abjure my ideals; I don't think you would prefer a son who is alive but a renegade to a son who has died somewhere or other while at least doing what he considered his duty . . . Moreover, what is certain is that once I've righted wrongs in Cuba, I will go elsewhere, and it's no less certain that it would be the death of me if I was locked up in an office or a clinic for allergic diseases. That said, it seems to me that this pain, a mother's pain, one that seems to have gripped you in your old age and requires that your son stay alive, deserves respect, and I have the obligation – and the urge – to recognize it for what it is; I'd like to see you, not only to offer you comfort, but also to comfort myself for my shameful and occasional bursts of homesickness. *Vieja*, I embrace you and promise you I'll come and see you if nothing new turns up. Your son, Che.

This letter, which various family members helped to decipher, convinced my parents that there was nothing else for it but to support my brother in his decisions. We knew how determined he was. He was going to be a follower of this Fidel Castro . . . whom my mother was now actually starting to admire. She had read his statement, a lyrical gem denouncing the tyranny of Fulgencio Batista and detailing the misery of the Cuban people. It was hard to find fault with it. As for Ernesto, he mentioned coming to see us, and we clung to this idea. In reality, he never returned to Buenos Aires except in August 1961 for a lightning visit of just a few hours, after a stay in Punta del Este. The whole family, aunt Beatriz included, then joined him at the Uruguayan resort. This was the last time we ever saw him. At the time, in 1961, Ernesto was minister of industry in the Cuban government and we had no reason to believe he was thinking of fighting far away from Cuba. But another letter to my mother, dated November 1956, three months after the previous one, was prophetic. He wrote: 'When the disease I suffer takes possession of you, I think it gets worse over time and only lets go in the grave.' This disease was his resurgent desire, or rather his need, to go off and fight against injustice.

Shortly after posting the letter of 15 July 1956, Ernesto embarked with eighty-one men (including Fidel and Raúl Castro, Camilo Cienfuegos, Juan Almeida and Ramiro Valdés) on the *Granma*, an old eighteen-metre yacht that Fidel had purchased for 15,000 dollars a few weeks earlier. The odyssey began with all lights extinguished in the Mexican port of Tuxpan on the night of 25 November, and lasted for ten days. The hardened crew immediately succumbed to terrible seasickness. Let Ernesto tell the story in his own words: 'The frantic search to find our antihistamines in our luggage began yet again; we sang the Cuban national anthem and then the anthem of the 26th of July Movement for maybe a total of five minutes and immediately the boat presented a tragicomic aspect, filled with men clutching their bellies, with woebegone expressions on their faces. Some of them had stuck their heads into buckets and others had ended up frozen in the weirdest positions, their clothes covered with sick.'[5] After four or five days, the food ran out.

The *Granma* reached Cuba on 5 December with some severely weakened men on board. The landing on the beach at Las Coloradas turned immediately into a disaster. The boat had been spotted approaching the island and Batista's army was ready to receive it, with its made-in-the-USA artillery. And scarcely had Fidel's men set foot on land than the air force swept in and machine-gunned them down, killing seventy of the eighty-two fighters who had embarked in Mexico. There were only twelve fighters and seven guns left to face 30,000 soldiers and an ultra-sophisticated battery of weapons including tanks, guns, planes, etc. And yet these starving troops would conquer the ferocious Fulgencio Batista. Ernesto would later tell the Argentinian journalist Jorge Ricardo Masetti, the first compatriot who interviewed him in the Sierra Maestra, that the movement owed its victory to the unshakeable faith of Fidel: 'He was an extraordinary man. The most impossible things were precisely those he faced and solved. He had an exceptional confidence in the fact that once he had embarked for Cuba, he would get there. Once there, he would fight. And once he fought, he would win.' While his men had just been slaughtered and the Cuban army was continuing to shoot at him, Fidel exclaimed: 'Just look at the way they're firing. They're terror-stricken. They're afraid of us because they know we'll finish them off!' Was this prophecy or self-confidence? No one will ever know.

Amidst the rout and carnage, Ernesto was faced with a dilemma. A comrade bearing a box of ammunition had fallen in battle right at his feet. Ernesto was carrying a box of medical equipment. At that moment, he had to choose between the two boxes, as he couldn't carry both. 'Either I'm a doctor, or I'm a fighter', he said to himself (he told the story in a letter to my mother). He grabbed the ammo box and slipped it under his shirt. A few minutes later, a bullet struck him in the chest. He was saved by the box and wounded in the neck. On another occasion, a bullet pierced his cheek and came out behind his ear.

The news of the landing in Cuba did not reach us immediately, but as soon as the papers relayed it, the nightmare began. We didn't even know he had embarked! He had talked about his commitment to Fidel Castro's cause without disclosing the details of their plan: he knew that the Mexican intelligence services were reading his mail.

The Argentinian press took an immediate interest in the 'revolutionary young Argentinian doctor'. And, for the first time, the news of Ernesto's death was announced in December, in *La Prensa*, a right-wing daily. 'Among the dead in this combat', said the article, 'was Dr Ernesto Guevara de la Serna.' That day, my father came home unexpectedly. He looked feverish and dismayed, which alarmed me. My mother was absorbed in a game of solitaire. My father stood stock still for a few moments without uttering a word. He was clearly not in a fit state to give her the news. My mother finally looked up and, on seeing him, asked: 'What's going on?'

My father said, 'I'm sure it's not true.'

'Ernesto?' she cried. In a second, her face became livid. He did not need to say any more. She jumped up, tore the paper out of his hands and, after reading the headline, rushed to the phone to call Associated Press. The agency knew nothing else. My mother was utterly despondent. The phone rang continuously. Family and friends wanted to know if it was true, if we had any news. Newspapers from around the world had announced the eradication of Fidel Castro's group. They were merely repeating the lies put about by Batista. For us it was pure horror. Once again, my father set his network of connections to work.

While we were waiting nervously for news from the Argentinian embassy in Havana, a letter that Ernesto had sent from Mexico before his departure reached us. It announced his irrevocable decision to fight for the independence of Cuba. We were helpless, not knowing what to think. Was he alive or dead? The uncertainty was excruciating. And then on 31 December, when we were all at home in calle Aráoz, an envelope appeared under the door. The postmark indicated 'Manzanillo, Cuba'. It was a very short message from Ernesto that said simply: 'Dear *viejos*, I'm perfectly fine, I've only spent two and I still have seven left [he was talking about his lives]. I'm still doing the same job; news is and will continue to be sporadic, but you can rest assured that God is Argentinian. A big hug to all. Teté.'[6] The joy we felt at that moment! The evening turned into a party, an occasion to remember.

After this episode, the international press would announce Ernesto's death on five different occasions. The Argentinian newspapers propagandized for the Batista regime. They told lie upon lie, claiming for example that the *guajiros* (Cuban peasants) were opposed to the revolution, that the dictator's army had neutralized the members of the 26th of July Movement, etc. Misinformation poured out. The reality was quite different. The *guajiros* wanted to sign up to the Movement in their thousands. If they couldn't join the ranks of the guerrillas, this was because the Movement had no weapons to give them. Yet its troops swelled every time the Ejercito Rebelde managed to carry out acts of sabotage, laying ambushes to seize the enemy's arsenal. While Batista was busy spreading misinformation, the revolutionary army was shaping up in the Sierra Maestra. Over the next few months, Ernesto would not only fight, but set up schools, field hospitals, bakeries, a bomb factory and a shoe factory. He also created a radio station and a newspaper, *Cubano Libre*, which was distributed thanks to an old photocopier: in it, he signed his articles 'The Irregular'. He was already applying the ethical principles that he later set out as follows: 'All we ask is that the narrator be sincere; that he will never, to clarify a personal position or make believe that he was in a particular place, say something untrue; we ask that, after writing a few pages according to his abilities, education and talent, the narrator subject himself to the most serious self-criticism possible so as to remove all the words that do not refer to a fact that is strictly true or of whose veracity he is not completely certain.' As if he was not busy enough already, Ernesto taught farmers to read and write, patiently helped them, listened to their grievances and nursed them. He even oversaw the construction of a landing strip for planes carrying weapons for the revolution. He seemed to have the gift of ubiquity: he was everywhere at once, and simultaneously sorted out a whole swathe of problems.

Che was the first fighter in the Ejercito Rebelde to be named *Comandante* by Fidel, even before Raúl. The celebrated guerrilla fighter Celia Sanchez sewed the famous red star on his beret.

The news reports of his death continued to shred our nerves – what if it was true? – but each time, they turned out to be a false alarm. We tried to pay less attention and stayed on the lookout for any positive information. The most reassuring news arrived late in February 1957 in the guise of a series of articles published in the *New York Times*. The US journalist Herbert Matthews had met Fidel in the Sierra Maestra. His report, published over three days, had a huge impact, and set the record straight. Castro was not a demoralized madman ready to lay down his arms, but completely the opposite. Nor was he a communist, but a Cuban patriot who wanted to rid his country of a bloody and oppressive tyrant. Castro's revolutionary army was organized, determined and growing. A cousin of my mother's, on holiday in New York, called us to pass on the story – an opportunity for us to celebrate at home yet again. A few days later, this same cousin called to say that, this time, she had seen Ernesto on television, in a CBS report, uniformed, bearded, cheerful, and absolutely confident in the victory of the Ejercito Rebelde! After the unspeakable torments we had endured, we were exhilarated.

A year later it was the turn of Jorge Ricardo Masetti to travel in the Sierra Maestra, sent by El Mundo, an Argentinian radio station. When he arrived at Che's camp after gruelling days walking through the perilous mountains,[7] he had this vision of my brother, as he later recalled in his report: 'He arrived by mule, his legs dangling, his back hunched, his legs prolonged by a Beretta and a shotgun with telescopic sights, which looked like two posts supporting an apparently slender body. When the mule approached, I could see that from his waist hung a leather cartridge belt full of ammunition, and a pistol. From his shirt pockets two magazines poked out, around his neck hung a camera and from his chin a few hairs trying to be a beard . . . The famous Che Guevara seemed a typical young Argentinian man from the middle classes.'

Radio Rebelde, the radio station installed on top of a hill in the scrub, allowed Masetti to broadcast his reports and interviews. After a long stay underground in the Sierra Maestra, he sent his exclusive recordings to Argentina. Unfortunately, once back in Havana, he learned that they had never arrived. So he returned to the Sierra Maestra in even more difficult conditions than the first time and met up with Fidel and Che, who seemed delighted to see him again. They had hit it off. His reports were eventually broadcast in four episodes. It was the first time that Argentina had heard Che's voice and obtained direct testimony of the Cuban revolution.

Back in Buenos Aires, Masetti immediately came to visit us. What he told us gave us new joy and hope. He handed over the tapes recorded for us by Ernesto. Hearing his voice after so many months was a pleasure and a huge relief.

Jorge became not only a close friend of the family, but a follower of Ernesto. Getting to know Fidel, Che and the other guerrillas, hearing their arguments in favour of the revolution, and seeing the atrocities committed by Batista had so stirred his conscience that, after founding the Prensa Latina agency with Ernesto – with the aim of disseminating reliable and honest information to counter the Yankee propaganda pumped out in Latin American countries – he gave up journalism to become a revolutionary. He first fought in Algeria for the FLN, then in the Argentinian province of Salta under the nom de guerre *Comandante* Segundo. His mission was to prepare for the arrival of Che and the expansion of the revolution on the continent. He disappeared on 21 April 1964. Masetti is the author of the best account of the Ejercito Rebelde ever written.[8]

Once the revolutionary army was firmly established in the Sierra Maestra, Ernesto managed to send us signs of life, albeit sporadic. He reassured us, saying that things were stabilizing. On learning of the existence of Radio Rebelde, my parents had immediately bought a radio equipped with a huge antenna to capture short wave and listen to the broadcasts of the news of the revolution that disproved Batista's misinformation.

After hearing yet again news of Ernesto's death, we were

comforted one day by a message from Radio Rebelde announcing: 'To reassure his parents in South America, as well as the Cuban people, we wish to assure you not only that Ernesto Guevara is alive, fighting in the front line, but that he is about to conquer the city of Santa Clara.'

Other journalists, like the Uruguayan Carlos Maria Gutíerrez, were now coming to visit us. Calle Aráoz had become an obligatory stopping-off point for reporters. They came at the request of Ernesto, who wanted to reassure us, but they were also starting to take an interest in us. Where did this Che come from, who were his parents, his siblings, cousins, aunts and uncles? One day Gutíerrez told my mother that the backpack Ernesto carried was filled with books and that he declaimed León Felipe poems from morning to night. She replied that only two things stopped her son from sleeping: 'The possibility that they might kill him and the certainty that he would kill others.'[9]

Journalists were not the only ones interested in us. My parents had formed a committee to support the Ejercito Rebelde. Our house had thus become a makeshift revolutionary centre. About this time, my father was approached by an American journalist, one Jules Dubois, who posed as the director of the *Diario de las Américas* magazine based in Florida, and claimed to support the revolution. Dubois made frequent trips between Miami and Buenos Aires. He never failed to call my father and arranged to meet him in cafés when he was in the capital. He asked questions about Ernesto, under the guise of wanting to protect him. The information he seemed most keen to obtain was where Ernesto might be in the Sierra Maestra. As he was so insistent, my father finally suspected him of being a CIA agent and broke all ties with him. We were vulnerable. General Pedro Aramburu – and his Liberating Revolution, mentioned above –

was in power. He had formed a repressive military government, and he was no friend to Cuban revolutionaries.

Beginning in June 1958, Ernesto briefly contacted us via Radio Rebelde. This appeal was providential for my mother. She was very lonely, very sad, and very worried about him. Soon after, she wrote him a long letter, though I don't know to what address she sent it. She probably entrusted it to a reporter bound for Cuba. I here reproduce the most touching passages:

Teté my darling,

I was deeply moved to hear your voice on the phone after so long. I didn't recognize it. You seemed like another person. Perhaps the line was bad or your voice has changed. It was only when you said *'vieja'* that I rediscovered the tone of your voice from the past. The news that you gave me is wonderful . . . Ana married Petit[10] on 2 April and has left for Vienna . . . Sergio bought the plane ticket for them. They plan to earn a living there so as to make the most of their journey.

It seems that a baby is on the way and he'll be an Argentinian.

How sad to see my children go! Their departure has left the house so empty. You know how Ana was always flitting and fussing around. Celia is still here, she's turned into a quiet little mouse, and very understanding too, since her sister left.

Roberto has two adorable little girls, both blondes, aged two and one. He's expecting an heir in August. He's working hard to support his big family. You know how able he is, a real go-getter. He looks happy . . .

Celia has just picked up a big prize with Luis Rodríguez Algarañaz, her husband, and Petit; the three of them together have won two or three million pesos. Certainly our Viennese travellers will have to come back and work here. It's a stroke of luck for me because I feel lost without my brood.

I'm full of pride to have such talented children.

Juan Martin, of course, has big feet: not because he's grown any taller, he continues to be as small as his siblings, and he's become a really charming teenager. He attacks life with gusto, but he won't be spoiled by it. Things come naturally to him and he receives them with the same simplicity. He is affectionate and sensitive. He has a funny voice that reminds me of Roberto, and a penetrating intelligence, but he doesn't have the same restless curiosity as you and Celia. I think he'll be one of those people who take flight as soon as they have wings; there are few young people who, like him, have such a desire to discover new horizons. Until then, he will be my companion . . .

As for me, I continue on the same path. A few years older and with a sorrow that is not as deep, but has turned into a chronic sadness, with a few great satisfactions from time to time.

The prize awarded to Celia has been one of these satisfactions; the return of the country will be another; and hearing your voice was an especially great joy. I've become very lonely.

I don't know what to write or say to you, I've got out of the habit.

I've still not received the inheritance. We want to do some more building, our plans have been approved, but we'll have to wait a bit longer: the proceedings on the evictions have been halted. Fortunately, this winter has been fairly mild so far. We'll have to put up with this old, cold, uncomfortable house for a while longer.

And as regards the house, we have a new occupant . . . He entered the house on his own initiative, without being asked . . . Things got seriously complicated when Juan Martin returned. With a great show of authority, I announced: 'In no case will I accept a dog here. Take it somewhere else, Juan Martin.' The dog's been sleeping in the kitchen for a week. Juan Martin calls it *Negrita* . . .

Having to look after the house is exhausting me. I've been my own cook for quite a while now, and you know how I hate housework.

The kitchen is my headquarters and I spend most of my time there.

I had a huge shouting match with your father and since then he no longer pops his head in at the door . . .

On 2 January 1959, Radio Rebelde announced Fidel Castro's victory. Ernesto was safe and sound in Havana. My brother, 'the Argentinian adventurer' as they called him, instantly became a national hero for his country. The good news was shared by the whole family.

8

Return to Buenos Aires

There was a before and after Che, a before and after the Cuban
revolution, for Latin America and for us. Once she was back
from Cuba, my mother rediscovered her militant energy. What
she had seen on the island had enchanted her. Her son had
emerged unharmed and wreathed in glory from the Sierra
Maestra, so she could finally relax and enjoy the victory and
the ensuing peace. No sooner had she come out of her long
depression than she formed a support committee for the 26th
of July Movement and became one of its most active members.
Now she was passionate, and indeed consumed, by the events
in Cuba.

My own activism had been consolidated by my stay on the
island. My mother and I had been the first to give my brother
unconditional support for his political career. It had not been
easy for my mother to digest the fact that he would never
resume his medical career or return to Argentina. But once
she had faced the facts, she devoted herself to defending him.
She abandoned once and for all her games of solitaire and
began to hold forth on the Cuban revolution and its goals.
She published a series of four articles under the titles 'Cuba

por dentro' ('Cuba from the Inside'), 'La tierra para el guajiro' ('Land for the Peasant'), 'Vivienda para todos' ('Housing for All') and 'Desarrollo industrial' ('Industrial Development') in the Argentinian magazine *La Vanguardia*. There she recounted her amazement at seeing so many young leaders working tirelessly for the common good: 'If the guerrillas learned to fight by fighting, now they are learning to govern by governing. They have all found within themselves hidden resources, which have risen to the surface from the latent depths of their personalities – resources that have rendered them capable of fulfilling the most diverse tasks.'

She did not stop there. When Vice-President Alejandro Goméz resigned from the government of Arturo Frondizi to form the Movimiento Nacional de defensa del petróleo y la energía (National Movement in Defence of Oil and Energy), with the objective of preventing foreign powers from exploiting our resources, she began raising support for this organization. When the intellectual Ismael Viñas, founder of the journal *Contorno*, launched his own Movimiento de Liberación Nacional (National Liberation Movement), she was the first to support it. She had moved out of a state of depression and paralysis into frenetic political activity. Over the next two years, she would twice go to Cuba for long periods, five months each time. The rest of the time she travelled to and fro between Argentina and other countries, giving lectures on the Cuban revolution, which had found in her its most devoted spokeswoman.

Despite my refusal to go to graduate school, I enrolled on a course in journalism. My mother had insisted, as had Ernesto – so I reluctantly agreed. I gave up after a year. I wanted to be a worker, and that's what I became. I found a job as a lorry driver.

My father, meanwhile, continued to live in his own world. He persevered in his mercantile enterprises. Thanks to Celia's architectural degree, he landed a contract to build a housing project in Buenos Aires, a huge apartment block for municipal employees. The building still exists, it's at the corner of avenida Rivadabia and avenida Donisetti. For two years, by some miracle, he had money.

Carried away by my mother's momentum and Ernesto's example, I began to campaign actively. The question the left-wing parties were starting to ask was whether they should take up arms to defend their ideals. They couldn't agree. The Cuban revolution was responsible for this break. It had led to deep divisions. My mother and I were for armed struggle. Ernesto had convinced us. He said that the only option was to fight and 'we needed to carry on fighting, as it was the only way to win'. My father was opposed.

If we were proud of Ernesto's fame and his exploits, his renown was not without consequences for us. It was a problematic time – indeed, what time was ever *not* problematic in Argentina? My parents had ceased being just members of the Guevara Lynch de la Serna family and become the parents of Che. A breach had opened up in the family. The Cuban revolution had initially seemed something to welcome with open arms. But as and when it took a left turn, our relatives began to show their opposition despite the great affection they felt for Ernesto. One thing, however, was unanimous: Che's exemplary integrity. *Ponia el cuerpo*: in other words, he had proved that he was ready to die for his ideals. His bravery had earned the respect of all, including his detractors. However, although all the members of the family without exception had boasted of their relationship when he became a hero of mythic proportions, the same was

not true in the 1960s. For one thing, Che was suspected of communism; for another, the mere fact of knowing him had become
dangerous. Cowards and traditionalists spoke ill of him, and criticized him. Two of my father's sisters, Suzana and Marta, were
particularly virulent. Not a single generous word ever came out
of their mouths. Everything they said was hostile. They had,
of course, married powerful men. Marta's husband was a distinguished surgeon. I've forgotten what Suzana's did. When
my mother died, Marta had the nerve to come to the wake. It
was a very hard time for us. We didn't know where Ernesto
was and my mother had died in great anguish. I asked Marta
what she was doing here and told her to leave immediately. The
Guevara family were reactionaries, except possibly my aunts
Beatriz and Maria Luisa. And yet my grandmother had been
an anti-conformist woman. The greatest irony in all this? The
Argentinian ambassador in Cuba when Che entered Havana
in victory was my father's cousin; this was the aforementioned
Raúl Guevara Lynch, who had helped us to get news of Ernesto,
and the same man who had signed Ernesto's birth certificate.
And he wasn't a supporter of the revolution!

We soon found ourselves isolated. On the Serna side of the
family, my uncle Jorge remained faithful and attentive. But
none of his children ever came to our house. My uncle Córdova
Iturburú and my aunt Carmen de la Serna stayed friends with
us, but Cayetano was now devoted almost exclusively to poetry
and art criticism.

In Cuba, Fidel, Ernesto, Raúl, Camilo and the others were trying
to put the revolution on a firm basis and organize their government. Of course, they still had it all to do: the task was daunting.
One of the biggest challenges was US hostility. Fidel declared

himself in favour of an entente cordiale with his powerful neighbour. He was not a communist. His revolution was above all patriotic and national. It had no international ambitions. However, his statements did nothing to placate the imperialists. The bloody Batista had been their man, their puppet. And they didn't like the fact that their man had been chucked out. They alone had the right to make and unmake governments, particularly in Latin America where they had a long tradition of oppression and opposition to democracy.

The first frontal attack occurred on 4 March 1960. Its target? *La Couvre*, a French ship anchored in the port of Havana carrying Belgian munitions from Antwerp. The explosion caused the death of seventy-six innocent people. Fidel saw the hand of the CIA in the attack, and denounced the United States – whereupon, hostilities between the superpower and the tiny defenceless island were declared. Before fleeing, Batista had emptied the National Bank of Cuba and deposited 424 million dollars in US banks, a sum which has never been returned to the Cuban people. So the country's coffers were empty. Led by Ernesto, the National Bank applied for a loan to support the Cuban currency. It was refused by the US National Security Council. Fidel then decided to speed up land reform and introduce social measures. He nationalized all properties bigger than 420 hectares for redistribution to peasants, tenants and the landless. He also nationalized all foreign assets and expropriated US companies. From that time onwards, the government of Dwight Eisenhower never ceased to obstruct the march of the Cuban revolution. Eisenhower's retaliation took the form of economic measures, starting with a drastic cut in Cuban sugar imports, followed by a partial embargo in October 1960 and finally a total embargo in February 1962. Sugar was central to the Cuban economy.

In August 1961, Che analysed the situation in an article that appeared in a (now defunct) journal published by the ministry of industry:

Naturally, there is no military power able to thwart the North Americans in the Americas; what worries them is the sudden appearance of popular powers and the possibility that these powers might acquire such strength that they can afford, as in the case of Cuba, to challenge US orders and implement an economic and social policy which the US would no longer be able to control; logically, they also cannot admit a foreign policy that is outside their control. That is why the imperialists are seeking new allies, new support, but without abandoning the old methods of economic and political domination.

The alliance of Yankee imperialism with local bourgeoisies means, in the economic field, that the 'new' methods for exploiting the Latin American peoples consist simply in transferring the national capital that comes from the land to industries that complement those in the US, or by replacing imported consumer products by other national products depending on technology and raw materials from North America.

There is another explanation for how the national bourgeoisie allies itself with foreign interests; together they create new industries in the country in question, obtain tariff advantages for these industries that allow them to completely exclude the competencies of other imperialist countries; the profits thus obtained can leave the country protected by favourable trade regulations.

Through this new and more intelligent system of exploitation, the 'nationalist' country is responsible for protecting US interests, promulgating preferential tariffs that make it possible to generate additional profits (that the same United States will re-export to their own country). Naturally, the sales prices of the items, unrelated to their quality, are set by the monopolies.

Fidel Castro had no alternative but to sign a trade agreement with the USSR. Cuba needed an ally. The United States refused all proposals. Diplomatic relations between the two countries were definitively broken. Ernesto was then minister of industry. He worked at a furious pace in the monastic office of a building that the journalist Rogelio García Lupo described much later:

> His office was in a fourteen-storey office block still under construction . . . The walls, in rough concrete, were dripping wet and our meeting took place in an atmosphere of intimacy that could only be explained, given such a dangerous political situation, by the confidence that the name of Tita Infante seemed to inspire in Che the minute it was uttered by her brother Carlos Infante. I have forgotten almost everything about the meeting but I remember the drink of *mate* passing from Guevara's hands to Carlos and a Bemporad map of the Argentinian Republic adorning one of the bare, undecorated walls on the verge of collapse – difficult to imagine as your everyday landscape.[1]

Indeed, the routine, the bureaucracy, and the stifling atmosphere in which he was supposed to be getting the revolution under way seemed to weigh heavily on Ernesto. During an official visit to Algeria in 1963, he wrote to my aunt Beatriz: 'From Thebes, the first capital of the dream, this poet who doesn't write poetry and has become a worthy bureaucrat with a respectable paunch and habits so sedentary that he walks around in a halo of nostalgia, slippers, and kids, sends you his best wishes.'

In 1960, my cousin Guillermo Moore de la Serna was approached by the Fiat-Someca group who had just set up in Argentina. Guillermo was a landowner. He was also an agronomist and divided his activities between Argentina and Nicaragua. He had just obtained his pilot's licence. Ernesto and he had spent many summers together at Galarza in their youth, at the home of my uncle Ernesto Moore and my aunt Edelmira. The Fiat-Someco group was at that time represented by Aurelio Peccei, the managing director of the Italo-consult group, a pool of Italian companies operating in Argentina. When he learned that Guillermo was about to buy a plane to get to the United States, Peccei said, 'Since you can fly, why not drop by to see your cousin in Cuba on the way back?' Guillermo realized that the mission Peccei was trying to give him involved convincing Ernesto to fill the gap left by the break with the United States by forging an alliance with Europe rather than the Soviet Union. He contacted Ernesto to inform him of his imminent visit to Cuba. On learning that he intended to arrive in an aircraft registered in the US, Ernesto exclaimed: 'You can't come in that plane, they'll shoot you down!' It's worth remembering that Camilo Cienfuegos had died in a mysterious and unexplained plane crash on 28 October 1959, and Ernesto was now wary of this means of transport. So Guillermo took a commercial flight. It so happened that my mother was in Havana at the time, and the prospect of welcoming her nephew and acting as his guide delighted her. Guillermo visited Cuba with the sharp eye of an agronomist. He wasn't very impressed with what he saw; he thought it would be a disaster. Huge tracts of land lay fallow, having been abandoned by the landowners. When he confided his doubts to Ernesto, Che replied, 'Let them go. This is a revolution. And tell your friends that it's too late for Europe. The die is cast.'

Guillermo spent two weeks in Cuba. Back in Buenos Aires, he told us that Ernesto was living in a very sparsely furnished house with Aleida; she was terribly jealous and possessive, especially of those who had been close to her husband before her, so it was sometimes difficult to speak to Ernesto. He was working hard, and only ever wore a spotless and immaculately ironed olive-green uniform, which had struck Guillermo as rather amusing given Ernesto's attitude to clothes as a young man. He rose at around 9 in the morning and drank a large cup of black coffee; in the evening, he often played chess, loved eating flan (his favourite dessert), drinking wine cut with water – an Argentinian custom of the time – and taking baths to relax; but what he had most enjoyed was getting Guillermo to talk about his family and Argentina. It was now seven years since he had been back there.

Aleida's jealousy was probably justified. Che was very popular with women. Personalities came from around the world to meet him, among them Simone de Beauvoir and Jean-Paul Sartre, the actor Gérard Philipe, the *New York Times* reporter Herbert Matthews, and an army of attractive women who flocked to Havana on various pretexts to talk to the handsome revolutionary.

While the young Cuban government was locked in struggle with the United States, my mother's political activism and her trips to Havana did not pass unnoticed in Argentina. They now had files on us as communists. The fact that Fidel Castro had stopped off at our home when he attended the Conference of the Twenty-One in May 1960 did not help matters. Fidel knew my mother and really liked her. He described her to his entourage as an exceptional woman, intelligent and cultured. For her part, my mother admired him. We all did. Whether you share his ideas or not, he was an extraordinary man, absolutely brilliant. Who would have thought at the time that he would resist the United States for over fifty years, without this great power ever managing to twist his arm!

In short, out of friendship for Ernesto and courtesy to my mother, he had announced his visit a few days earlier. A very funny thing then happened. To start with, my father flatly refused to allow the visit to take place in our dilapidated house in calle Aráoz. My mother didn't care, and let him do as he wished. She lived very austerely and knew that Fidel wouldn't mind. Fidel surely couldn't have cared less, but my father did! So he had organized the festivities at his sister Hercilia's. She lived in a luxurious apartment in calle Republica de la India, in the exclusive part of the Palermo neighbourhood, near the park. My aunt and her husband were fiercely anti-revolutionary, but not for all the world would they have missed out on the opportunity to receive Fidel Castro in their home! They were bursting with pride! It was a tremendous honour! In any case, the apartment was filled with about thirty people: uncles, aunts, cousins and friends mostly opposed to the spirit of the Cuban revolution.

Fidel arrived at the end of the road with all the dignity of a head of state – escorts, bodyguards and all the rest of it, but he came into the house alone. On entering, he announced with a smile: 'I'm in my brother's house.' Then, greeting my mother: 'You're like my mother. Che and I have talked so much about his "Mama"! In all our adventures, he talked about you with so much love that I love you as much as he does.' My mother was radiant.

Fidel was welcomed as a hero and mobbed by the guests.

Everyone wanted to talk to him, listen to him, speak privately with him. Women seemed to want to eat him raw. You should have seen how they devoured him with their eyes! Fidel was Fidel! A victorious revolutionary, a legend, thirty-four years old, wearing a handsome uniform, an attractive, highly charismatic and very charming and affectionate man. Whether he was a revolutionary or not, the eyes of the women seemed to be saying: 'How dishy he is! How nice to have his powerful arms enfold you!' But the only women Fidel stared at were a cousin and my sister Celia. They were both beautiful. It was an unforgettable evening.

The visit soon led to a whole series of reprisals. One day, our house was sprayed with bullets. Guevara de la Serna had become a difficult name to bear. Too bad. I now shared my brother's ideas; I understood and supported his fight. Perhaps I wasn't much of a student, but I read a lot. I built up a store of knowledge. And I would soon have the opportunity to show Ernesto that I was not a dunce.

In July 1961 Ernesto informed us that he would be in Punta del Este in early August for the Assembly of the Organization of American States (OAS). The whole family set off for Uruguay. The reunion was very emotional and intense. My aunt Beatriz, who had missed him terribly all these years, gazed at him with such adoration! She wanted to bring him back to Buenos Aires. We all had the vague feeling that this meeting might be the last. Unfortunately, we were right; only my mother would see him again in Havana a few months later. Ernesto was Cuba's representative in the Assembly. So it was very difficult to catch him alone. However, he took all his meals with us, and always sat between my mother and my aunt Beatriz, a protective arm around each of their shoulders.

The journalist Rogelio García Lupo has related that Punta del Este was crawling with Secret Service men, spies, security officers in disguise, Americans, Cubans, Russians, and women who wanted to see Che. It was hell. The Bay of Pigs had only just happened.[2] I was too young to be aware of this confused background noise, more suitable to some story of espionage, but I had matured enough to want to have meaningful conversations with Ernesto. I wanted to discuss socialism, the changes in the world, the future of the American continent and Cuba. He answered my questions with good grace. But he still insisted on my studies. We just went round in circles as far as this was concerned. Eventually, he gave in and handed me a book written in the Stalin era, the *Manual of Political Economy*, produced by the Academy of Sciences of the USSR, asking me to immerse myself in it. The funny thing is that he became violently critical of this same book three years later: 'There are many assertions in this book that resemble the dogma of the Holy Trinity; they are incomprehensible but faith solves them . . . The chapter "Building the socialist economy in European countries where there is a people's democracy" seems to have been written for children or idiots. And where's the Soviet army in all this? Scratching its balls?'

However, in 1961, Ernesto still had faith in the USSR. And I was young and innocent. Later, he would cease to believe in it, would mistrust it and even criticize it harshly. During his last stay in Prague in February 1966, before leaving for Bolivia, he would discuss delicate matters with visitors in his hotel room. He thought he was being bugged. In the final analysis, the USSR was just as unwilling as the US to have an agitator fomenting revolutions and disturbing the established order. Indeed, I suspect that KGB agents collaborated with the CIA to eliminate Che in Bolivia, though of course I can't prove this.

A few days after our return to Buenos Aires, we learned from the daily paper *La Nación* that Ernesto had breezed into the capital before returning to Cuba via Brazil. He had told us nothing about this whirlwind tour. He had become as silent as the grave with us. Two missions had brought him to Buenos Aires: the serious illness of my aunt Maria Luisa Guevara Lynch, and an audience with President Arturo Frondizi.

He had left Montevideo on the morning of 18 August for San Fernando, a suburb near the Argentinian presidential residence of Quinta de Olivos, along with the former MP Jorge Carretoni. The meeting with the president needed to remain confidential. It was imperative that the military be unaware that Frondizi was about to grant a hearing to the Marxist revolutionary. So as not to attract their attention, Carretoni had first been ordered not to take the same plane as Che in Montevideo. But, fearing a CIA ambush, Ernesto had refused to fly alone. Carretoni had yielded. When they landed at the airfield in San Fernando, they were greeted by two soldiers of the Helicanes Brigade. Seeing Che, the soldiers stared wide-eyed: they were not in the loop. His presence on Argentinian soil was completely unexpected and problematic. Not knowing what to do, they called their superior, who gave the green light. Che was then escorted to Frondizi. The two men talked together for three hours. No one ever knew what they had said. Once the meeting was over, Ernesto went to my aunt's in San Isidro. He took the opportunity to eat a *choripan*.[3]

The latest events related to Che and Cuba had apparently annoyed quite a few people. My mother received several death threats. One morning, on arriving at our house, our maid Sabina Portugal discovered a bomb on the stairs. She ran into my room to warn me that a strange box with a smouldering wick had been placed on a step. I grabbed my mother and a pair of scissors hanging around in the kitchen. We raced down the stairs four at a time and I cut the wick. Out in the street, my mother discovered that she had forgotten her dentures and rushed back into the house to get them. Not knowing if the bomb was disabled or not, I pointed out that it would be crazy to go back indoors. I was wasting my breath! She insisted and eventually headed towards the door. My mother was like that, stubborn, brave. She was prepared to die to get her dentures! Of course, I didn't let her go in: I went up instead. We called the police. It was TNT. The culprits were never arrested.

I had a second cousin, a fascist named Juan Martin Guevara Lynch. I was sometimes confused with him. So we received anonymous calls from both opponents and supporters of Ernesto. Some said: 'Nazi son of a bitch'. Others: 'Piece of communist shit'. It was an ultra-politicized time.

My mother was very discreet even though she could also be very noisy. At meetings or conferences she attended, she never revealed that she was Che's mother. She simply called herself 'Celia' and purposely omitted her last name. Some knew, others guessed; others didn't make the connection. In any case, she refused to take advantage of her family relationship to obtain any privileges or special treatment. On the contrary. She felt more at ease in ordinary places, surrounded by simple people. But at the same time she held forth constantly about the Cuban revolution.

On 23 April 1963, while she was returning from a six-month trip to Cuba, Europe and Brazil, she was arrested in Concordia, a town on the Uruguayan border. She had been identified as 'dangerous'. She had wanted to return to Buenos Aires by car from

Rio de Janeiro to 'see America close up'. She was fifty-seven years old and in frail health. Placed under the control of the executive power, she was accused of violating the higher decree 8161/962 by bringing communist propaganda into the country. The 'communist propaganda' my mother had with her comprised a photo of Che, a few books, a manuscript of Ernesto's and a little flag of Cuba.

My aunt Carmen, my father, my brother Roberto, my sister Celia, her husband Luis and I immediately left for Concordia. The tabloids were already gloating over my mother's arrest: she had travelled via Czechoslovakia and some newspapers accused her of spying. The judge asked for her release, which was granted. But the Argentinian president, José Maria Guido, of the Unión cívica radical intransigente, overruled this decision and ordered her transfer to the Reformatorio del Buen Pastor, a women's prison in the San Telmo district of Buenos Aires.

For the offence of having produced Che, she remained in jail for two long months. She could have spent ten months or ten years there: the sentences were completely arbitrary. We went to see her almost every day. She never complained. From the filthy cell she shared with other inmates, she wrote to Ernesto: 'It's a wonderful *deformatory*.[4] Both for common law prisoners and for political prisoners. If you're lukewarm in your beliefs, you become active, if you're active you become aggressive, and if you're aggressive you become relentless.' After a few months, the executive power gave her a choice: stay in jail or leave the country. She opted for the latter. We escorted her to the Uruguayan border but she did not stay in Uruguay for long: yet another change of government soon allowed her to return to Buenos Aires.

By this time, I had started working at the La Bohemia bookshop. Its owner had left it to me. I had renamed it La Pulga (The Flea). I was selling all kinds of activist books and publications such as *Pekin Informa* (*Peking Informs*), *Lenguas extranjeras de Moscu* (*Foreign Languages of Moscow*), *El Obrero Monthly Review* (*The Worker's Monthly Review*), the *Monthly Review* of Huberman and Paul Sweezy, and the works of Jorge Alvarez. La Pulga had quickly become a meeting place for revolutionary organizations of the time. People came to read magazines and books they couldn't find elsewhere. They settled down among the bookshelves for hours on end. I read a lot too. It was at this time that I came into contact with Marxist militancy. And then I got married at nineteen, and started to have children too. If I had seriously considered joining Ernesto in Cuba, the illusion had now faded. I had really put down roots in Argentina.

9

'This letter might be the last'

I learned of Ernesto's death from the newspapers on 10 October 1967. At that time, I was a lorry driver in charge of delivering dairy products. The day had not yet dawned in Buenos Aires and I had just arrived at my place of work. There it was, the headline of the daily *Clarín*, with a photo of Ernesto smoking a cigar: 'Bolivia announces that Che has died.' I was devastated. Page two of the newspaper showed the famous photo of Che lying stiff and dead, shirtless, his eyes open, his arms lying along his body and his tousled hair, resting on the cement slab of the wash house in the Vallegrande hospital. It was a dreadful shock. Everyone was discussing the event. My colleagues were unaware that he was my brother. I said nothing.

I didn't for a single moment doubt that the lifeless body and the fixed stare were those of Ernesto, although I did not know he was in Bolivia, so close to us. The family had lost track of him since he left Cuba. Nobody knew where he was, with the exception of Fidel and those who were fighting with him in the Ñancahuazú region. Two and a half years earlier, on 18 May 1965, my mother had died of cancer, distraught at his disappearance. A few weeks before she passed away, without revealing that she was dying, she had told Ernesto of her desire to return to Cuba as soon as she could. 'It's impossible', he had replied in a letter. 'You'll have to arm yourself with patience. I'm going off to cut sugarcane for a month.' He added that he had left the ministry of industry to devote the next five years of his life to running a business. My mother knew my brother better than anyone. This response had deeply disturbed her: far from stopping her coming, Ernesto generally insisted that she join him Cuba. She was convinced he was concealing something. Nobody could get her to shake off this idea. She didn't for a moment believe that he had really resigned his post in the ministry, nor that he was running a business, let alone cutting sugarcane, even if he had one day told her that he loved to 'help with the harvest – it's an escape, a form of mental relaxation as well as physical exercise'. Che had launched the voluntary work system. This involved sending the townspeople to work in plantations and factories once a week to recharge their batteries. Moreover, everyone – including himself – had to contribute to the building of the revolutionary society he dreamt of: he wanted this society to be one of solidarity, altruism and generosity. Volunteering was one of the factors that would allow the new man to be born: a reconstructed human being whose thinking, customs, habits and values would be radically transformed by self-denial, for the good of all. To set an example, Ernesto often joined in the hard work in the fields or factories on a Sunday. He even spent a few hours every night volunteering in a factory. So for him to devote all his time to sugarcane when there were so many important things still to do ... She remembered with terror one thing that Ernesto had told her in Punta del Este when she asked him to be careful: 'Rest assured, *vieja*, I won't die in bed.' Ernesto's negative response regarding a fourth stay in Cuba had reached her in early April. From then on, she had frantically tried to join him by all means possible, in vain. She was dismayed. It was a painful period.

The birth of my son Pablo on 2 April did nothing to cheer up his grandmother. She couldn't understand Ernesto's silence; it obsessed her. It was just not like him. He was always so considerate to her. How could he leave her so ignorant of his movements? The misinformation conveyed by the Argentinian and international press only served to increase her torment. The wildest and most libellous rumours were circulating. Some asserted that Che was suffering from a severe heart disease due to asthma; that an irreparable break with Fidel had forced him to take refuge in the Mexican embassy to avoid being executed or imprisoned; that Fidel's harsh criticism had driven him mad and that he was locked up in an asylum in Havana; that he had been shot for his pro-Chinese and anti-Soviet positions; that he was very ill, had travelled to the USSR for surgery, and there been liquidated for his Trotskyist views; and finally, that he had sold military secrets to the US for 10 million dollars and was in fact a CIA agent, sentenced to death by Fidel . . .

Cuba was going through a difficult time. Before his mysterious disappearance, Ernesto's critiques of the Soviet Union had intensified. His last speech in Algiers on 24 February 1965 created an enormous stir.[1] He blamed the USSR for behaving like a capitalist country, holding the carrot of materialism under its citizens' noses. 'Everything starts with the misconception that seeks to build socialism out of the elements of capitalism without really changing their meaning. Thus we arrive at a hybrid system that leads to a deadlock difficult to perceive immediately but requiring further concessions to economic elements, i.e. a step backwards', he wrote.[2] Now the USSR was Cuba's main

1 1902. The Guevara Lynch family, the paternal side, in Argentina.
2 1908. The de la Serna Llosa family, the maternal side, at the coastal resort of La Perla, in Mar del Plata, Argentina.
3 1928. The Guevara de la Serna family in Misiones in Argentina. *Left to right*: two friends, Ernesto Guevara Lynch (father), Celia de la Serna (mother) and Ernesto in his buggy.
4 1928. The married couple Ernesto Guevara Lynch and Celia de la Serna in Rosario, Argentina.

5 1928. First photo of Ernesto with his parents in Rosario. **6** 1929. Ernesto with his childminder Carmen Arias, a young Spanish woman from Sarria. **7** Ernesto and his mother on horseback in the sierras de Córdoba in Argentina.

5

6

7

8 1935. Ernesto on a bicycle in Ireneo Portela (province of Buenos Aires). **9** 1938. Summer holiday in Mar del Plata. *Left to right*: Ernesto, Ana Maria and Celia (sisters). *Behind*: Ernesto Guevara Lynch. **10** 1935. The children and their mother reading in Alta Gracia (province of Córdoba). *Left to right*: Roberto (brother), Ernesto, Celia, Ana Maria and Celia de la Serna. **11** 1938. Family holiday at Mar del Plata. *Left to right*: Roberto, Celia, Ernesto, Ana Maria and their mother.

12 1928. The first house of the young Guevara couple (*La Calesita*) in Misiones. Here, Ernesto took his first steps.
13 1938. Ernesto and his sister Ana Maria playing with doves in Alta Gracia. **14** 1940. Ernesto, Ana Maria and Roberto with friends from the neighbourhood, in Alta Gracia.

13

14

15 1940–41. Out for a walk in the sierras de Córdoba. *Left to right*: Carmen Córdoba (cousin), Roberto Guevara (cousin), Fernando Córdoba and Ernesto. *Behind*: Carmen de la Serna (aunt) and their mother.
16 1940–41. Ernesto, Celia, Ana Maria and Roberto in Alta Gracia.

23 1952. On the balcony of the house in the calle Aráoz, Buenos Aires, with Jorge de la Serna (uncle), Carlos Figueroa (friend), Roberto, Luis Rodríguez (friend), Juan Martin and Ernesto. **24** 1953. In Guatemala on Ernesto's second trip across Latin America with Gualo Garcia. **25** 1953. Juan Martin in the house in the calle Aráoz.

20

Guevara, un Joven Raidista, Cumplirá una Extensa Gira

SANTIAGO DEL ESTERO, 2 (Especial).— Hoy llegó a esta ciudad, el joven ciclista Ernesto Guevara de 21 años, estudiante, que se propone cumplir un extenso raid de ciclismo.

Inició su gira en Buenos Aires, pasando por Santa Fe y Córdoba. Ahora se dirige a Tucumán. de londe seguirá a Catamarca, La Rioja, San Juan, Mendoza y San Luis, donde emprenderá el regreso a Buenos Aires.

Viajeros. De Córdoba la señora Zulema de Marinucci.
—Del mismo punto la señorita Josefa Castiñeiras.
—De Buenos Aires la señorita Rosa Romeo López.
—A Córdoba el joven Jerónimo Cornet.
—A Ceres la señorita Ilda Monkarzel.
—A Buenos Aires el señor Fernando Berraondo.

21

22

20 First article to mention Ernesto, at the time of his arrival in Santiago del Estero on a Solex bicycle.
21 The newspaper *El Gráfico* which published the letter sent by Ernesto to the manager of Amerimex, congratulating him on the quality of the Micrón engine that had enabled him to travel over 4,000 kilometres across the poorest provinces in the north of Argentina.
22 1949–50, in Córdoba. *Bottom to top*: Ernesto, Celia, Carlos Ferrer, Roberto and a friend.

17 and 18 1943. Juan Martin in the arms of his big brother Ernesto, under their parents' attentive gaze, in Córdoba. **19** 1945. The Guevara de la Serna couple on holiday in Mar de Plata with their five children. *Left to right:* Juan Martin, Ernesto (father), Ernesto, Celia (mother), Ana Maria, Roberto and Celia.

26 Mexico, 1955. Ernesto with his first wife, Peruvian Hilda Gadea, and his first daughter, Hilda Beatriz Guevara. **27** Cuba, January 1959. Che's command headquarters in the Sierra del Escambray. Celia de la Serna, Celia Guevara de la Serna, Luis Rodrìguez and Juan Martin next to local people and fighters of the 26th of July Movement.

28 1959. His family's first visit to Cuba. Che sharing a joke with his mother and his younger brother Juan Martin. **29** January 1959. Che together with Aleida March, a fighter in the 26th of July Movement who later became his second wife, and Harry 'Pombo' Villegas in Santa Clara, Cuba. **30** 1960. Ernesto taking part in the fishing tournament at La Aguja in May 1960, with his mother.

31

32

33

31 14 May 1960.
With Fidel on
the second day
of the Ernest
Hemingway
fishing
tournament.
32 1960. Fidel
Castro visits Che's
family in Buenos
Aires.
33 1961. Che
with his family in
Punta del Este,
Uruguay, where
he attended the
Conference of the
Organization of
American States.
Left to right: Celia
de la Serna,
Juan Martin,
Ernesto, Roberto,
his friends Julio
César Castro and
Carlos Figueroa.

34 1961. Celia de la Serna (*left*), with her daughter Ana Maria and her son Juan Martin, holding her grandson on her knees in her house in the calle Aráoz, Buenos Aires. **35** The death of Che announced in the Argentinian daily *Clarín*. **36** 1976. Pamphlet designed by Celia Serna (sister) demanding the freeing of Juan Martin, a political prisoner of the Argentinian junta for his militant activities in the Partido Revolucionaria de los Trabajadores (PRT).

Photo credits: 1 to 27, and 32–36: Private collection, Guevara de la Serna family. 28: Oficina de Asuntos Históricos. 29: Alain Nogues/Sygma/Getty Images. 30, 31: © Alberto Korda © ADAGP, Paris and DACS, London 2016.

ally. So it was inadvisable to make an enemy of the Soviets. Fidel was not fundamentally opposed to Ernesto, but he was under pressure. He was the head of state. On Ernesto's return from his last official tour abroad, the two men had had a long conversation. Ernesto had announced his desire to head off and foment revolution elsewhere.

In his biography *El Che Guevara*, the Argentinian author Hugo Gambini relates that Fidel tried to convince Ernesto to stay. Che apparently replied: 'The Cuban revolution needs to have an ally in Latin America it can count on, so as to have another point of support and consolidate itself. The ally I have in mind can be found only if we start a revolution somewhere else, and for that, we must place a leader at the helm, a leader with extensive experience of guerrilla warfare and with the prestige necessary to ensure the leadership of the political movement. That leader is me. *You* can't start a revolution elsewhere because you must carry on as leader of this one. *I* can, and I will, damn it!'

It remained to be seen in what Latin American country the next revolution would begin. The insurgency launched in the Argentinian province of Salta by Jorge Masetti, meant to be the starting point of a wider movement, had been dismantled. Masetti had gone underground in September 1963. Seven months later, he was missing. Nobody has ever seen him since.

Without necessarily believing the absurd rumours, my mother had spent the last weeks of her life in a state of continual anxiety. She wondered whether Ernesto wasn't just angry with her. Had he dug his heels in as a result of the letter she wrote to him on 14 April 1965, filled with bitter reproaches? She entrusted this letter to Ricardo Rojo, a compatriot and old friend of Ernesto's: at that time, diplomatic relations between Cuba and Argentina had been suspended, so we entrusted our correspondence to safe messengers. Rojo was to deliver the letter to an intermediary bound for Cuba, but his trip had been cancelled at the last minute and the letter had remained in Buenos Aires. So Ernesto never learned of its existence. This letter was given to the family much later, after my mother's death.

In early May, I took my mother to my grandmother's in Portela, hoping this would provide her with some relief. After a few days, her condition suddenly worsened. She suffered terribly. So I took her back to Buenos Aires where she was hospitalized. She had only one thought: to see Ernesto, or at least talk to him.

After several attempts, she finally managed to get Aleida March on the phone. My sister-in-law tried to reassure her: she didn't need to worry, Ernesto wasn't in Havana, she couldn't reveal where he was, but he was well, and working. This enigmatic explanation was of no comfort to my mother. She died tormented by anxiety, wondering about Ernesto's whereabouts and the reasons for his long silence.

At her funeral, her coffin was covered with the Argentinian flag, a Cuban flag and the banner of the Movimiento Nacional liberación (National Liberation Movement).

The mystery of Che's disappearance was unsolved, including in Cuba. No one had seen him since his last trip which had taken him to New York, then to Mali, Ghana, Algeria, Dahomey, Guinea, Congo and Tanzania. Cubans were particularly surprised by his absence from the funeral of Aníbal Escalante, an important member of the government. At that time, people were unaware that Che had handed Fidel a letter of resignation and farewell during his last secret visit to Cuba. The letter, which I reproduce here, would be read out in public by the *Líder Máximo* on 3 October 1965:

Fidel,

I am remembering so many things right now: the day I met you at Maria Antonia's, where you asked me to accompany you and all the tension that surrounded the preparations.

One day, we were asked who should be notified in case of decease, and the possibility of death suddenly struck us like lightning. Later, we learned that this possibility was perfectly real and that in a revolution (if it is genuine) you must conquer or die. Many of our comrades fell on the road to victory.

Today, our tone is less dramatic, because we are more mature; but the situation is repeating itself. I have the impression that I have done my duty for the Cuban revolution on its own soil, and I am taking my leave of you, of my companions, and of your people which is now also mine.

I formally resign my duties to the Party leadership and my post as minister, I renounce my rank as commander, and my status as a Cuban. No legal relationship now connects me to Cuba. What does bind me are links of a different nature: deep links, which do not break in the way a title or a rank do.

As I look back over my life, I believe I have worked with sufficient honesty and dedication to consolidate the triumph of the revolution. Perhaps the only serious mistake I have made is not having had more confidence in you right from the start in the Sierra Maestra, and not having been able to discern your qualities as a revolutionary and leader earlier. I have lived through some magnificent times and at your side I have been proud to belong to our people in the bright and melancholy days of the Caribbean Crisis. Rarely has a head of state been so brilliant in such circumstances, and I am pleased to have followed you without hesitation, to have shared your way of thinking and of seeing and assessing dangers and principles.

Other countries in the world are calling for the support of my modest efforts. I can do what is denied you due to your responsibility at the head of Cuba. The time has come to separate.

You should know that I do this with a mixture of joy and sorrow; I leave here the purest of my hopes as a builder and the dearest of all those I love . . . and I leave a people that has adopted me as a son. It is heart-breaking. On new battlefields I will carry inside me the faith that you have inculcated within me, the revolutionary spirit of my people, the feeling of accomplishing the most sacred of duties: to fight against imperialism wherever it may be; such a mission always comforts us and heals the deepest wounds.

I repeat once more that I relieve Cuba of any responsibility except that of setting an example. If one day, under other skies, my final hour should come, my last thought will be for this people and more especially for you. Thank you for your teachings and your example; I will try to stay true to them, right to the furthest consequences of my actions. I have always been in total agreement with the foreign policy of our revolution and I will remain so. Wherever I find myself, I will always bear the responsibility of a Cuban revolutionary, and I will behave as such. I leave nothing material to my children and my wife, and I do not regret this; on the contrary, I am happy this is the case. I ask nothing for them, because I know that the state will give them what they need to live and learn.

I still have so much to say to you and to our people, but I feel that there's no point, because words cannot express what I feel, and it is useless to blacken paper in vain.

Until victory, always! The Fatherland or Death!

I embrace you with all my revolutionary fervour.

So, instead of cutting sugarcane, Che was training for combat and was planning the next stage of his life. To my parents, he wrote the following farewell letter on 1 April 1965:

Dear old folks: once again I'm getting itchy feet; I'm heading off again, my shield under my arm. Almost ten years ago, I sent you another farewell letter. If I remember rightly, I lamented at the time that I wasn't a better soldier and a better doctor; the second doesn't interest me anymore, and I'm not such a bad soldier. Nothing has basically changed, except that I'm much more aware, my Marxism is rooted and uncluttered. I believe in armed struggle as the only solution for peoples fighting for their liberation, and I am consistent in my beliefs. Many will call me an adventurer and so I am, only of a different kind – one of those who risk their lives to demonstrate their truths.

This letter might be the last. I do not seek death, but it is part of the logical calculus of probabilities. If so, may this letter be a last embrace: I really loved you, but I couldn't express my affection, I'm extremely rigid in my actions and I think you didn't always understand me. I wasn't easy to understand. On the other hand, don't just believe me today. Now, a powerful desire that I have polished with an artist's delight will support tottering legs and tired lungs. I will do it. Remember from time to time this simple *condottiero* of the twentieth century. A kiss for Celia, Roberto, Ana Maria, Patatín, Beatriz, and everybody. A big hug from a prodigal and recalcitrant son.

Held up in Havana, this highly personal letter did not reach us before my mother's death. Ernesto heard the terrible news in Congo on 20 May, and in her honour wrote the magnificent text *La Piedra*, of which I here reproduce a short excerpt:

He gave me the news [of my mother's death] in the way these things have to be told to a strong man, a responsible man; I thanked him for this . . . What can I do? I really don't know. I only know that I feel a physical need to see my mother appear, to put my head on her thin lap so she can say '*mi viejo*' with a dry, intense affection, to feel in my hair her clumsy hand stroking me with rapid jerky movements like a puppet, as if tenderness was pouring from her eyes and her voice, because her strings are damaged and don't allow her to reach the end of my hair. And hands tremble and touch more than they stroke but the tenderness flows out of her pores and envelops my hair and I feel so wonderful, so small and so strong. I don't need to ask her for forgiveness; she understands everything and we know this when we hear her say '*mi viejo*'.

Che had flown to Africa sometime in late April–early May 1965[3] under an assumed identity, as Ramón Benítez. He arrived in Congo-Kinshasa three weeks later with twelve Cuban companions[4] – a hundred others would join them later – whose aim was to assist the Simba rebel movement led by Laurent Kabila. Congo had been gripped by a civil war since gaining independence. On the ground, it was a terrible chaos. The weapons that arrived were damaged, information was imprecise, men spent part of the money meant for the revolution on prostitutes and were suffering from venereal diseases, there was latent alcoholism and logistics were virtually nonexistent. For an ultra-disciplined fighter like my brother, such disorganization was difficult to tolerate. As for Laurent Kabila, he first impressed and then disappointed Ernesto. He lacked seriousness, and was never where he was supposed to be. He was a dilettante. Disenchanted, Ernesto left the Congo in November with the feeling of having accomplished nothing really concrete and with his health weakened by the climate. He had lost twenty kilos. Feeling that he could not return to Cuba now that Fidel had publicly read out his farewell letter, he spent the next six months under a false identity in Dar es Salaam in Tanzania, where Aleida, also under a false identity, had gone to join him, and then in Prague where he re-established contact with Tania Bunke, an Argentinian revolutionary of German origin based in La Paz, Bolivia.[5] 'I never felt so alone on the path I was following', he wrote in his diary.

In Buenos Aires, we were still without news of him, and worried sick. Later, we learned that Fidel had finally convinced him to return incognito to Havana before setting off again. The events are well known. He returned to Cuba under the name of Ramón Benítez via Switzerland, probably Paris (some maintain that they saw him walking near the Sorbonne wearing his famous beret, heedless of being recognized), Germany and Moscow where, to confuse potential spies, he had shaved off his beard, cut his hair and grown a moustache. Ernesto had made himself unrecognizable by adopting the look of a respectable travelling salesman. The disguise was so effective that his children Hilda (ten years old), Aleida (six), Camilo (four), Celia (three) and Ernesto (one) had not recognized him when he paid them one last visit before leaving for South America. He had introduced himself as a friend of their father's and they had believed him.

When I heard the terrible news of Ernesto's death, I went to my father's in calle Paraguay, clutching the newspaper. The family immediately assembled at Celia's. Only Ana Maria was missing: she lived in Tucumán and had five young children. Her friend Olga was present. We scrutinized the photo in the newspaper together. Nobody wanted to believe that it was Ernesto. Celia kept saying: 'What do *you* think? It must be a trick photo.' My father thought the same. It was too horrible. I was convinced that it was indeed him, not a fake photo. Olga thought the same thing without daring to say so. She peered at the hands in the photo and recognized them. We all had the same hands. We also all had the same bearing, she kept saying. Celia couldn't accept the fact that Ernesto was dead. The idea caused her terrible pain. My father intoned: 'I tell you that the photo is fake, it's not Ernesto.'

One of us had to leave for Bolivia immediately to be sure. We found it very difficult to decide which of us would go. My father and Celia were too deeply affected. That left just me, or Roberto. They chose him: he was thirty-five and a lawyer.

Going to identify Che's remains in Bolivia was not without its practical consequences for him. It amounted to being an act of rebellion, as well as an extremely sorrowful duty. Argentina was living under the military dictatorship of Juan Carlos Onganía. You needed guts, and Roberto certainly had guts.

My brother flew in a private plane to Vallegrande on the morning of 11 October, two days after Ernesto's death, accompanied by two journalists from the magazine *Gente*. It was raining heavily over Buenos Aires and visibility was nil. Most flights were cancelled because of the weather. But Roberto's trip couldn't wait. He needed urgently to arrive in Bolivia and find out. Was Ernesto really dead?

This simple trip quickly turned into an epic. The plane first had to land in Salta where Roberto, the pilot and the two journalists were forced to spend the night. It was already 5 p.m. and Bolivian airports stopped operating at nightfall. In Salta, Roberto gave his name to a hotel employee who hastened to alert the press, whereupon a swarm of reporters soon descended. The news of the death of the most wanted guerrilla in the world had, of course, travelled all round the world.

The front pages all showed the same thing: Che's corpse. Roberto stared at them, examining every detail of the bruised body, trying not to recognize his brother in them. To the journalist who asked him for his opinion after seeing him struggling mentally over the photos, he replied: 'Indeed, it's very disturbing but it's inconclusive. When I have the body in front of me, I'll be able to give you a definite reply.' But he wouldn't be able to see Ernesto's remains due to the series of obstacles that the Bolivian army put in his way.

Arriving in Vallegrande the next day, Roberto asked to see the man responsible for Ernesto's capture, Colonel Joaquín Zenteno Anaya, but he had gone away. In the street a vendor selling the local paper was shouting the headlines: 'Che was buried yesterday at dawn'. Roberto was incredulous. How had they dared to bury Che so quickly without informing his family? When the colonel returned, he confirmed the story. Che's burial had indeed taken place in the greatest secrecy and he was not allowed to reveal the place of burial. Only the high command of the Bolivian army knew, as part of a policy applied to all guerrillas. Zenteno Anaya also claimed to have evidence of Ernesto's identity. The army had found his diary on him, the fingerprints matched, and, above all, Che had admitted his identity before dying. Roberto asked for the body to be exhumed on the grounds of his rights as a brother. The colonel replied that he was not empowered to take such decisions. He advised him to go and see the head of the army, General Alfredo Ovando Candía, in La Paz. So Roberto left for La Paz and, on his arrival, went directly to the barracks. Ovando Candía was not there. Roberto knocked at the door of his private residence. He was starting to believe that he was being led down the garden path, and that the Bolivian military leaders were deliberately avoiding him. 'The general's policy is never to receive official visits at home', he was informed by a lieutenant who opened the door. Roberto gave his name and insisted. The general came to welcome him with these words: 'I am truly sorry. I would have preferred a hero like your brother to come out of the Bolivian scrub alive.' Roberto repeated his request to have the body exhumed. And thereupon, the general invented another story: 'I authorize you to return to Vallegrande but you will certainly arrive too late. I wouldn't be surprised if he has been cremated.'

The commercial flight to Santa Cruz, the airport closest to Vallegrande, did not leave until the next morning. So Roberto spent the night at the Hotel Crillon. Coincidentally, he was given the room occupied a few months earlier by the parents of French philosopher Régis Debray, when they had come to visit their son in prison. Debray was arrested on coming out of the scrub in Ñancahuazú with the guerrilla Ciro Bustos, who had just deserted with the agreement of Che.

Roberto was less and less inclined to believe that Ernesto was dead. Each story seemed to contradict the last. The Bolivian army was gaining time by making him go on endless futile return trips. Why? However much he scratched his head over it, he couldn't fathom the situation. He had also just read a report which claimed that the teeth of the 'dead guerrilla' were in a perfect state, apart from one missing molar. This wasn't true: in our family, we all had rotten teeth. By the age of thirty-six, Roberto already had dentures. Ernesto's teeth had begun to decay from the age of ten. Everything seemed such a muddle.

Roberto didn't manage to book his flight to Santa Cruz.

Everything conspired against him. At dawn he appeared at La Paz airport. The airline staff at first claimed that the plane was full, and then that it wasn't full but that it was too late to buy a ticket. Whatever the real reason, it was apparently impossible to take the flight – until Roberto came up with the idea of offering to pay almost triple the price, and then seats miraculously became available. From Santa Cruz, he took another flight to Vallegrande. The runway was guarded by an army of 200 soldiers. On leaving the plane, Roberto found himself face to face with Zenteno Anaya who had come hurtling along the track in a jeep. The colonel seemed both surprised and annoyed to see him. He thought he'd got rid of this other Guevara once and for all. As he could hardly ignore him, he invited him to the barracks to meet General Juan José Torres, who confirmed repeatedly the lie of his colleague Ovando Candía, namely that Che's body had been cremated that same morning. The general advised Roberto to return to Argentina.

Five guerrillas had managed to escape the ambush and were still alive somewhere in the region: Harry 'Pombo' Villegas Tamayo, Daniel 'Benigno' Alarcón Ramírez, Leonardo 'Urbano' Tamayo Núñez, David 'Dario' Adriazola and Guido 'Inti' Peredo Leigue. Roberto was now convinced that Ernesto wasn't dead, that he had slipped through the net with them. His death had been announced so often, only to turn out to be a false alarm! Plus the Bolivians had told him too many conflicting stories. He also felt that, in the photo, Ernesto looked too thin and pointed. Ernesto had a flat nose.

Short of ideas and support, he left Bolivia, still undecided. Rather than go directly to Buenos Aires, he decided to go and see my sister Ana Maria in Tucumán. She had obviously seen the pictures and was not under too many illusions.

The trip to Bolivia had all been for nothing. Roberto knew hardly any more than he had before he set out. Upon his return, the family met again. We didn't know what to think. There was some evidence to indicate that Ernesto had died, and some to suggest the opposite. It was Fidel who put an end to our doubts by calling us the next day to confirm Ernesto's death. He wanted to show us the evidence. So Roberto flew to Havana. He was received by Fidel with these words: 'Forgive me, but we can't deny the obvious. We have all the evidence to show that it's him.' A Bolivian soldier had sent Che's diary and hands to Cuba. His hands had been amputated to preserve his fingerprints. Roberto collapsed in grief. This time, he returned to Buenos Aires convinced that our brother was indeed dead. The news crushed my father. In the wake of all this, we were informed that Ernesto had not fallen in combat on 8 October as the Bolivian army had initially claimed, but was assassinated on 9 October (photos of him as a prisoner in the school in La Higuera would be published only much later). Nobody believed he had really been cremated. It was a fable intended to prevent people digging him up. The Bolivian army had refused to wait for the arrival of the federal police to identify the body. They had even sent the secretary of the Argentinian embassy in La Paz, Miguel Cremona, packing.

We were all in a terrible state of shock. Without a word being exchanged, a silent decision was made: we would now never talk about Ernesto except amongst ourselves. Roberto and Celia kept their word. Until her death, Ana Maria said repeatedly that she would never talk about Che. As for me, I will explain below the reasons that finally impelled me to speak.

In Cuba, Che's death was announced by Fidel on 15 October. Three days of national mourning were declared. Three days later, on the Plaza de la Revolución, Fidel gave a long homily on his dead friend to a million Cubans, a vibrant tribute that ended with these words:

> If we have to say who we wish to be our revolutionary fighters, our militants, our men, we will say without hesitation: let them be like Che! If we want to express how we want the men of future generations to be, we declare: like Che! If we wish to say how we want our children to be educated, we must say without hesitation: we want them to be educated in the spirit of Che! If we want the model of a man who does not belong only to the present time but to the future, truly, I say to you that this model, without blemish in his exemplary behaviour, his attitudes, his way of acting – this model is Che! And with all our heart, as zealous revolutionaries, we want our sons to be like Che!

We finally learned the truth about Ernesto's burial at the end of 1995, thanks to the American journalist Jon Lee Anderson.[6] He had come up with the idea of meeting with the retired Bolivian general, Mario Vargas, armed with a bottle of whisky. A few glasses did indeed help the soldier unburden himself: he revealed the truth. Anderson learned that Che had not been cremated but thrown into a mass grave near the cemetery and airfield of Vallegrande with the six companions arrested with him: Orlando Pantoja Tamayo, Aniceto Reinaga Gordillo, René Martinez Tamayo, Alberto Fernandez Montes de Oca, Juan Pablo Chang Navarro and Simeon Cuba Sarabia. Only two witnesses had attended the clandestine night-time 'burial': the truck driver responsible for transporting the body and the tractor driver who had dug the hole. Threatened with death, they had sworn to keep the secret.

The Bolivian government authorized the exhumation a few days after the general's revelation. Tongues were suddenly loosened. A surprising amount of contradictory evidence was then made public. Excavations began. Argentinian and Cuban teams of geologists and forensic experts arrived in Vallegrande, preceded by a squad of 110 soldiers instructed to watch their every move. The excavations lasted more than a year. The remains of seven bodies were dug up on 28 June 1997. One of the dead men had had his hands cut off. The colonel of the squad then called us to inform us of the discovery. The forensic experts who set to work identified all the remains, including those of Che.

In Cuba, the man responsible for handling the case and verifying Ernesto's DNA was Ramiro Valdés, the old companion from *Granma* and the Sierra Maestra. He called us and asked us what we wanted to do with Ernesto's remains. This was a pure formality to show that our feelings were being taken into consideration. Unfortunately, there was no way to bring Ernesto to Argentina. This would have been pointless: the country was not ready to receive him as he deserved. His body was transferred to Havana on 12 July 1997, then to Santa Clara, the site of his victory, where he was buried officially in the presence of the members of his family: his four living children (Hilda Beatriz had died two years earlier), Aleida March, his wife, Roberto, Celia, my Guevara Erra half-brothers, and myself.

To the pain of my brother's death was added the pain of a failed revolution. Some described the Ñancahuazú campaign as a suicide mission. According to them, Che was a nihilist who had stated: 'I'm here now, and if they take me out of here, it'll be feet first.' They were wrong. Bolivia was not an end in itself.

It was to be a starting point, the springboard to a new revolution which would extend to all of Latin America and liberate the sister nations from Yankee imperialism. Its geographical position made it a strategic region 'to extend the revolution to neighbouring countries', Che said (Bolivia has five borders: with Chile, Argentina, Peru, Brazil and Paraguay).

Nothing in Ernesto's diary provided any evidence that he was knowingly throwing himself into the lion's den. He kept hoping for a victory until the end. Some, including myself, as I said before, thought the KGB had collaborated with the CIA to capture him. The USSR had no liking for revolutionaries. It was also said that the Bolivian miners had not come to his aid and that the Bolivian Communist Party had abandoned him. Certainly, its general secretary Mario Monje wanted to break with Che despite his initial promises of assistance. When he went to see him in the scrub and demanded to lead the Ejercito de liberación nacional de Bolivia (ELN – Bolivian Army of National Liberation) himself, under the pretext that Che was a foreigner and the ELN needed a Bolivian to head it, he knew full well that Che would never accept. Monje had no experience of guerrilla warfare. To enable him to betray Che without seeming to betray the cause of communism, he had to find an excuse; and this was Monje's excuse. Guido 'Inti' Peredo, one of Che's companions, later explained that the desertion of the Communist Party had cut the rebels off from the cities and the potential logistical support crucial for the survival of the movement.

Che had come to create a hotbed of insurgency in Bolivia, developing what was already latent. The whole of Latin America was in turmoil at the time, with protest organizations active in several countries. Ernesto had, as is well known, a special attachment for Bolivia because of our maid Sabina Portugal. He had visited the country for the first time in 1953, in the middle of a revolutionary period, when Víctor Paz Estenssoro's government was in power. He wrote us long letters describing what he had observed of the mobilization of the people in the streets and progressive measures such as nationalizations and land reform. He believed in the Bolivians' capacity for rebellion.

We can assume that Ernesto overestimated the support he could get from the peasants. Most were poor and of indigenous origin. They spoke in Quechua and Aymara rather than Spanish, which they could hardly speak. They had only one idol, Pachamama (Mother Earth), and lived in another dimension. Cut off from the world, they lacked the perspective to appreciate a revolution. Every Hispanic was a stranger to them, treated with suspicion. They had obviously never heard of Che Guevara, whose fame had not reached their lands. It was very difficult in this context to make allies of them.

It was indeed a peasant who alerted the army to the presence of guerrillas in the Quebrada del Yuro. Yet the rebels treated the *campesinos* with respect and affection. Ernesto took care of their sick children, and taught them to read and write. He set up mobile schools and chose his best-educated fighters to give lessons daily from 4 p.m. to 6 p.m., in grammar, arithmetic, history and geography. Ernesto himself played a part in this educational effort and gave extra French lessons to interested parties. His lectures on political economy were mandatory. After the victory, he said, educated people would be needed to assume power. And he repeatedly said that a guerrilla couldn't just be a 'mere shooter': he needed a broad general knowledge.

Che released prisoners from the Bolivian army after bandaging their wounds. My brother was a great humanist. 'At the risk of appearing ridiculous', he had said one day, 'I say that the true revolutionary is primarily guided by great feelings of love. It is impossible to think of a genuine revolutionary devoid of these qualities . . . It takes large doses of humanism, justice and truth not to fall into dogmatism, in a cold scholasticism, and isolation from the masses.'[7] Before he left, he gave Aleida a list of books he wanted to take with him. They included the works of Sophocles, Demosthenes, Herodotus, Plato, Plutarch, Euripides, Aristophanes, Aristotle, Dante, Racine, Goethe, Shakespeare and Pindar.

The Ñancahuazú campaign lasted eleven months. Forty-five gruelling weeks, in constant movement. Ernesto suffered from increasingly frequent asthma attacks that weakened him even if he didn't let them slow him down. He never allowed others to treat him with more respect or give him more food.

He had arrived in La Paz in the greatest secrecy in early November 1966, in his famous travelling salesman disguise. On 27 November, the Bolivian revolutionary Guido 'Inti' Peredo laid eyes on him for the first time in the scrub; he described this initial contact in his book *My Campaign with Che*: 'Che was sitting on a tree trunk. He was smoking, and obviously revelling in the scent of the tobacco. He was wearing his beret. When we arrived, his eyes sparkled with joy. The man most wanted by imperialism, the legendary guerrilla, the strategist and theorist of projects of international ambition, the banner of struggle and hope: here he was, sitting quietly in the heart of one of the most exploited and oppressed countries on the continent . . . His trip to Bolivia was one of the most fascinating secrets of history.'[8]

The first clashes with the Bolivian army had not been sought by the rebels, who were forced to initiate them when they were discovered. They were only fifty or so men. But in the first months of 1967, as they managed to win a few battles, they bluffed the Bolivians into imagining that the rebel army was larger than it actually was. In response, the Bolivians strengthened the means to combat it. Duly alerted, the CIA moved into the palace of the puppet president René Barrientos and ordered the neighbouring countries to close their borders to the rebels and prevent any aid from reaching them.

By the end of September, the ELN was reduced to a column of seventeen men; they were exhausted, tormented by hunger and thirst, and lacking protein. On the morning of 8 October, it was very cold in the Quebrada del Yuro. Because he knew he was surrounded, Che sent three groups of two sentries each to locate the positions of the Bolivian army. This was how some of these men evaded the ambush.

I can't go into an analysis of the failure of the Ñancahuazú campaign. The only certainty I have is that it ended in a rout. I can't give specific reasons: they are beyond me. Everyone seeks them in his or her own convictions. Some argue that Fidel Castro let the campaign down, others that the miners did not support Che, or that he deceived himself about the peasants, or that captured combatants and deserters spoke. It is a proven fact that the captured guerrilla Ciro Bustos, as he admitted, produced an identikit portrait of 'Ramón Benítez' under questioning, and that this portrait finally convinced the military that Ramón was indeed Che, as they had suspected for some months and were seeking to confirm. The most important lesson is that we experienced a continental defeat of the revolutionary project represented by Che. For me, the failure in Bolivia is deeply puzzling.

Another certainty is that there were five survivors, named above. Despite the massive presence of the army, Guido 'Inti'

Peredo was one of those who managed to get out of the scrub; he took refuge in Cochabamba. From his hideout, Inti contacted a man from the Bolivian Communist Party. And what did this man tell him? That he should under no circumstances reveal his presence in Cochabamba to the leader of the Party, as the latter would betray him. Inti remained in hiding for several weeks. He was assassinated in 1969 by the security forces. Had he actually been betrayed by a member of his circle?

10

Eight years, three months and twenty-three days

On 3 May 1974, I was walking quietly down calle Córdoba when, for the first time, I was arrested by men in uniform. I was returning from Havana where I had been to drop off my wife Maria Elena and our three children. I feared for their safety in Argentina. The political climate was becoming alarming and unhealthy for activists like us, let alone the fact that Che was my brother. We had entered into one of those accursed periods when bearing the Guevara name was not easy. Despite the danger, I decided to return home, determined to continue my political and militant activities. I had impelled my father to emigrate to Cuba the year before. Knowing that my family was safe, I could get more involved.

I was an activist for the Partido Revolucionario de los Trabajadores (PRT), a major politico-syndicalist organization encompassing several movements. I belonged to the wing known as the Frente anti-imperialista por el Socialismo (Anti-imperialist Front for Socialism). Juan Perón was very weak physically, but he continued to govern. He was back from exile thanks to an agreement with the military government of Alejandro Agustín Lanusse, who had allowed him to return home to block the advance of the revolutionaries. But Perón's days were numbered. He was seventy-nine and suffered from heart disease. He died on 1 July 1974 and was replaced as head of state by his third wife Isabel,[1] a former cabaret dancer who had been to school for only five years but still occupied the envied position of vice-president. Unable to govern alone, she was assisted, or rather dominated, by a sinister character, a high-ranking policeman fascinated by the esoteric: José López Rega, alias 'El Brujo' (The Sorcerer). López Rega had schemed for years to get close to Isabel and had devoted considerable energy to consolidating their friendship. The effort had paid off: he was invited to join the Perón couple in their Spanish exile as a private secretary.

On the death of the general, he naturally assumed the role of Isabel's adviser. Now a widow, she no longer took any decision without consulting him. So Rega's influence increased considerably. He took advantage of his power to found the death squad known as the Argentinian Anti-communist Alliance – better known as the Triple A – with the goal of 'eradicating the Marxist infiltration of Peronism', embodied among others by the Montoneros movement, the Fuerzas Armadas Revolucionarias (FAR) and the Ejercito Revolucionario del Pueblo (ERP). My country was again heading towards a new era of repression now known as the 'dirty war' and the 'years of lead'. I should make it clear that the political context of the time was extremely complex. Unless I take the trouble of explaining this, it will be impossible to understand my two periods of detention and the gradual banishment of all the Guevaras to Cuba.

Basically, Peronism was a working-class, trade-union movement. 'Neither Yankees nor Marxists. Peronists!' as its supporters chanted. More than a party, it was a movement that allowed everyone to find what they were looking for. Juan Perón was an idol of the masses, fought over by supporters of all stripes. Whether they were on the right or the left, they struggled to exist without his blessing, including and especially during his exile. Peronism had given birth to two opposing trends: a left-wing movement, represented by the young Montoneros, the Juventud Peronista (JP) and the Argentinian Confederación General del Trabajo de los Argentinos (CGT) under the leadership of Agustín Tosco, and an 'orthodox' movement represented by the powerful CGT union.[2] Both trends were convinced that they embodied authentic Peronism and fought for the love of their leader. But whenever Peronism seemed about to take a turn to the left, Perón nipped the initiative in the bud. When Héctor José Cámpora, alias El Tío (Uncle), was elected president in March 1973, Perón forced him to resign two months after his inauguration even though he himself had appointed him as the Peronist candidate.[3] El Tío had committed three unforgivable mistakes: he had declared an amnesty for members of revolutionary organizations; he had restored diplomatic relations with Cuba; and he had appointed young socialists to government posts. In other words, he had favoured leftist elements.

The Peronists stopped chanting 'Cámpora in government, Perón in power'. Cámpora's resignation on 13 July – he had obeyed without batting an eyelid – allowed the general to organize new elections and win. He reassumed power on 12 October and named Isabel as vice-president. The 'rightward shift' of the political base was now a reality.

Some Peronists attempted to distance themselves from the tragic events that shook our country, notably the military coups of 1955 and 1976, by placing the blame on others. However, some of the responsibility for these tragedies does lie with them. When Perón went into exile three months after the bombing of the Plaza de Mayo on 16 June 1955, he came up with countless justifications to explain why he was abandoning ship. He was fundamentally opposed to any genuine process of social trans- formation. For example, he profoundly mistrusted the youth movement represented by Montoneros. Having courted both trends and cultivated ambiguity, he finally put his cards on the table on returning from exile: he despised the left wing of the movement.

The final break with Montoneros was the bloodbath of 20 June 1973, the day of his return from Spain. To greet Perón in style, his faithful on both sides had planned to gather at an inter- section of the road from Buenos Aires to Ezeiza International Airport (later, their number was estimated at three and a half million people). Some supporters came armed, so great was the animosity between the two factions. They had not managed to agree on the places they would respectively occupy on the road the general would be taking to reach Buenos Aires after eighteen years of exile. Without consulting Montoneros, the 'orthodox' supporters had hastily mounted a platform. They had the advantage of height. When the Montoneros support- ers approached it, snipers fired on them, leaving thirteen dead and 365 wounded. Far from denouncing the killing, Perón declared: 'You don't create a fatherland by screaming. We, the Peronists, must take over the leadership of our movement, set it in motion and neutralize those who want to deform it from top to bottom.' The massacre marked the outbreak of real hostilities. The Montoneros had been betrayed by their idol, and so had the young people of Argentina.

So Isabel had inherited a regime conducive to revolutionary

action. Some have suggested that Perón had been bewitched by López Rega.[4] This is quite untrue; it's a story made up to hide the fact that Perón was deeply reactionary, a lackey of imperialism. He was a right-wing nationalist capitalist and populist who wanted nothing to do with Marxism, communism, socialism or a revolution. Towards the end of his life, it was this persuasion that dictated his actions. He approached the military and orchestrated an interim period of power for his wife so as to give the armed forces time to prepare for the coup of 24 March 1976.

Under the influence of López Rega, Isabel intensified the repression. In addition to his dabbling in esoteric practices and his anti-communism, 'The Sorcerer' followed orders to rid Peronism of its leftists, stop the demonstrations and halt any potential working-class or revolutionary advance. Pursued by the Triple A, which imprisoned and assassinated Montoneros members with total impunity, the latter gradually transformed itself into an armed group. Rebellion was brewing. Other factions were formed. Attacks became ever more common. One of the other targets of the Triple A was the PRT. In the face of this turn of events, our meetings now revolved around one central question: should we take up arms and if so, was this the right time? We were divided. Across the continent, the climate favoured armed confrontation, with revolutionary movements in Uruguay, Bolivia, Chile, Venezuela, Colombia and Brazil. Their model was Cuba, the cradle of the victorious struggle, the flagship of the American continent. This island represented hope for a real change in society.

In Argentina, conflict between left and right worsened every day. We witnessed a huge mobilization on the part of the working class and the trade unions. The proletarian masses, workers and students formed organizations. They were opposed by an alliance between economic groups, the secret services of Argentina and elsewhere, the armed forces, conservative politicians and right-wing trade unions. Their main enemy was the left, and their ultimate objective its disappearance. So our companions started to be swallowed up in ever more alarming numbers by the clandestine detention and torture centres that had arisen throughout the country. They disappeared without trace or sometimes reappeared in the form of mutilated corpses. The situation was more critical in Córdoba than in the rest of the country. Since the military coup of General Juan Carlos Onganía in 1966 and the enactment of his repressive anti-communist legislation, the city had been transformed into Argentina's capital of political struggle. An already well-established tradition of protest had preceded the appearance of López Rega's death squad. The rebel movement had a name: the Cordobazo. It brought together students, workers and trade unionists in an endless series of revolts, protests and attacks, and organized its first major riot in May 1969. From his exile, Perón declared Córdoba 'the centre of the infection'.

It was in Córdoba that the Triple A emerged; here, too, occurred the fatal break with institutional legality in the name of repression. I had arrived there a few months before my arrest, just before the regional coup of 28 February 1974. On that day, the army colonel and police chief Antonio Domingo Navarro stormed the government palace and arrested the governor Ricardo Obregón Cano and his lieutenant governor Atilio López, both on the Peronist left, and twelve of their colleagues. Obregón Cano and his running mate had picked up over 50 per cent of the vote in the previous elections. No matter: they were incarcerated. There was no doubt that the order came from the highest levels of the state. Moreover, the same thing had happened in the province of Buenos Aires a month earlier. Governor Oscar Raúl Bidegain had been sacked from his post by right-wing Peronists who distrusted the young progressives in his government.

It was in this poisonous and explosive atmosphere, then, that I was arrested on 3 May 1974. Two men in uniform that I had not seen coming suddenly loomed up in front of me. They each grabbed me by an arm. When I tried to fight back, they pointed their guns at me. They bundled me into a police van. We shot off to the prefecture. En route, they told me that my apartment had been searched while I was at the factory. They had found PRT documents and 'incriminating' books. I was a worker, an active member of the PRT, and my name was Guevara. I was carrying false papers as it was so risky to use my real name, but they had still picked me up. However, I didn't know if they were aware of my true identity. I might have been arrested for the mere fact of belonging to the PRT.

Even my party comrades didn't know who I really was. For them, I was nobody's brother, just Juan Martin. I didn't proclaim my family relationship to Che from the rooftops: it was too dangerous not only for me but also for my friends and for the PRT. Nowadays, I seek to spread Che's ideas; but not at that time. Also, we suspected that the Triple A might have infiltrated the party; we had to be constantly wary. Several armed groups, which later merged, were rampant in Córdoba.

I was jailed in the San Martin prison for three months and eighteen days. At his own risk, my brother Roberto acted as my lawyer as soon as he learned of my arrest. He immediately came to Córdoba and defended me with all his might. So, though I was beaten, abused and interrogated, I was not tortured. I was accused of 'falsifying official documents', the only charge they had managed to bring against me. I deduced that they did in fact know my real identity. I was given a conditional release, but I was now on their files. Meanwhile, my companions who had been arrested the same day as me remained in prison. I later learned that others had been shot, or tortured to death. You never knew why one prisoner was released and another shot.

After the coup of 24 March 1976, people were no longer released or even simply jailed: death became the most common sentence. This was the fate of José René Moukarzel, who was thrown naked into the inner yard in sub-zero temperatures and repeatedly doused with freezing water because he had accepted a sachet of salt from a common law prisoner.

I thought I could escape the forces of repression after my release in August by moving to Rosario, the capital of the province of Santa Fe. Here, things seemed calmer, less explosive than in Córdoba. I found a job in a *yerbatera* factory. This was where I met my wife Viviana Beguán, aka La Negra, the mother of my daughter Dolores. Viviana was, like me, an activist in the PRT. We started to campaign together. We attended meetings and went into the universities to try and unify the movement before the imminent military coup – we were convinced that the armed forces would seize power by force. This is what they had done in each period of unrest in Argentina – and in the course of history, we had had our fair share of such periods! In the PRT, discussions continued to revolve around what strategy to adopt. The party leadership was leaning more and more towards armed struggle, but some members were opposed to it, believing that it might precipitate a coup rather than prevent one. In the final analysis, we were all at sea; we doubted whether we would be able to prevent the coup simply by resorting to activism, and we were unsure of the appropriate time to act. Perón's death had really complicated things. Isabel's government was enacting increasingly repressive measures that limited our room for manoeuvre.

At the end of September 1975, under the chairmanship of Italo Luder, the Senate authorized massive repression by passing the so-called anti-communist and anti-subversive national security law 20840. Its fourteen articles allowed the government to arrest people under the false pretext that they were in possession of subversive materials – leaflets, newspapers, books, etc.; to criminalize union activity and labour movements; to prohibit the publication of certain newspapers and imprison anyone who was suspected of engaging in indoctrination. At the same time, the federal government sent a fascist Peronist, Brigadier Raúl Oscar Lacabanne, to Córdoba to organize 'ideological cleansing'.

A year after the coup, the dictator and leader of the military junta, Rafael Videla, would not hesitate to declare: 'If necessary, all those who oppose the attainment of peace in Argentina will die.' On his orders, the military repression group GT4 dedicated itself to hunting down supporters of Guevara and Castro. Fortunately for me, if I may say so, I was already in prison when the crackdown became systematic.

My second detention occurred on the night of 5 March 1975 in Rosario. Viviana and I were sleeping at the home of some friends in calle Tucumán, when four men in plainclothes, armed to the teeth, woke us with guns to our heads. They'd broken down the door. Viviana was pushed into a corner, with the barrels of several Sten MKII machine guns trained on her. Meanwhile, they put a hood over my head. We heard a burst of gunfire outside. I thought it was the end, that they were staging a fake scenario in the street to make people think we were armed and putting up a fight. This was their usual modus operandi: they would invent some pretext to shoot down 'subversives' without further ado. That's not what happened this time. They made us climb into a black car that roared off, tyres screeching, to a secret detention centre. I couldn't see anything but I could hear the silence of the empty streets. The Triple A liked to act in secrecy, generally at night time.

Once we'd arrived, they threw me into a room at the foot of a staircase, a basement, I imagined, with a musty smell. Hooded and disoriented, all I knew was that I was in the hands of the secret police. I had been separated from Viviana and didn't know where they'd taken her. After a few minutes, men came in to interrogate me. I was subjected to psychological torture. They threatened to kill me, break me, destroy me. They wanted to know the name of my contacts and my responsibilities within the PRT. I revealed nothing, nothing at all. They then sent in an official from the Federal Police. Faced with his questions, I continued to say nothing. I didn't even ask to see a judge. Silence was the best way of saving my life. For several days, they took turns to interrogate me, without success. Tiring of this, they eventually brought me before a judge, for a quick hearing. The National Security Law laid down penalties for 'subversive activities of every kind'. The definition of such 'subversive activities' was kept vague so as to facilitate the arrest of anyone opposed to the government of Isabel Perón. After the coup and the National Reorganization Process launched by the military junta, the generals saddled people like me with an acronym (they loved acronyms): BDS (*banda de delincuentes subversivos*, 'group of subversive criminals'), which allowed them to ignore the Geneva Convention for the treatment of political prisoners; thanks to this new label, we became common law prisoners. In the same Orwellian style, they named the secret detention and torture centres LRDs (*lugar de reunión de detenidos* – a meeting place for inmates).

The trial, or rather farce, that took place lasted half an hour and was completely informal. Faced with the absurd charges brought against me, I merely answered that I was a member of an organization that fought against injustice. Full stop. End of story. The judge asked me if I accepted the charges. I replied in the negative. 'Yet, in your apartment, we found . . .', he insisted. I retorted: 'It's not my apartment.'

I was then transferred to the penitentiary in Villa Devoto, calle Bermudez, in the suburbs of Buenos Aires. This was an insalubrious place, a succession of high concrete buildings dating back to 1927. I had the pleasant surprise of seeing Viviana upon arriving. We didn't realize it yet, but we were fortunate to now be official prisoners, with our own files. Once we were in the system, it became more difficult – though not impossible, as we shall see – for them to make us disappear. Our relatives at least knew what had happened to us and where we were, in contrast to the thousands of families of future victims of the dictatorship who would never know and would be tormented by uncertainty for years. We had the enormous luck to have been arrested before the coup: the junta would industrialize the domestic repression put in place by the Triple A. We thought we had already supped full with horrors. What awaited Argentina in the late 1970s was much worse.

Despite the risks associated with our name and my status as a subversive, my sister Celia immediately rushed to Devoto on learning of my incarceration. As for my brother Roberto, he decided once again to become my lawyer. It was a perilous decision. The repressive apparatus was already attacking the relatives of inmates. Since my first detention, the terror had intensified. The lawyers representing political prisoners were being exiled or disappearing. Some of them were shot down like dogs in the street; others were jailed. Indeed, the military would come down on them so heavily during the years of lead that there would soon be none left to defend us. Two of the last lawyers to have been courageous enough to confront the junta were Enrico Germán Broquen and Angel Gerardo Pisarello. The latter was seized on 24 June 1976 and then became one more of the 'disappeared'. His mutilated body, hands tied behind his back, was discovered a few days later. The fact remains that Roberto teamed up with another lawyer from Rosario, Delia Rodriguez Araya, a woman of extraordinary courage, to prepare my defence. It was useless. A trial could just as easily last a thousand years as not occur at all. We had no recourse, no rights. We were nobodies.

One day, I saw Viviana. Friends had chosen us to be godparents for their newborn baby. This required them to have him baptized in prison, so we would be reunited, if only for a few moments (this kind of subterfuge would soon no longer be possible). We came together again at the font of the chapel. After that, I didn't see Viviana again for the eight years, three months and twenty-three days that my detention lasted.

Argentinian prisons were harsh, sickening places. Conditions in Devoto were particularly appalling. One of the main causes of death in prison was pulmonary oedema. Guards would beat a prisoner so hard that the blows created deep lesions in the lungs. Several of us were crammed into each cell, mixed with common law prisoners. The corruption was terrible. The huge budget received by the state prison was supposed to cover the needs of the 3,000 prisoners, but the authorities pocketed the money and left us to starve. The meat that was supposed to be for us was sold to local butchers. Homosexuals were sold off by the guards and handed over to wealthy inmates for rape. Political prisoners were revolted by such vile behaviour. We denounced it but nothing changed. So we decided to begin a hunger strike. In order to break this, they transferred us to other prisons. To some degree, the political prisoners put a spoke in the wheel of this juicy trade. We could create a stir; we still had contacts outside who could publicize what was happening and condemn the situation. This pissed off the corrupt prefect and his clique, who preferred the common law prisoners as they were more malleable.

I was transferred with other companions in a Hercules plane to Rawson Penitentiary, near Trelew,[5] in Patagonia. This 'move' marked the beginning of what I have called my tour of the prison system. In eight years, I was transferred five times: from Devoto to Rawson, from Rawson to Devoto, from Devoto to La Plata, from La Plata to Sierra Chica, then from Sierra Chica back to Rawson. Prison conditions deteriorated with each transfer.

Rawson was a penitentiary for the convicted, a sort of penal colony lost in the depths of a hostile land battered by the icy winds of the Atlantic Ocean, 1,100 kilometres south of Buenos Aires. Its isolation made it difficult, not to say impossible, for anyone to visit. Cutting us off from our loved ones was precisely the purpose: they wanted to destroy us both physically and psychologically.

Religion was represented at Rawson – in an unusual way!

The chaplain (who had a military rank) was a sadist who called us terrorists, murderers and filthy leftists, and even took part in harsh interrogation sessions . . . all in the name of God. Luckily, he was replaced by the Archbishop of Comodoro Rivadavia, Monsignor Moure, with whom I became great friends.[6] Argimiro Moure was a genuine Christian. The first time he called me into confession, I confessed my atheism. He replied that this didn't matter. He wasn't here as a proselyte but as a man offering us the opportunity for some pleasant human dialogue. The majority of prisoners began to go to Mass every week to hear him.

The repressive apparatus kept visitors under increasingly close surveillance. Being the relative of a political prisoner was enough to sign someone's death warrant. Viviana's parents never paid her a visit. She had not been transferred as I had (in fact, she spent her eight years in prison in Villa Devoto, in cell 90, on the third floor in wing number 5, without ever seeing the sun or the moon). With the hardening of the regime and the echoes of the mass disappearances which reached her in prison, she was anxious about her parents and asked them to leave the country immediately. They lived in Córdoba. Instead of going into exile, they secretly moved to Avellaneda, a suburb of Buenos Aires – she never knew in what street – and went underground. One day in October 1977, a woman friend of Viviana, Stella, who had known her since childhood and shared her cell, was visited by her three young children. They had come from Avellaneda, and recounted a nightmare: their father had disappeared, swept away by the repression, followed a few weeks later by the female friend who had taken them in. A retired couple from the neighbourhood had then taken care of them after this double tragedy. A few days later, they had in turn met with the same fate. Traumatized by this succession of disappearances, the children had forgotten the name of the couple. But on hearing their story and their descriptions, Viviana had a terrible presentiment: the couple they were talking about were her parents. So her warning to them had been useless. They were in their sixties and had never been involved in politics. Upon her release, Viviana was informed that they had been seized, taken to the Campo de Mayo secret detention centre, tortured and thrown alive out of a plane into the Rio de la Plata. These events had taken place in September 1977. I learned this when I was released from prison.

The memories of my various detentions have merged into one. Each day was more or less identical to the previous. I especially remember certain key dates and a few striking anecdotes. The reader will forgive me if I relate them in no particular order.

There was a before and after the coup. In 1975, we were allowed radios, newspapers, visits, and time to take a stroll around the prison yard. As of 24 March 1976, these rights were abolished. We witnessed a tangible hardening in the treatment of political prisoners. Groups of soldiers now stood in the prison yards and aimed their weapons at the skylights of the cells. Beatings, searches, threats and insults all intensified.

I was in Rawson twice. I never understood what I was doing there, or what the point was in transferring me so often. On my second stay, they locked me in a cold cell with no mattress and no blanket; as result I developed rheumatism which I still suffer from today, and the hepatitis that I had contracted before my incarceration worsened.

I spent a total of three and a half years in isolation. My longest period of solitary confinement lasted six months. I walked up and down and thought; there was nothing else to do. They fed me so little that I didn't have the strength to exercise. I lost track of time and space and what was happening not only outside the prison, but down the corridor a few metres from me. From time to time, information did reach me. When we were placed in isolation, we sometimes managed to communicate with others either via the toilets or through the cracks in the walls, or in Morse code. If those listening understood the message, they banged once on the wall; if not, twice. These interactions, however brief and infrequent, prevented us from going completely crazy. I still suffered, for a while, from hallucinations. One cell in which I was confined was dark, with round corners, and I wasn't allowed out. There was a basement window that just about allowed me to see if it was day or night. In some prisons, the food came in through a crack. You couldn't see who had brought it. In others, a guard opened the door but it was better not to see his features. Victor Hugo said somewhere that the most wretched man isn't the prisoner but his guardian. There were doubtless some who were less bad than the rest, but they were all horrible. What a twisted mentality you must have to choose a profession like this!

When we were not in isolation, we were crammed into a shared cell. Nobody came to visit us at that time. There were no more lawyers. Some parts of the prison had common rooms where, randomly, we were allowed to spend time. It sometimes happened that a guard left a newspaper in the toilet. It was usually a daily, several days old, but it allowed us to glean snippets of information. We were also alerted to massive waves of arrests by new inmates who had also been seized and ended up from time to time in prison. Some had the opportunity to become official prisoners. They told us about the disappearances, the killings. Others vanished into thin air. They were never seen again. We gradually started to realize the scale of the repression.

At regular intervals, torturers entered the cells to interrogate us. Or else they escorted us into a torture chamber. We had a method to avoid talking: it was called 'Poker face, give nothing away'. It meant we adopted a blank expression – we never knew what was going to happen. When they asked us, 'Have you read this book?' we replied, 'No'. 'Do you go to the gym?' – 'No'. 'What a slacker! You don't do anything!' concluded the torturer.

One day, a colonel in uniform entered the cell I shared with another inmate. He asked him: 'Are you a Montonero?' – 'No, I'm a Peronist', my companion replied. It was an important distinction. Montoneros was an armed group while Peronism was a movement. The interrogator frowned and repeated his question. My cellmate stuck to his guns: he was a Peronist, he said. Suddenly, the interrogator turned to me: 'And you, you're PRT, right?' – 'No, I'm a socialist', I replied, following my friend's example. The trick was to remain vague, not to admit to any party affiliation.

On occasion the interrogators would raise the question of my relationship with Ernesto. Those who learned that I was Che's brother came to see me. It seemed to perplex them. I became an object of curiosity. That could play in my favour or work against me. It was difficult to anticipate the reactions. It depended on the guard or the soldier.

One day when I was alone in my cell in Sierra Chica, the door opened to reveal a guy in uniform, an officer. He asked the guard to leave us alone. The bench I slept on was a concrete slab. They would bring in a mattress at 10 p.m. and remove it at 6 a.m. It was bitterly cold. When a soldier or a guard entered a cell, the prisoner had to stand against the back wall, hands behind his back. The officer looked me up and down and said, 'At ease, sit down'. He sat next to me. He initiated the conversation by asking me if I was doing any exercise, what I thought of the food, etc. I answered 'no' to each question, as usual. I wanted him to leave; I had nothing to say to this creep. When he realized that I wasn't going to break my silence, he tried to break the ice, exclaiming: 'So what do you know, you're Che's brother!' And he started to discourse at length on Ernesto. He told me about the art of guerrilla warfare, and what Che represented, and he concluded by saying: 'What an incredible guy, that fantastic brother of yours!' I was stunned. This soldier was a specialist in counterinsurgency, he knew that Che had dedicated his life to fighting against brutes like him; in short, Che was an enemy for whom he was professing great admiration! Another time during an interrogation, the soldier started by talking about Che. He said: 'What a pity that your brother chose the wrong side! He was a great guy.' And he went on telling me everything he knew about Ernesto, everything he'd read. Nobody could say he wasn't well informed about the subject . . .

One night, during my first stay in Rawson, they came for four of us. They told us they were taking us to the Almirante Zar naval air base in Trelew for an 'administrative transfer'. We were convinced they were going to shoot us. At this base, six leftist political prisoners had been murdered on 22 August 1972. One of the methods used by the military to shoot prisoners 'legally' was to pretend they were attempting to escape. The junta had passed legislation on runaways to justify this kind of killing. The vehicle carrying us towards the base suddenly stopped in a deserted place. There was another vehicle on the roadside, with all its lights off. We were told to get out. We looked at each other and nodded: our goose was cooked. They'd accuse us of having fled so they could shoot us.

In fact, we were ordered to get into the other vehicle. On arrival at the base, we were pushed towards a small plane. And I found myself back in Villa Devoto. I was put in a cell with other prisoners. Over the years, we'd learned that the military had divided political prisoners into three categories: the recoverable, the just about recoverable, and the unrecoverable. I belonged to the third. It has to be said that I wasn't a model prisoner. I was forever protesting. What else could I do with the upbringing I'd had and my brother as an example! So I found myself in solitary. Here, every three or four hours, they came for me and dragged me under a cold shower until I was dying from the cold. Then they brought me back to my cell, soaking wet and half naked. Meanwhile, they'd taken away my mattress, and they gave me nothing to eat. Any trifling infraction resulted in punishment, usually a beating, to unhinge you and break your spirit. But for most of us this didn't work as we had strongly held convictions: we weren't criminals. We knew why we were imprisoned. Also, we managed to maintain contact with each other. They were never able completely to prevent our communication or destroy us. We were organized inside the prison. We sometimes even managed to get in touch with inmates who were doctors.

On my fourth transfer I was taken to La Plata, located in the province of Buenos Aires. I can't really describe the outside of the prison, I arrived there at night, in a van. We were greeted with a hail of blows. It was a terrible prison, a place of torture and detention for the 'disappeared'. They separated me from the others and led me to the prison director's office. He'd selected me as a delegate of the inmates so he could tell me he didn't want any problems, he'd keep us alive and respect some of our advantages – unlike the military – at least if we watched our step. He wanted to reach retirement age without any problems. In fact, he would soon be replaced by a soldier. With the intensification of the repression, prisons gradually came under the control of the army. A large number of political prisoners, such as the Montoneros Horacio Rapaport and Angel Georgiavis, had been murdered in La Plata; it was claimed they were trying to escape. Wings 1 and 2 were reserved for irrecoverable inmates like me. It was summer, scorching hot, and we had to wear thick cloth uniforms that stuck to our skin. It was, of course, forbidden to remove them. I protested and found myself in solitary. I was getting used to this. The following winter, they did the opposite. We were handed thin uniforms in which we froze.

On the night of 22 August, guards came for five inmates in the isolation wing. The date was symbolic: it was the anniversary of the Trelew massacre mentioned above. We concluded once again that we were about to be shot, and lost all hope when the soldier escorting us asked the guard where our personal belongings were, and the latter replied that we wouldn't be needing them again. We came from different cells but we recognized each other. We realized that we'd all been very active politically. There was a Brazilian comrade, a Montonero leader, a guerrilla who had fought with Fidel in Cuba and a PRT leader. They put us in a van that came to a stop in open country. Once again, there was a vehicle, headlights on, by the roadside. This time, we were sure we were going to die. Not at all! We were transferred to Sierra Chica. I later learned that there *had* been a massacre of prisoners that night and our little group had been saved at the last minute by the military; to this day I don't know why. We never found out why we'd been spared, but we came

to the conclusion that, when we were going to be shot, a coun-
termand was issued. The military had spheres of influence, four
in number in the whole country; these in turn were divided into
nineteen sub-zones and 117 sectors and sub-sectors. A general
was head of each zone, and had the right of life and death over
the prisoners under his control.

I spent three years in Sierra Chica (also located in the province of Buenos Aires). It was a fan-shaped prison, very old and
sinister, with twelve wings, each of them 100 metres long. It had
been built in 1890, before electricity, near a small town called
Olavarria, among fields and mineral quarries which employed
the prisoners. In the centre of each wing was a courtyard overlooked by the cell windows. One of the particularities of the
prison was that, to prevent inmates filing the bars, the windows
were fitted with iron shutters that made an unbelievable racket
and gave the impression you were in a penal colony. The cells
were concave, their walls were 80 centimetres thick and their
doors were made of wood with an opening for passing food
through. They were equipped with a WC and a tap. You could
spend weeks without leaving your cell. I shared mine with
the leader of the Juventud Peronista, Juan Carlos Dante 'El
Canca' Gullo, who later became a pro-Kirchner MP, and whose
mother and then brother were illegally arrested and 'disappeared' during our detention.

Wing 12 was the 'punishment wing'. It was completely isolated from the others. Wing 11 was the 'death wing'. We no
longer had individual names: we had become mere numbers. I
was 449. For a while, we were allowed out into the central yard
three times a week. However, we didn't have the right to walk in
groups, to approach a window, or to stop walking. When some
detail derailed the machine, the guards entered the cell, ran-

sacked everything, beat the inmates and doused them with ice water, the only 'bath' to which we were entitled in Sierra Chica. One 24 or 31 December in I forget which year, I shared a cell with other prisoners. The guards came to see us. They found some sweets. I don't remember how they had come into our possession. This enraged them; we were confined to solitary, of course.

Outside, the dirty war was in full swing. Some armed groups like the Montoneros had become radicalized, and treason was punishable by death. By 'treason' they meant, for example, denunciation, even under torture. Argentina was going through a period of atrocities, a downward spiral where each death was followed by others in reprisal. One day, they brought in a 'disappeared', a member of an armed group. He had spoken under torture. The organization to which he belonged had sentenced him to death. The military dropped him into the lion's den, amidst the inmates, for them to kill him. He became a human wreck, between torture on the one side and the death threats on the other. A group of prisoners including myself found this so cruel that we decided to protect him by keeping him apart from the rest, and serving as his shield. The guards waited impatiently for the others to murder him. But we were vigilant. We never left him alone. Gradually, he regained his strength. Then one day he committed suicide by cutting his jugular. A psychiatrist cellmate explained that it had been necessary for him to perk up before he could decide that his life was no longer worth living. We were shaken by his death.

My health was declining. I had a hernia and appendicitis in addition to rheumatoid arthritis. I was operated on twice, once in Sierra Chica and again in Rawson. I had a heart attack while I was in hospital.

Messages were passed from one inmate to another by writing tiny letters on sweet wrappers that we kept in our mouths. These messages were often exchanged at the infirmary. We waited for the right moment when no one was watching us and we passed on the sweet. Communication was slow but it worked. When they took me to the infirmary to operate on me for the first time, I had one of the sweets in my mouth. I was very weak. I was anesthetized. When I woke up, flanked by two guards, the first thing I wondered wasn't whether the operation had gone well but if I still had the sweet in my mouth. It was under my tongue!

I was transferred again to Rawson, the last and longest stage of my tour of the prison system. This was 1979 and the military had ordered a massive transfer of prisoners between Sierra Chica and Rawson. The Hercules plane carrying us landed again at the Almirante Zar base in Trelew. When we arrived at the prison, a guard exclaimed, 'Ah, I can see that you were treated well in Sierra Chica!' This was a cruel joke: we were starving.

Yet despite all the mistreatment, we started to believe that we would one day escape this hell. The question was when. Purgatory could last for a long time but things were moving in the right direction. Thanks to the activism of my sister Celia in Europe, I received three visits in quick succession: from the Austrian consul in Buenos Aires, a human rights organization, and the Red Cross. While the scale and barbarity of the repression seemed to escape the expert notice of the national press, it was not the same abroad. Argentinians in exile struggled tirelessly for our cause, highlighting the inhumane conditions in the prisons. So much so that the junta was finally driven to allow partial prison inspections. The military thought they could kill two birds with one stone. The detention of so many political prisoners would prove, or so they thought, that the rumours of illegal arrest were false. Of course, our presence did nothing to explain the disappearance of tens of thousands of people who had never been seen again and were not down on file as being held in any prison. The 'disappeared' had indeed . . . disappeared.

The Falklands War – which began on 2 April 1982 – marked the beginning of the end for the junta. Everything was going from bad to worse in the country. The policies of José Alfredo Martínez de Hoz, the minister of the economy under the dictatorship, had led to disaster. The generals tried to awaken the patriotism of the country's citizens by rallying them behind an idiotic and irresponsible invasion of the British-held islands, hoping this would make them forget the repression, rampant inflation and huge social problems that were then affecting the country. After seven years of military dictatorship, Argentina had been bled white. In addition to being murderers, the generals were incompetent fools. It was a dismal failure. And the absurd Falklands War ended in a dismal, humiliating defeat seventy-four days later. The junta had seriously misjudged the reaction of the British and the Americans, convinced firstly that Margaret Thatcher would have other fish to fry than defend the distant Falklands, and secondly that Ronald Reagan would support his South American ally, or, at worst, would remain neutral, which was not the case.

The fate of the junta was sealed with the collapse of its invasion force; some soldiers died of hunger as their commanders failed to supply them with food. Our fate was about to improve. However, we did not know this, as the incessant propaganda to which we were subjected obviously talked of the repeated triumphs of our army, claiming that victory was imminent.

Following the invasion, we suddenly had the right to listen to the radio again!

The most surreal thing for me was to see several political prisoners defending our tormentors, out of patriotism, just as the junta had predicted. The invasion of the Falklands had divided us. Those prisoners said we needed to support our army against British imperialism; there were even some who wanted to volunteer for the front! It was totally crazy! The invasion was another act of madness on the part of the fascist clique in power!

After the defeat, we suddenly started receiving visits from lawyers, human rights organizations, and so on. We realized that there was now a détente, a stepping down of the repression. And then, on the morning of 10 March 1983, a guard came to tell me: 'Get your personal effects. You're leaving.' I thought it was a bad joke, a lie. But a few minutes later, they brought my belongings. I didn't know it, but they had travelled with me. Nothing was missing.

11

Days of liberation

I came out of Rawson with twenty-six pesos in my pocket and a Trelew-Rosario bus ticket provided by the prison administration. Nobody was waiting for me at the exit. My whole family was living in exile, in Cuba or Spain. From the Iberian Peninsula, my brother Roberto ran an organization called MODEPA (Movimiento Democratico popular antiimperialista), one of the last surviving branches of the old PRT, which had ceased to exist due to the repression. My sister Celia was still actively campaigning in Europe for the release of political prisoners.

Twenty-six pesos was next to nothing. I spent them on a bottle of wine and took my bus to Rosario. Thanks to a contact, I knew where to find Viviana. She'd just been released and was now faced with the tragic death of her parents.

We were on parole, so we didn't have the right to move about in the country, let alone abroad, without judicial authorization. In Rosario, I contacted a female lawyer who arranged for me to settle in Buenos Aires, then go to Cuba to see my family. Viviana and I moved into the old quarter of San Telmo. One of the first things we did was go to the apartment of Viviana's parents in Avellaneda. We found it just as it had been on the day they were seized. It was a terrible moment for Viviana.

We were watched day and night. A car occupied by two men was stationed permanently in our street. The military were still in power, with their National Reorganization Process,[1] even if their days were numbered. The repression had been stepped down, but every now and again still bared its teeth: a few days after my release, two companions were abducted and reported disappeared.

I was haunted by a sense of hopelessness and bankruptcy. Every revolutionary effort had been destroyed. It was a total failure. The junta had 'disappeared' 30,000 people; 10,000 were imprisoned for their ideas; tens of thousands of Argentinians had gone into exile. State terrorism had spread the most appalling fear and fostered a climate of dread. There had been so many informers!

Argentina had changed profoundly. Young people were terrified, overwhelmed, lacking any sense of identity. They had no future, no hope, no desire: a terrible loss of energy for the country. Our political and trade union organizations were pale, wan affairs. In prison, we had a vague idea of the disaster that was occurring in our absence, but we had nothing concrete to confirm it. We had lived through the years of lead locked up, cut off from the world. Also, Viviana and I had gradually become aware of how lucky we were to have been arrested before the mechanization of the repression kicked in. Detention was very tough, but less tough than for those who were kidnapped, tortured and thrown alive from airplanes into the ocean or the Rio de la Plata, those whose entire families had been decimated just for having a 'subversive' as a member. Faced with the barbarity that these tens of thousands of victims had just lived through, our detentions didn't amount to a hill of beans. As far as the military were concerned, political prisoners were war booty.

We learned that, before the invasion of the Falklands on 30 March 1982, there'd been a huge spontaneous mobilization in the country. Everything was going wrong. The annual rate of inflation had reached 924 per cent. The numbers of mothers of the disappeared, the famous *Madres de la Plaza de Mayo*, had swollen. It had become impossible to ignore these courageous women circling the Plaza de Mayo with their white kerchiefs on their heads. They were demanding to have their children returned back to them alive. In the worst cases, they insisted on knowing what had happened to them, under what conditions they had died, at whose hands, and where their remains were. For their part, the workers' forces were on the move. The unemployment rate had soared, wages had not increased for several years, and there was still galloping inflation. The Falklands invasion was an attempt – an unsuccessful one – to gather strength and regain the initiative. Power was slipping through the fingers of the military.

Imprisonment had been a learning experience for the political prisoners. We had two options: either we felt worn out and defeated and relapsed into inactivity, thus aggravating the extent of the debacle; or we remained optimistic and loyal to the ideas that had inspired us before the disaster. Ultimately, both options had their followers. There were a lot of suicides and nervous breakdowns in our ranks. Many comrades abandoned the struggle and the ideas behind it. But not the majority.

Back in Buenos Aires, I went to visit my cousin Hercilita, the daughter of one of my father's sisters. She was married to a wealthy man from the upper bourgeoisie, a certain Casares, the owner of a dairy company called La Martona. Learning of my release, they invited me to dinner. They had a damn nice house in a very chic part of town. When I arrived at their place, Hercilita asked me a question which I found unbelievably cynical: 'Now that the military government is about to leave, what are you subversives going to do?' I didn't get it. I was too shocked by her sly suggestions. I had spent more than eight years in prison, her cousin Ernesto was dead, the rest of the family was exiled, including her uncle (my father) and this was all she could think of to say to me! I replied: 'The military carried out a coup. It seems to me that *they* are the subversives, don't you think? So why don't you call someone from the military and ask them?' And with that, I slammed the door. A few days later, I received a call from an uncle. He was old and dying and had behaved like a bastard after the death of Ernesto and during my detention. He was summoning me to his bedside to obtain my forgiveness. 'Let me find the way into heaven', he begged me. I told him to go and fuck himself. I had lost all patience with this kind of character.

My twenty-six pesos had been spent, and I didn't have a penny left. My sister Celia put me in touch with a man named Chevalier, a Swiss who had supported her when she was campaigning on behalf of political prisoners. Chevalier sent me a cheque for 50 Swiss francs. I was so disoriented and unaware of the different currencies after eight years of detention that I walked into a branch of the Swiss Bank in Avenida Corrientes, thinking I could exchange my cheque for banknotes. I got into a lift and was surprised by its modernity and the light that came on when you entered it. I was convinced that this light needed to be turned off before sending the lift towards its destination; I didn't understand how it worked. At the bank, I spoke to a very serious gentleman in a suit, saying that I had Swiss francs. 'How many?' he asked me, probably thinking it was a large sum. 'Fifty.' He looked at me incredulously. He clearly took me for a simpleton and sent me to a bureau de change. Chevalier continued to send me money until I'd got back on my feet.

Once I received the official authorization, I went to Cuba. My children Martin, Pablo and Ana had been raised by their mother, without me. They were close to Ernesto's children. My father had got married again, to a younger Argentinian artist, and had three young children. I spent a few weeks in Havana, during which I made contact with publishers through Celia who had several connections. It was a bittersweet experience. During my absence, Che had become a historical figure, a mythical character whose exploits were taught in schools. Being his brother opened all doors to me, the complete opposite of in Argentina!

I had decided to publish and sell Cuban books, which hitherto had not been available in Argentina. My family had very strong, close ties with Cuba. Fidel treated us as if we were family members. It was his way of honouring his dead friend. These special relationships gave me access to the Cuban cultural world.

I returned to Buenos Aires shortly before my children, though in fact they very quickly headed back to Cuba: this was where their lives now were. Meanwhile, the military dictatorship in Argentina collapsed.

So I started working in a bookshop on Avenida Corrientes, one of the busiest shopping streets in Buenos Aires, with my friend Carlos Damian Hernandez, a publisher and bookseller. I was then contacted by a sales rep from the Cuban embassy and that's how I started selling new Cuban books; I became the representative of the Cuban Book Institute. We then opened a cultural centre named Nuestra America. It was an immediate success. It had been forbidden to talk about the Cuban revolution for so long that the Argentinians were athirst with curiosity. They wanted to rebuild their memory. I organized a book festival; it attracted big crowds. People came and leafed through the books in silence, unable to speak or to express themselves. Repression had taught them to keep quiet. We had had so many dictators and waves of persecution that they didn't yet know whether the new democracy would last. It was scary.

Hearing of the festival's success, the Soviet Union asked me to do the same thing in Moscow. I declined the invitation. I didn't want anything to do with that sectarian country. Also, Che had denounced the USSR and even predicted its collapse. He had called it 'La Cortisone', after the name of the analgesic. According to him, Soviet communism had strayed from the right path and lost its meaning. 'If communism is not interested in matters of ethical awareness, it can be a method of distribution but it is no longer a revolutionary morality', he had told the journalist Jean Daniel.[2]

Gradually, I began to sell other Cuban products: rum, guava jam and cigars, primarily those things that were not sold in Argentina. From then on everything started to speed up. I became the first importer of Havana cigars. The Cuban company Habanos S.A. offered me a full partnership and later I became one of its vice-presidents. I was travelling between Buenos Aires and Havana. Selling cigars allowed me to continue selling and publishing books. I became a kind of businessman. I imported millions of cigars that sold in 1,500 outlets, from north to south, as far down as Ushuaia in Tierra del Fuego. I learned marketing and advertising. I had the idea of installing humidors in service stations, duty free shops, kiosks and supermarkets. I brought over *torcedores* (rollers) from Cuba, to give demonstrations; I made the way the cigars were presented more attractive, selling them in attractive aluminium tubes or wrapped in cellophane.

In 2000, after 40 per cent of Habanos S.A. shares were sold to the Spanish (Altadis), I ended my collaboration. I didn't agree with the sale. The situation in Cuba at the time was very complex. One day I discovered by chance a smuggled product in a shipment of cigars coming from the north of the country and bound for Europe. I believe it was cocaine, though I was never sure. I asked a friend who had connections in Customs if he could request an investigation. Customs replied that they needed money to launch an investigation. I gave them the sum requested. Three days later, my friend gave me an appointment. He returned the money and said: 'They don't want to have anything to do with it.' It was strange that the Customs sniffer dogs hadn't detected anything. I also realized that the cigars weren't even genuine: they were smuggled cigars! It was worrying.

With the money earned from Habanos S.A., I decided to open a place in the Las Canitas neighbourhood in Buenos Aires, called Epicúreos, which served as a restaurant and a wine and cigar shop. It was a ramshackle project which lasted six years, swallowed a huge part of my life and cost me all my savings. The business foundered for lack of customers. It wasn't so much the money I lost that hurt as the feeling of failure. A few months after I left prison, I was selling the equivalent of 600,000 dollars' worth of cigars per month, travelling and meeting lots of interesting people. I naively thought I could repeat the experience with Epicúreos. I was wrong. Selling cigars isn't at all the same as running a restaurant. I'd just suffered my first professional defeat.

12

Flying to Havana

My father had been the first member of the family to go and live in Cuba, in 1974. He had serious money problems. He lived in his studio in calle Paraguay with his new wife Ana María 'Tutti' Erra and their two children Maria Victoria and Ramón. At the time, his wife and he were painters. They didn't make much of a living. My father had also decided to publish a memoir about Ernesto. There were complex copyright issues to be resolved. Roberto, Celia, Ana Maria and I didn't think he should publish this book, which seemed to us to stem more from my father's ego than from his duty to remember. It seemed to me that the project was for him a way of saying: 'I am who I am, the father of the famous revolutionary, and I'm cashing in on what is mine by right.' The book didn't live up to my brother's ideals, as my father changed some things and embroidered others. For instance, he wished to include letters from Ernesto while removing passages that revealed the quarrels between them. I personally considered that it was necessary to publish all the letters, including the paragraphs that were not very flattering. In short, this project irritated me. My father knew he could say whatever he wanted: we would never contradict him publicly.

When Ernesto wrote to us about his travels, he often clashed with my father politically. He kept talking about 'your friends the Yankees'. But when Ernesto became a myth, my father completely changed his tune and began to criticize the United States, those imperialists. I never knew if it was by calculation or out of conviction. He was certainly entitled to change his mind. Who knows? Ernesto had perhaps managed to convince him. After all, he had great powers of persuasion.

Roberto doesn't agree with me and we still sometimes argue about my father. My brother believes I'm too harsh on him. Maybe. I'm the youngest and I've had a different set of experiences from my siblings. I spent years alone with my mother, seeing her suffering from the separation and then falling ill. My father was an extremely complex man, difficult to define. He had lots of friends and relations: he could adapt to all situations and was often very highly appreciated. But he couldn't find his niche. *What was his niche?* That was the 64,000-dollar question. I spent my time quarrelling with him. I berated him for his immaturity. For a time, I hardly spoke to him. In fact, in the 1970s things had gone particularly sour between us. I realized that we couldn't continue like this if we wanted to maintain a semblance of family unity. I had to make a decision: to accept him as he was or to stop seeing him. I chose the former.

And so, at the advanced age of seventy-three, he was in Argentina, struggling with intractable problems and having to fight on many fronts. His two young children were ignored, and suffered as a result. To complicate matters, he was campaigning on behalf of the communist organization the National Movement for the Defence of Petroleum and Energy (of which my mother had been a member). Juan Perón was in power and persecuting the leftists. We felt the noose tighten around our family. Not only was the political situation problematic for a Guevara, but the way my father responded to it aggravated the risks. We never knew what fateful words he'd blurt out, how irrationally he would react. At the beginning of 1974, the terrible Triple A was in full swing.

I came up with the idea of sending him to Cuba. His problems would disappear once he had set foot in Havana. He was, after all, the father of Che. Roberto refused to interfere. It was risky for him to take up a position in favour of the island. Ana Maria had already moved there: her husband Fernando Chaves had been expelled by the military dictatorship of Alejandro Agustín Lanusse[1] in 1972. Fernando was a university professor and also an activist, for the PRT. He had been arrested and released on condition that he leave the country. On the day of their departure into exile, the whole family had accompanied them to the airport at Ezeiza. We had all been searched. There was an army of police officers and probably henchmen from the Triple A. My sister Celia had flipped the bird at them, an extremely compromising gesture, but Celia was like that: a reckless, rebellious loudmouth.

I mentioned the idea to my father, or rather, urged him to leave so as to free us from the headache that his presence in Buenos Aires now caused us. He didn't argue. I then contacted Fidel, who prepared for his arrival. As I've already said, Fidel has always treated us like family and helped us out in difficult times. I organized the departure, and one day in February 1974, my father and his new family flew out to Havana. They were first put up in the hotel Habana Libre, the former Hilton, where we had stayed in 1959. Fidel then gave them the run of a house located at 7617 calle Septima in the Miramar neighbourhood.

Cuba was going to look after my father in thanks for his having sacrificed his son to the island.

In Havana, Ernesto Guevara Lynch naturally slid into the skin of the 'father of Che', a state that would soon become a full occupation, almost a profession. Extremely proud of Ernesto, he was ready to reap the benefits from his eldest son's status as a national hero. When the Cubans learned that Che's father was among them, they came to honour him as a VIP. In the continual flow of visitors, there were foreign tourists on a political vacation. They usually came unexpectedly and knocked on his door. My father welcomed them all! They asked him if he was an architect and he replied 'Yes!' An engineer? 'Yes!' The father of Che!? 'Yes, yes, yes!' In Cuba, being Che's father was out of this world. This immediately gave him an exceptional stature. When I was there myself, I never said I was Che's brother. However, when people discovered it in spite of everything, they came over to talk. Ernesto was revered. A part of this cult reflected upon us. It was impressive.

My father lived off the Cuban state, which solved all his problems. He even had a third child, Ramiro, at the age of seventy-five! A year later, with Argentina continuing its inexorable march towards a new dictatorship, I sent my wife and three children to Cuba. This exile had the advantage of bringing my children closer to their cousins, whom they hardly knew.

Roberto and his family were the next to leave. Roberto had already been greatly impressed by his stay in Vallegrande in 1967. Ernesto's death had deeply shaken him and simultaneously boosted his convictions. His support for the militant left had been strengthened. His activism had deepened. My successive arrests and the brutal repression had finally convinced him to commit himself to the fight. His older brother had lived, fought and died for his ideas; his younger brother – myself – was jailed for his. He couldn't remain impassive. Despite the risks, he tried, as we have seen, to defend me and had contacted another lawyer specializing in criminal law, who was also an activist for human rights, Gustavo Roca,[2] a friend of Ernesto. The other colleagues with whom he had established regular contacts were also seriously compromised by their defence of Montoneros and members of other revolutionary groups.

I asked Roberto to flee, to drop my defence. He at first refused point blank. I didn't want to lose the only brother I had left. Neither did he. Our desire to protect each other led us into an impasse. He had the hardest time imaginable abandoning me to my fate. At the same time, he had a wife and five children who also needed his protection. At my insistence he finally complied. The threats had increased. Roberto then understood that there were, for him, only two possible outcomes: to disappear like the others or to go into exile. He first flew to Cuba and then to Spain. He travelled extensively, trying to mobilize foreign countries against the junta and its atrocities. He campaigned for the PRT, of which he was elected president by Argentinians in exile.

In October 1981, while attending a conference in Mexico City, he was arrested. The Mexicans accused him of involvement in the kidnapping of a niece of the Partido de acción nacional (PAN) candidate running for president, Pablo Emilio Madero. The alleged reason for the kidnapping? To raise funds for the PRT. He was released a few weeks later for lack of evidence. It goes without saying that my brother Roberto has never kidnapped anyone. However, with a name like ours, it seemed only fair to blame us for everything and anything. We were dangerous 'subversives' by default; and the more we were wrongly accused, the more disgusted we were with the system and the more we felt we needed to oppose it.

Celia was the last to flee. Already labelled a subversive like the rest of us, she had aggravated her case by making regular visits to me in prison. She had even had the impertinence to go to Rawson, a highly symbolic gesture that showed her determination, her courage and her rebellious spirit, qualities that the repressive apparatus could obviously not tolerate. In 1975, the horrors of the Triple A were in full swing. Out of defiance, and because she could not bring herself to abandon me, Celia had maintained the pace of her visits. After the coup, I begged her to stop coming. She was unbelievably headstrong, and refused. In March 1976, we felt the repression hardening. By monitoring the comings and goings of visitors, the military was aiming at families and supporters, who instantly became guilty in their eyes. They made them disappear. Massive kidnappings began at that time and they gradually homed in on our circle. One day, a friend of Celia's was abducted from her street in front of witnesses. From that moment, I was certain she would be the next victim. Now I was the one scared of losing a sister. She was also imprudent enough to come and tell me in prison about her friend's abduction. And I just had to tell her off: 'But you're crazy! What are you doing here? I'm already in prison, while you're not! You can't do anything for me! Get out of here, make a run for it.'

I was relieved when she finally decided to leave in August 1976 after the ransacking of her apartment by the military, organized in cells of repression called *Grupos de tareas* (Action Groups). They took everything they could and destroyed what remained. The forces of repression sometimes also attacked innocent people whose property they coveted. I'm not suggesting that there were guilty and innocent people here, I'm talking about people who were not political and yet found themselves being swept away by the wave of repression.

Celia had been the subject of intimidation and anonymous phone calls since November 1975. When she visited me in prison, the guards also threatened her. She campaigned loudly for the release of political prisoners. At the time, she was alone. Her husband Luis, from whom she had separated, had died.

She fled on foot across the border into Uruguay (Ezeiza airport was under tight surveillance). Making it into Uruguay didn't necessarily mean she was free: our northern neighbour was also a landmine. Argentina had signed agreements with neighbouring countries to extradite 'subversives'. She managed to stay there unnoticed.

Accompanied by her husband Carlos, our friend Olga found the courage to go to Celia's home just after her departure. She would see what she could save from the looting. While she was weighing up the damage, the phone started ringing. After a few seconds of hesitation and a furtive glance at Olga, Carlos picked up the phone. During the years of lead, the most trivial decisions could tip someone's life into horror. A man posing as Roberto asked if Celia was there. Carlos immediately knew that it wasn't my brother's voice. The men of Action Group obviously knew that he often phoned Celia from Cuba or elsewhere. Thank God they seemed unaware that Celia had crossed the border and was already far away. Carlos pretended he thought it was indeed Roberto and said she was out on an errand, and would be back soon. Olga panicked. They fled without taking anything.

By the end of 1976, my family had all gathered in Havana, except for me. I was in Rawson, happy to know they were beyond the reach of the military junta. Celia did not settle in

Cuba, she left almost immediately for Spain in search of lawyers willing to defend political prisoners. From 1976 to 1982 she travelled around Europe to try to raise awareness, giving interviews and lectures wherever she had the opportunity. She spent several months in Paris and Switzerland. She spoke French like Ernesto but soon tired of speaking in a foreign language every day. Exile was very difficult. She was completely broke, couldn't practise as an architect, and lived on the generosity of good souls. She often slept on sofas, always in the homes of other people. She had had a poster of me made, and she carried it everywhere with a photo of Ernesto that she placed each night next to her bed and gazed at before going to sleep. I think she was very lonely.

She returned from exile a few months after the election of Raúl Alfonsín on 30 October 1983. Roberto followed her. Ana Maria and my father preferred to stay in Havana. After my release, I saw them regularly since my professional activities forced me to make regular round trips between Argentina and Cuba. My father had become very close to my children and also to Ernesto's children, especially the youngest, who had hardly known his father. They asked him loads of questions about Che and he was happy to tell them about his childhood, his youth, his loves, his travels.

My father died in 1987 at the age of eighty-seven from a brain haemorrhage that took weeks to finish him off. The day of his stroke, I was myself hospitalized in Havana, in a really bad way. I had fallen seriously ill in Argentina without any insurance, and was transferred to Cuba a few days before my father's death, at Roberto's insistence. The ten-hour flight was horrible and interminable. I was given three seats so I could lie down. I thought I'd never get there. I was suffering from a very rare disease, Guillain-Barré syndrome, something that affects one in a million, attacks the peripheral nerves and is characterized by progressive weakness or even paralysis.

When we finally landed in Havana, a team of doctors was waiting for me at the airport with an ambulance. I was very ill for three months. Meanwhile, my father was dying by inches on another floor of the hospital. Too weak to get out of bed, I never saw him again. He was, in any case, barely conscious. I learned of his death one morning, from the television. The nurse who was in my room at that time ran to turn off the TV. It was too late. I wasn't able to attend his funeral, either. He was buried in the Military Pantheon in Havana, as was my sister Ana Maria, who died three years later of bone cancer.

I argued so often with my father! After my release, he had the crazy idea of wanting to publish the correspondence from my years of detention. According to him, my letters were of particular interest: I wrote in code to escape repression and censorship. I had become expert in the art of expressing things indirectly. My father thought my letters were excellent and wanted to share them with the public. When he suggested publication on my release, I exploded. I couldn't understand how he could have such an idea. It was a private correspondence between him and me. I think my rage scared him. He gave up the idea.

After his death, I continued my round trips between Buenos Aires and Cuba. I had drawn a lot closer to my nieces and nephews. But – and I bitterly regret this – I never got close to Fidel. I never wanted to benefit from our relationship, except in exceptional cases. Perhaps I thought that this would do no honour to my brother, a man of such integrity who had a pronounced aversion to privileges.

However, I did know Raúl Castro and his wife Vilma Espín

Guillois. Vilma was a very important woman in Cuba. She came from a powerful and influential family (her father was one of the lawyers of the Bacardi group), and was a brilliant student at MIT where she obtained a degree in civil engineering. On her return to Cuba, she joined the 26th of July Movement in the province of Oriente and fought bravely, revolver in hand. She was chair of the Federation of Cuban Women from 1960 to her death in 2007. Vilma was a very strong woman, very combative, a feminist who did wonders for the rights of women and homosexuals. Before Fidel, Cuba was a country of diehard macho men. Vilma helped to transform mentalities. Her daughter Mariela is director of Cuba's National Sex Education Centre; her son Alejandro is a colonel in the interior ministry. Mariela is much more like her mother than her father. Raúl is primarily a soldier! He doesn't speak, he barks orders. I spent a great deal of time with their family. For years, it was their little inn that I stayed at when I was in Cuba.

On the other hand, I don't know Fidel's current wife, Dalia Soto del Valle. She has also long remained unknown to the public. Fidel has always led a very discreet private life. He seemed to have no social life, rarely going out apart from his official duties, in which his wife never participated. It has long been said that he was very close to the Cuban revolutionary Celia Sanchez. May be. I think Fidel was obsessed with security issues. His children emerged from the shadows only once they were adults. We hardly knew who they were or even how many there were. Fidel Castro has eleven children from seven women, two of whom were his wives. I've had occasion to meet his son Alejandro.

The only time I directly contacted Fidel to obtain a favour was when I wanted my daughter Ana to return to Cuba in 1984. She had spent several years there before returning to Buenos Aires with her mother, but she couldn't adjust to Argentina. I wrote to Fidel. He immediately responded with a very affectionate letter, a lovely piece of writing, accompanied by several gifts: he not only agreed that Ana should move to Cuba, but said he would ensure that she had accommodation and a job. I was very grateful.

After the fall of the military dictatorship, the other two children from my union with Maria Elena Duarte, Martin and Pablo, also returned to live in Buenos Aires for a time. But nine years had passed since their departure into exile and their lives were now in Cuba. So they returned there too. My son Martin and daughter Ana are now living in Spain. My son Pablo still lives in Cuba.

I stayed in touch with Ernesto's former fellow fighters, Harry Villegas and Leonardo Tamayo, who survived not only the guerrilla war in the Sierra Maestra but also that in Ñancahuazú, and occupied important positions in the Cuban government. They confided something to me that touched me deeply. While they were fighting in Bolivia, Ernesto often talked about me. One day he told them that, of all his siblings, he regarded me as his spiritual heir, the one who could continue his fight and bring it to a successful conclusion. That's what I think of today, while writing this book.

13

'Until forever, my children . . .'

One day, chance led me to a restaurant in Havana with Alejandro Castro, the son of Fidel, and Celia, the daughter of Ernesto. One thing led to another, and we started talking about what our kinship with these illustrious men meant for each of us. I don't know his brothers and sisters, but we realized that Alejandro was the one who had suffered most from his parentage. He had been overprotected and surrounded by bodyguards his entire life. Fidel's security has always been a key aspect in the life of his family. The repeated acts of aggression from the United States made him fear that they might take it out on his offspring. So his children grew up without the right to go out alone. And then, being Fidel's son, what a weight to bear! Alejandro has a great admiration for his father, but he can't express it openly. He's a photographer and does portraits of . . . Fidel. While he's an excellent photographer, the important thing in his photos isn't him, but Fidel. The poor man has lived his life in the shadow of the *Líder Máximo*.

Celia, my niece, is a veterinarian, a big specialist in dolphins. She works at the aquarium in Havana. Years ago, she decided never to speak of her father. She is separated from her Chilean husband and leads a very quiet life with her children. She has no desire to look after the Centro de Estudios Che Guevara in Havana, the museum whose mission it is to compile Che's archives: writings, books, speeches, articles and photos. The Che Centre is run by her brother Camilo, now a photographer after holding several positions in the Cuban government.

I never really knew my niece Hilda, Ernesto's eldest daughter. When I came out of prison she was twenty-seven, married to a Mexican, and was a librarian by profession. She was already suffering from depression. She died of cancer at the age of thirty-nine.

Aleida is a paediatrician, a specialist in childhood allergies. She practises in a hospital in Havana. She has conducted numerous humanitarian missions in Angola, Ecuador and Nicaragua. She campaigns a great deal for human rights and also runs two centres for disabled and abused children. Aleida travels tirelessly to promote free access to health care. She says that her father is her inspiration. She also publishes a journal, *Paradigma*, with her brother Camilo.

My nieces and nephews hardly knew their father.[1] When he was absent, he sent them postcards illustrated with drawings. They kept the beautiful farewell letter written before his departure for Bolivia:

To my children, Hildita, Aleidita, Camilo, Celia and Ernesto,

If one day you hold this letter in your hands, I shall have ceased to be with you. You will barely remember me and the younger ones will not remember anything. Your father was a man who always acted in accordance with his ideas and one thing is certain: he was true to his convictions. Grow up as good revolutionaries. Study enough to master the technology that will allow you to dominate nature. Never forget that the revolution is what is important and that each of us, alone, is worth nothing. Above all, always be able to feel deep within your being all the injustices committed against anyone, anywhere in the world. This is the most beautiful quality a revolutionary can have. Until forever, my children, I have not lost hope of seeing you again. A huge kiss and a big hug from your Dad.[2]

Ernesto was very tormented by his inability to play his role as a father. He loved his five children and lamented not being able to show them more of his affection because of his prolonged and repeated absences. He was torn between the well-being of his children and the well-being of the world. Who needed him most? Aleida March was a very attentive mother and he counted on her to bring them up properly. 'My children say "papa" to the soldiers they see every day, and they never see *me*', he complained. And: 'Sometimes we revolutionaries are very lonely, even our children consider us almost as strangers. They see us less than the sentry, the one they call "uncle".' Having to be far away from his family was, for him, a huge sacrifice. In January 1965, while he was in Paris, he wrote to Aleida: 'You know, I'm really getting old. I'm more and more in love with you, and I feel powerfully drawn to our house, to our children, to that whole little world that I imagine more than I experience it. This advanced mental age I bear is very danger-ous; you are becoming necessary, while I am just a habit.' For the children, growing up without this father in Cuba, where he is so revered, was very difficult.

I never spoke to Aleida March about Ernesto's absence. The day Fidel publicly read his farewell letter in a theatre, she was dressed in black and crying silently in the circle. She was very much in love with my brother, she felt a real passion for him. She later embarked on a new life with a government cadre. The Cubans have never forgiven her. They thought that she should remain faithful to Che in widowhood, devote herself to sustaining his memory and nothing else! I realized as much when I talked to people. And yet, in a certain way, Aleida *is* dedicating her life to her dead husband. She too works at the Centro de Estudios Che Guevara. I have often wondered, indeed, how her current partner put up with it all.

I have a great affection for my nieces and nephews. I try to help them in life, to see them as often as possible, to advise them. At the same time, I'm not a therapist, I'm not here to ask them too many questions or to analyse them. There are topics I address with them only if they ask me. We sometimes talk about Ernesto, but always in a light-hearted way. They make jokes. For example, Che's son Ernesto likes to joke that his father forgot to transmit his neurons to him. You sense that it's a complicated field for them, so they make fun of the situation. I imitate them. There is a void in their lives that I try to fill as best I can. When they come to Argentina, I do my best to make them feel at home. Ernesto feels more Argentinian than his brother and sisters, but ultimately, his life is in Cuba. He's the one I am closest to. He's an interesting character who refused to live up to the expectations of his family, a nonconformist who pretended to go with the flow and then did as he pleased.

Ernesto speaks Russian fluently: he studied law in the Soviet Union. He became a lawyer, more out of obligation than desire. He wanted to be a mechanic, but Aleida could not countenance her son, especially a son of Che, not going into higher education. So she sent him to the University of Moscow. He occupied his leisure time with mechanics, his great passion. He specialized in motorcycles and then Harley-Davidsons in particular. There is no doubt that the blood of my uncle Jorge de la Serna flows in his veins! He acquired such expertise that he is now considered one of the best Harley-Davidson mechanics in the world, which is of course ironic. He has two old vintage Harleys, relics that he has kept in a good condition. In Cuba, you have to be a damn good mechanic to get these bikes to work! But even with his many talents, his two Harleys just allow him to ride around in town, not to make trips out into the countryside. His mother doesn't always approve. She's also annoyed by his refusal to get involved in the Centro de Estudios Che Guevara. But Ernesto is in his fifties and has decided it's high time for him to do what he likes. Recently he had the idea of buying twelve Harleys so as to organize a tour in partnership with a travel agency. He named the circuit La Poderosa Tours, after Alberto Granada's motorcycle[3] on which Ernesto and Mial roamed around South America in 1951. The route passes through the most emblematic places of the Cuban revolution. When it got wind of the project, the Cuban community in Miami virtually choked with rage. They thought the plan was insulting.

Of my brother's five children, Ernesto is the one who finds it most difficult to bear the weight of his illustrious parentage. I always joke that there are two titanic tasks that it's impossible to carry out: convincing my sister Celia and my nephew Ernesto to talk about Che. It seems to me that it would be easier for them to climb Everest!

One day, Ernesto asked me to accompany him to Santa Clara, where the Mausoleum of Che is situated – an imposing monument with an almost religious feel that I don't like. It was October, the month of Che's death and the accompanying commemorations. I didn't want to go on the actual day of the ceremony, which usually takes place on 8 October; I preferred to avoid the crowds and the press. Ernesto agreed to wait two days. Unfortunately, there were still a lot of people on 10 October. A woman journalist who must have recognized me approached me. I suggested she talk to the son rather than to the brother. As she moved over to Ernesto, he recoiled. He soon found himself literally up against a wall and she took this opportunity to stick a microphone into his face. He was forced to say something. He still hasn't forgiven me for this 'betrayal'!

14

People are often wrong about the Cubans

Since the announcement of the historic rapprochement between the US and Cuba, many Argentinian television and radio journalists have contacted me. They want to know my opinion. As a brother of Che? Or simply as an Argentinian with a profound knowledge of the island and some important connections? I've never found out and I don't care. I'm close to the Cuban rulers and to the proletariat, too. I have links with government leaders and with a large number of ordinary workers. But none of this makes a Cuban of me. The fact that I'm Che's brother maybe gives reporters the impression that my opinion is more valuable than someone else's.

First, I want to clarify this much: my support for the Cuban revolutionary process is unwavering, and the Cuban-American population is almost unknown to me.

As chance would have it, just before the announcement of the thaw, I was helping my nephew Ernesto to acquire the twelve motorcycles required for his tourist circuit. Some people immediately deduced that I was involved in the secret negotiations and knew that American tourists would soon be heading to Cuba. TN, the Argentinian television channel, invited me to appear for an informal discussion about Barack Obama and Raúl Castro. While I know Raúl, I am not his spokesperson, and it goes without saying that I have never personally met the US president! But I sardonically replied that Obama had of course called me to ask me to launch La Poderosa Tours. Joking aside, this project began with a succession of chance occurrences, and as my friend Orlando Fundora used to say: 'Whatever happens has to happen.'

Still, I told the TN journalist this much: Cuba is, in my view, much more important than a mere subject of international politics. I feel close to Cuba, it's my other homeland, my other family, my other home, although I've never spent more than three months at a time there and have no official position. Cuba welcomed in my family without asking any questions when Argentina was persecuting them. It is a beloved and familiar place. I've been there regularly since 1959, I've travelled it from north to south and from east to west, and I'm deeply attached to it. For all these reasons, I think have a fairly accurate picture of events.

In general, when people want to know my opinion on the thaw, I start by saying that it needs to be placed within a political and diplomatic context: the changes we are witnessing are the result of a long process experienced by the Cubans of Miami and Havana, even if the world did not know until recently that this process was ongoing. In fact, there have always been contacts between these two countries that have a love-hate relationship. Sometimes it's love that takes the upper hand and sometimes it's hate.

Many Cubans on the island have close or distant relatives in the United States. On one side or the other, the old guard practise a double discourse: saying one thing in public and doing another in private. Those on the island who chose to remain have long regarded the exiles as traitors to the fatherland, as *gusanos* (worms, worse than nobodies). 'If you jumped into the sea to get to Miami and you managed to get there, that's your choice', they said. 'Now that you're over there, you dare to criticize us? No way! Shut your mouths!' At the same time, those who remained in Cuba accepted the money sent from Florida and all the countries where the Cuban diaspora settled. As for the members of this diaspora, they criticize Cuba but ultimately help by sending money there.

In the 1990s, I knew a family whose grandmother had lived in the same house since before the revolution. Her eldest son had gone to live in the US while her younger son had remained in Cuba. He was an official. The grandmother continued to communicate with her son and her grandchildren in Miami. The younger son considered that his brother had gone over to the enemy. The grandmother defended her exiled son. Time passed and the younger son's criticisms gradually turned into compliments. It was with this family that I personally experienced the way that minds could change.

The Cuban exiles have always tended to believe themselves better informed. They imagined that their compatriots on the island knew nothing. This isn't true! I concede that the Internet is slow in Cuba and that the press is not pluralistic. But everyone has a satellite dish and watches television programmes from Miami. CDs and DVDs circulate. Information also passes through what is called *radio bemba* (word of mouth) and in communication with those who have left. In Havana, you can see young people looking for the best places to connect to Wi-Fi, such as La Rampa or the Presidente Hotel. Modernity and technology allow them to stay informed. Also, the island-ers read widely. They are cultured people, and they know and respect their history. They have a much broader view of the world than people imagine. When they land in Florida, they are already educated and prepared. They have studied thanks to the free education system. They come to organize, build, and start up businesses. It's not by chance that they often become successful quickly.

The Cuban lobby in Miami is losing momentum. I imagine this is because young people want to normalize relations, to go to visit relatives in Cuba. They are not extremists like their parents or grandparents. Fighting a rearguard action is not for them. They don't recognize this as their struggle because they have not had the same experiences. They do not want these conflicts, which seem to them ridiculous and unnecessary. The same thing happens in Cuba.

The Cuban government has always changed its regulations and jurisdiction as the country changed. It adapts to the fait accompli. There is an incredible amount of money under the mattress, sent by the diaspora. Since charter flights from Miami and New York have been allowed (the José Martí airport in Havana has a special terminal to accommodate these passen-gers), about 1 million Cuban exiles have visited the island over the last ten years. If we suppose that each visitor brought 10,000 dollars, the authorized amount, 10 billion dollars have come into Cuba, not counting the money sent via Western Union. The United States has just allowed airlines to open up commercial flights between the two countries. It is estimated that there will be 110 daily flights (in comparison, there are about twenty-five charter flights per day).

For years, then, the islanders have accumulated money, without any real opportunity to spend it. They could not officially buy houses (many Cubans own their old family residences), but they did have the right to trade. So what did they do? They pretended to swap a two-room property for a house with fifteen rooms, paying the difference off the books. It was an open secret. Who would believe that the owner of a manor would swap it for a two-room dwelling?

Noting not only that it could not prevent this black market but was actually losing money, the Cuban state finally legalized property transactions and subjected them to tax. This simply confirmed an already well-established process.

There was a Bureau of Cuban Affairs in the US playing what Cubans called 'roulette'. From time to time, it authorized a Cuban from Miami to visit the island. Over time, it allowed more and more such trips. Now that trade has been liberalized, money is coming out into the open. Whenever I go to Cuba, I see enormous changes. Hair salons, restaurants and auto repair shops are mushrooming!

Obama acknowledged that the time had come to change policy. Fifty years after the embargo was imposed in 1962, it had yielded no results. And I think he was also influenced by changes in the Latin American countries that have become more left-wing and moved closer to Cuba.

One story has stuck in my memory. I was in Cuba at a very difficult time for the island. I stopped at a service station. The employee took me for a Spaniard because of my clear complexion. He immediately started complaining as he filled up my tank. 'Oye, Pepe,'[1] he said to me, 'just try to imagine what it's like for us to live in this country. It's terrible! We have nothing to eat.' I examined him from top to toe. He was fat, almost obese! I replied: 'Are you kidding me? You dare to tell me you have problems getting enough to eat! I don't mind listening to you moaning but find something else to moan about!'

I love the Cuban people. They're admirable and stoic and do what they like at a pace that suits them. In terms of heroism and bravery, they have no equal! They're among the first to have taken to a skiff to get to a better life. They're experts in the art of talking the hind leg off a donkey while saying absolutely nothing. They can smoke a cigar under water. They're full of life, they dance, they laugh, they joke, they have a propensity for happiness, a cheerful temperament, a great sense of humour, and they can laugh off their misfortunes. A sad story that would be the subject of a haunting tango in Argentina becomes a joke in Cuba. Blackouts are frequent, and indeed the norm. Cubans laugh at them. When there's light, they go into raptures: 'Oh, light!' They like to repeat the following joke: capitalism comes to the edge of the abyss and looks down. What can it see at the bottom? Communism, already lying there in ruins; and capitalism is about to go the same way . . .

The Cuban's door is always open. Hospitality and solidarity are two of their great qualities. They continue to consider human beings as just that – humans, not objects or machines. They're not out to get one over their neighbours, to see what they take from them. They don't have Ferraris, Mercedes or private planes. So what? Are they any unhappier as a result? I know a young Cuban woman of twenty-six who's just moved to Buenos Aires. She's a pretty girl from Havana, well-educated, cultured, astute and intelligent; she'd never before left Havana. The first time she went shopping here, she was shocked. She wanted a pair of white ballet shoes. What did the woman in the shoe shop tell her when she asked to try on some white ballet shoes? That the new fashion was wedges, adopted by all Porteñas,[2] and that she ought to wear these if she wanted to avoid making a fashion gaffe. My friend is a stranger to the notion of fashion and what's in or out of style: these are notions that she deems frivolous. There's no fashion in Cuba. We dress in a cheap, utilitarian way.

Cuba is admittedly a poorer society than most developed countries, but it is fairer, less materialistic, with well-developed criteria of equality and fairness. A Cuban has a certain sense of morality, brotherhood and justice. Here, woman is the equal of man. She does what she wants with her body. She has access to abortion. Nobody will force her to give birth to a child she doesn't want. Crime rates are extremely low. The justice system works. The violent death of a human being, whether a man or a woman, usually results in the arrest of the culprit the same day. The sense of security that stems from this is the result of changes that the revolution has wrought in society. There is no organized crime in Cuba.

A proportion of the state's income funds public health, another education, yet another social programmes such as family allowances, nursery schools, etc. Social and human values dear to the Cubans might be lost with the return of US influence to the island. The US wants to win the ideological war. For fifty years their goal has been to transform Cuba into a capitalist country. But capitalism destroys equality – you need only look at what is happening in China with its 100 million millionaires and the privileges enjoyed by Party officials and business leaders there. And yet the changes I observe in Cuba are needed.

To create and sustain social programmes, the Cuban state has had to balance wages. What is a fair wage? The sum of the wealth of a country divided between its inhabitants. Cuba does not experience the insane levels of inequality found in other countries such as the United States, where a top CEO earns 300 times more than a typical worker. The US plunders the resources of other countries but does not redistribute wealth to its own citizens and even less so to the inhabitants of the plundered countries. Meanwhile, the Cubans send their best doctors abroad to save lives. Don't forget that they were very active in West Africa during the Ebola outbreak.

Cuba is a small country of eleven million people who have bravely resisted the biggest power in the world for more than five decades. This fighting spirit is admirable. Cuba survived – with difficulty, but it still survived – the 'special period' that succeeded the Cold War. After losing the support of the USSR, when the Berlin Wall fell and Cuba was left with nothing, it was able to survive, in part by developing tourism. No one seriously believed that Cuba could survive the dissolution of the USSR. It demonstrated that it could. It rallied around Fidel. Cubans continue to defend the concept of solidarity and fairness while approaching the much more selfish capitalist model. I call this mixture of capitalist and socialist systems 'capisol'. This is a contradiction, but what nation doesn't have such contradictions? Cubans are eagerly awaiting the US cruise ships but are at the same time afraid they will be irremediably polluted by them. They want the gringos to come and spend all their money while knowing that the changes made by this new revenue will transform mentalities, and not necessarily in a positive way. They are both excited and nervous about the human tide that is sure to land on their shores. France is not getting left behind: since the announcement of the thaw, President François Holland has been to Cuba with the aim of developing diplomatic and trade relations. He arrived in Havana accompanied by several businessmen, including representatives of Pernod Ricard, the hotel chain Accor, Air France, Carrefour and Orange. And one can easily imagine that a lot of the revenue from these projects will go to the French.

People are often wrong about the Cubans. They have never defined themselves as Marxists, but rather as supporters of Castro and revolutionaries. A friend recently told me: 'Cuba depended on Spain for four centuries, then the United States, then the USSR, and it is now preparing to yield to American influence again. They've come full circle.' The problem is that Cuba has no choice. It can't fend for itself and confront the millions of investors specializing in resource development and the opening of new markets. What do people want from Cuba? Do they expect it to be Switzerland or France? It's always being compared with developed countries. Why not compare it instead with its neighbours, Haiti or the Dominican Republic, or Honduras? Which of these nations is doing best? Which gives its citizens health care and an education for free? Which has less crime? But as for being the locomotive of a triumphant socialism and changing the world . . . it's not easy when the US is just 180 kilometres away! The fate of world socialism cannot depend on Cuba.

Is its business model a success? It depends on your point of view. Che foresaw the problem of industrialization in 1963, stating in the famous interview with Jean Daniel: 'Our difficulties are mainly the result of our mistakes. There have been many of them. What caused us the worst problem was the way we did not make the best use of our sugarcane.' He also said on another occasion: 'What I most dislike, sometimes, is our lack of courage in facing up to certain realities, economic or political . . . Sometimes our companions follow the politics of the ostrich, they bury their heads in the sand. Regarding our economic problems, we have laid the blame on drought, imperialism ... Sometimes we didn't want to disclose a piece of news, we couldn't decide to go ahead, and then only the American version remained.'

What would have happened if Che had remained in Cuba? It is obviously impossible to know. He thought the whole island was on track, in good hands, and that he could therefore go off and reproduce the experiment elsewhere. Has Cuba remained true to the spirit of Che? And, conversely, is Che responsible for its failures? This is a dialectical trap. Ernesto wanted to industrialize the country and diversify its production. That is why he set up the ministry of industry. He wanted to extend binary trade: basically, Cuba exported sugar and imported meat. But this could never be enough to enrich the country. It needed to become more independent to pursue its revolution.

The image of Ernesto is ubiquitous on the island, but it is difficult to measure its actual impact on Cuban politics. In Cuban schools, students are taught about Che's exploits, they speak of him as a hero of the country, but his thought is not studied. Few people know it in any depth. The ministry of industry no longer exists, nor does the volunteer work programme Che set up, which was primarily what I call a 'conscience generator', since its vocation was not economic in nature but social and humanitarian.

Cuba is accused of being a repressive country. The United States dares to denounce its human rights violations even though they have run the prison camp at Guantánamo in Cuba since 2002 – an extra-judicial detention centre where inmates are locked up for an unlimited time! In reality there is no real political repression in Cuba. We now know that the fifty-three inmates so often described as poor political prisoners were actually CIA agents unmasked by the Cuban services! Besides, a large number of so-called dissidents in Cuba are mercenaries supported by the US. What is Cuba supposed to do? Let them do what they want? If the CIA wants to destabilize the island via US anti-Castro organizations, the country is obviously going to defend itself! How many times has the CIA tried to assassinate Fidel? Cuba was attacked for fifty-four years while it has never attacked the United States. And all that time people tried to convince us that it was Cuba that was a danger to world peace! What did Che say in 1964, in an interview with CBS's *Face the Nation*, when reporters asked him how he envisaged Cuban-American relations? 'What Cuba wants above all is for the United States to ignore it. We do not want conflict. We want you to forget us. That's all we ask and it's pretty simple.' But the United States couldn't forget Cuba. They turned it into an obsession, spreading lies about it over the last several decades. They claim, for example, that people can't express themselves there. In Cuba, we are free to talk at ease in the street without anyone hassling us. What we can't do is express ourselves freely in newspapers. Another little-known fact concerns elections: there are more elections in Cuba than in any other country. There is no presidential election but there is a plethora of municipal, regional and parliamentary elections. The National Assembly of the People of Cuba has 612 members elected by the people. And nobody puts a gun to their heads to force them to vote a certain way.

Did Fidel betray Che by abandoning him in Bolivia? Did he send him off to wage war elsewhere so as to get rid of him in order to satisfy the Soviets, who Ernesto had started to criticize in his speeches? Nothing is further from the truth. Fidel and

Che shared a view of the revolution necessary to put an end to the misery that capitalism and its alter ego imperialism impose on societies. Fidel had to remain in Cuba and Che wanted the freedom to go and plant the seeds of independence, equality and socialist ideals in other countries. He left Cuba voluntarily. His correspondence and his writings could not be clearer on this issue. Ernesto was an enemy of big industrial groups, multinationals and capitalism, as was Fidel. But as Che is dead and buried, they attack Fidel, who is still alive and kicking. Fidel plays the role of the fall guy, the scapegoat. He becomes a traitor, a quitter. But Fidel takes care of Ernesto's children who call him *tio* and really love him. As proof of his care for our family, the Cuban government has prevented the publication of the famous photo of Ernesto dead, the one that traumatized me on 10 October 1967, and the photo of his hands cut off. He did so out of decency towards us, and because it was too painful.

One day, Fidel gave a very important speech in Havana in the presence of the Soviet ambassador Yuri Petrov. It was in 1987. Fidel looked Petrov in the eye and said: 'I think it wouldn't hurt you to spend some time reading the thoughts of Che. You'd realize that, here in Latin America, we also have our thinkers.'

15

What can I do but sow seeds?

Chance sometimes does things well. If my venture with the café-restaurant turned out badly, it at least gave me the opportunity to meet the French journalist Armelle Vincent and write this book with her. For it was at a table in Epicúreos that our friendship sprang up, in 2007. An Argentinian woman friend had told her about me after reading an interview – my very first – in the daily *Página/12*, in which I demanded that the government pay the reparation promised to political prisoners in recompense for their incarceration, as it was being slow to honour its promises. When she learned of my existence, Armelle immediately wanted to meet me. Like most people, she had never considered the possibility that Che might have a brother, and one who was still alive! She immediately set out to look for me in the Las Canitas neighbourhood (the interview did not include the name or the address of Epicúreos) and finally found me. She introduced herself and asked me for an interview. I refused. At the time I wasn't ready. But I invited her to have a cup of coffee. She was accompanied by her Argentinian husband. We talked a lot. I told her a bit about my family. Armelle seemed interested, and we met the next day for lunch. During the conversation, I learned that Claudio, Armelle's husband, had fled Argentina in 1974 after being arrested for his revolutionary activities; he was active in a Guevara-inspired movement. That inevitably forges a bond between people. So I ended up granting an interview to Armelle. She produced a portrait of me for the French magazine *L'Amateur de cigare*. We stayed in touch. When we met up again in Buenos Aires in March 2015, I told her I now wanted to honour my brother's memory and she suggested the idea of a book. This is how this book came to be published, in France.

I refused to talk about Ernesto for years. Out of modesty, a tacit agreement with my brother and sisters, as a reaction against my father who overdid his role as Che's father in Cuba, and probably, too, out of fear. Why would I say that I was his brother? So they could assassinate me? The fact of the matter is that, after the dictatorship, when the danger had passed, I didn't really ask myself why I still felt so uncomfortable with the idea of mentioning the fact that I was related to him. It was a very personal subject. Che was my brother before he was the hero crowned with glory. I was afraid of exploiting his memory as so many others have done. So I kept silent while finding myself constantly confronted with his image in streets all around the world where he continued to exist as a legend. I couldn't stand this myth; I still can't.

One day in October 1973, I was in Cuba with my family when my son Martin had a very severe asthma attack. I guess it's in the family; his uncle Ernesto and his brother Pablo both suffered from it. My two sons are asthmatic – unlike me. I had some unusual lung problems when I came out of jail, but it wasn't asthma. I took Martin to the emergency ward in Borras, a hospital complex in Havana. His case was so serious that the doctors decided to hospitalize him and put him on a serum drip. He could barely breathe.

Probably due to my name, the woman doctor recognized me. The next day she took me aside: 'Mr Guevara,' she said, 'we want to invite you to participate in a ceremony to be held tomorrow. We have to present awards to the best employees, in the name of Che, and we are counting on your presence.' October is the month of commemorations of the deaths of Ernesto and Camilo Cienfuegos. I declined, explaining that I preferred to keep quiet: I had come to the hospital because my son was sick. The doctor, who was small, slight but extremely authoritarian, did not see it that way! She looked at me with blazing eyes and, in a tone that brooked no reply: 'You listen to me, Mr Guevara. You have every right to speak or not to speak. But in my view you're acting in a very selfish manner. Everyone knows that you're here, you have no idea of all the things you could say, and that you have buried deep within you. If you prefer to keep it to yourself, it's your choice but I don't think it's right.' I was stunned.

She was inexhaustible and relentless. Weary of her remonstrations, I gave in. What could I do? I asked her for the time and place of the ceremony and I turned up without having any idea what I was going to say. They had placed a long table in a large room. The director of the hospital was there, with doctors, nurses, porters . . . I didn't know anyone from those circles. They put me at the end of the table, and to my relief they forgot all about me as they gave out the prizes. I was thinking. Nobody had ever asked me to do this. What was I supposed to say? Suddenly, the woman doctor picked up the microphone and announced: 'We are honoured to have with us tonight the brother of Dr Ernesto Che Guevara, the heroic guerrilla fighter . . .' Before she could finish her sentence, the whole audience rose to its feet and began to applaud wildly. This came at the right time for me because I had a huge lump in my throat, and I was shaking; I had to calm down and think about what I was going to say. They were weeping! Che had been dead for only five years and he was still painfully missed in Cuba. The audience was obviously emotional, and this touched me deeply.

Someone put the microphone up to my face and I started talking. The words came out naturally. As I spoke, I felt like crying too. There was still a lump in my throat and yet I was talking. I've forgotten what I said, but my words came from the heart. The audience kept breaking out in applause. This was the first time I'd spoken publicly of Ernesto. I kept a very fond memory of the occasion, but I didn't do it again for thirty-six years.

As for giving interviews to the media, I had a miserable experience in 1965 or 1966 (I don't exactly remember the date) that put me off for a long time. The whole world, my family included, was wondering where Che was. He had vanished. I wasn't talking to any of my relatives and in any case I knew nothing about Ernesto's movements. One day, a journalist from *Gente* magazine appeared at my bookshop. He wanted to interview me. I replied that I never gave interviews. He insisted. 'I just want to know if you know where your brother is', he said. I again told him that I didn't give any interviews. I added that, even if I had known where my brother was, he was the last person I would have revealed it to. There was a photographer with a telephoto lens that I had not seen on the other side of the street. He photographed me without my consent. The next day, *Gente* published a picture of me accompanied by the following caption: 'Juan Martin Guevara claims not to know where his brother Che is, but the tone he used to say this suggests he actually knows perfectly well.' These methods were all the more shocking in that they put me in danger. I went looking for that bastard of a reporter and told him: 'What do you want? Do you want the SIDE,[1] the FBI, the CIA and the KGB on my heels? Are you off your head?' He couldn't have cared less so long as he had his fake scoop. The damage was done. If the secret services had not noticed me before, which I very much doubt, they now had me in their sights.

Over the years, I changed, and the journalists finally left me alone. I'd discouraged them. But they returned to the attack after my first interview, in 2007 for the Argentinian daily *Página/12*. This interview wasn't about Che but about the indemnities the government had promised to political prisoners. It was slow to keep its promise and I stepped into the breach. The public thus learned of my existence. They'd forgotten that Che had brothers and sisters. The Argentinians were amazed. This shows how little they knew of his story. However, it took me two more years to decide to speak of Che. I was a victim of self-censorship!

When the Argentinian press made a renewed attempt, in 2009, I was finally ready, without having formally decided to go ahead. It happened naturally. One day, I just agreed to give an interview. I had many things to say that I'd kept to myself. And then there were the many conversations I had had with Roberto, Celia, and Ana Maria before her death. Since Celia had returned from exile in 1984, followed by Roberto, we had talked a lot about Ernesto and the need to express ourselves or, instead, to be silent. Ana Maria and Celia stuck to their positions and continued to remain silent. Roberto expressed himself frequently in public, especially about his movement, the MODEPA.

Celia knows nothing about this book. When she learns of its existence, she may never speak to me again! She disagrees with me on this issue. So we steer clear of the subject so as not to argue. She is fiercer, more single-minded, than ever. Roberto has resumed his anonymity and, at the age of eighty-three, doesn't want to talk about these things any more. He knows I'm very active, very involved in defending the memory of Ernesto, but he never asks me any questions. His wife, in contrast, gives me a great deal of encouragement.

My desire to talk stems from more than personal considerations. Between 2001 and 2003, Argentina experienced a cataclysm. Politically, it was a period of extreme instability: after the two disastrous terms of the Peronist Carlos Menem, five presidents succeeded one another in the Casa Rosada in four years; a couple lasted just forty-eight hours.[2] At that time, I realized that young people were rediscovering Che. They thirsted for knowledge. They asked questions. There was a need, a necessity born of the chaos following the catastrophic economic and social crisis that overwhelmed us in 2001. We were already in a dangerous recession. We were pushed into the abyss by the drastic economic measures imposed by the International Monetary Fund (we were Greece before Greece). Whole sections of the population went from being middle class to being impoverished overnight: their savings had suddenly been devalued – when they had not completely melted away. People had to resort to barter to survive. They had no cash left: the banks had closed or imposed limits on withdrawals. We started swapping food for services. It became clear that wild capitalism was not the promised paradise. There were mass protests. We had to find a remedy, enable a new society to rise from the ashes of the old one. Young people turned to Che. What did he have to say about capitalism? What solutions did he advocate? Gradually, I began to answer their questions. I got involved. I felt I had a responsibility to him, a duty of memory that requires me to talk about him. What steps had led him to become the Che we know?

At the same time, three old friends decided to open museums: the sister of a cellmate, and MP for the province of Misiones, Julia Perié, in Puerto Caraguatay, where Ernesto spent his first two years; the woman in charge of tourism, Carina Chuicicich, in Alta Gracia, where Ernesto lived as a young man; and Dario Fuentes in San Martin de Los Andes, in the Patagonian province of Neuquén, a place of spectacular beauty that so captivated Ernesto that he spoke of spending the last years of his life there. Julia, Carina and Dario asked me to participate in the venture. They were making such a huge effort to honour the memory of my brother that I couldn't refuse. We launched a cultural tourism circuit called *Los Caminos del Che* linking the three museums, with a programme promoted by the Argentinian ministry of tourism. Our first public meeting was held in 2009: it marked my debut on the national and international scene. In 2013, I founded the association Por Las Huellas del Che (In the Footsteps of Che) with the aim of spreading his ideas. I always say that they wanted to put Che on a cross and crucify not only his body but his ideals. The association began by making a detailed study of how Che's image had been treated since his landing with Fidel on Las Coloradas beach. We wanted to understand how he was perceived. What did we discover? That his image is definitely multifaceted: the Communist Argentinian doctor indoctrinating young men from good families; the film hero (*Che!* directed by Richard Fleischer with Omar Sharif in the leading role, and, more recently, Steven Soderbergh's *Che*, with Benicio del Toro[3]); the psychopathic murderer who goes around shooting people at random; the heroic fighter and defender of widows and orphans, etc. In reality, who is Che?

I would like this book – and the association – to accomplish several objectives. The important thing is to get people to know Che as more than a myth. People have a distorted view of him. Under the mask of the icon or the guerrilla, however attractive, there was a content that needed to be publicized. Who knows about Che's ideas? Almost nobody! Yet he was one of the great Marxist thinkers of the twentieth century. People need to realize that this man was not just good at taking up arms. He said he was an adventurer, but he was of the kind who do not think twice about sacrificing their lives to live in harmony with the truth, and are prepared to die for their ideas. It is important to understand that Ernesto began as a normal and even ordinary person, who became an exceptional person that others can and should emulate. Great men are rare but they do exist! And this man was Argentinian. Hence my second objective: that Argentinians recover the figure of Che as a symbol. No offence to the Cubans, but his customs, culture and sense of humour were Argentinian. I recently gave a lecture at a major university in Havana and I had the misfortune to evoke Che's 'Argentinism'. This didn't go down very well. Indeed, several people stood up to contradict me. Che was not only Cuban, they assured me, but *santaclareño*[4] too; there was nothing Argentinian about him, not even his accent, a mixture of Mexican and Cuban. I didn't insist, there was no point, but I was still left speechless.

Ernesto never stopped feeling Argentinian and loving our

country. In Havana, he went regularly to the news agency Prensa Latina to find out what was happening in his homeland; he followed Argentinian affairs with enormous interest. He knew the names of all the politicians, all the important members of the military and trade unions. Nothing of what was happening in Buenos Aires escaped him. Jorge Masetti – who had interviewed him at length in the Sierra Maestra and had become his friend – sent him all the news about Argentina every morning.

One day a female journalist whose name I've forgotten asked Ernesto about our country. At one point, he said: 'Enough about Argentina, let's move on to another topic.' 'Why?', she asked him, 'if you love your country so much?' – 'Precisely for that reason!' replied Ernesto. The truth is that he was very homesick for his country.

In Cuba, Che is perfection itself, he is sanctified and nobody has the right to criticize him. But Ernesto had his faults, like everyone else. He often found it difficult to express, verbally or physically, what he felt for other people. They deduced that he was distant, like my mother. She loved us dearly but she never took us into her arms. And yet we all knew the love she had for us. That's why the long hug between mother and son at Havana airport was so moving and spectacular for us. In his letters, Ernesto was much more expansive. He wrote wonderful love poems to Aleida, and before that to Chichina. His heart was full of tenderness. One of his favourite sayings was 'Grow hard without ever losing your tenderness.' That was true in his case.

I would like to make him better known. I am neither an intellectual nor a journalist, but I'm his brother and that simple fact has an impact. When people learn who I am, they don't believe me; they doubt my word and treat me as a storyteller. They examine me insolently from head to toe. I am an enigma. Once they've accepted the fact that I might be telling the truth, their next response is to look for similarities. They scrutinize my eyes, my nose, my mouth, my height. I'm smaller than Ernesto. We are vaguely similar, but not obviously alike. We have the same voice. When someone pours out his or her emotions on meeting me, like the Japanese woman in Vallegrande mentioned at the beginning of this book, I am well aware that these feelings are not for me. I'm only the vector. Each time, I wonder: what is this person feeling? Why such a strong emotion? I have met people of all nationalities who bear Che within themselves.

In Argentina, the phenomenon is almost the opposite of that in Cuba. Ernesto was long vilified and then ignored. He made people feel too uneasy. Imagine: a country that has seen seventeen military dictatorships, where freedom of expression has been violated so often, where cronyism is encouraged, internalized! While the provinces of Córdoba, Neuquén and Misiones honour Che today with their museums, not a single street in Buenos Aires bears his name. The city council refused. Recently, a school asked permission to be renamed Escuela Ernesto Guevara: the request was refused on the grounds that 'he was a murderer'. No matter that dozens of streets in the capital are named after dictators and perpetrators of massacres!

Still, attitudes are changing. Today Che is a symbol that many Argentinian people adopt for themselves. The Kirchners adorned one wall in the Casa Rosada with a portrait of him. Politicians, often unaware of Che's real ideas, exploit his image, forgetting that their corruption is an affront to his integrity.

However, I sometimes have pleasant surprises. I was recently looking for an out-of-print book about my brother. After a fruitless search in the capital's bookshops, I finally found it on a website for second-hand books. The seller gave me an appointment, in a working-class part of town, on a street corner. He didn't know who I was. He'd simply come to sell a book to a stranger. He was a man in his thirties. He seemed quite poor. He arrived, handed me the book and immediately apologized for parting with it. He told me he had a big collection of books on Che, he was a great admirer, he had read almost all of his writings, I should do the same, etc. He was only reluctantly parting with this book because he was broke. He gave me an improvised lecture on Che at the entrance to a supermarket whose security guard, walking up and down, stared at us suspiciously! I finally revealed my identity. At first, he was incredulous. For one thing, why would I be looking for this book if I really was Che's brother? Shouldn't I already have owned a copy? (I did actually have one copy, which I took out of my bag to show him, but I wanted another.) He asked me what my name was, and asked questions about my family, trying to confuse me. As he couldn't catch me out – for good reason – he accepted the evidence. He was so happy to meet a close relative of Che! I had made his day!

This man was well versed in the thought of Che, which in Argentina is quite rare. There is a terrible lack of information. It is essential that new generations take a look at Ernesto, as a child, a teenager, and a young man. At present, my companions in the ATE union (Asociación de trabajadores del estado) are working with the University of Buenos Aires and the Centro Che in Cuba to amass all the documents relating to Ernesto in Argentina. People will discover him as brother, son, friend, nephew, grandson, doctor, chess player, intellectual, politician, strategist and fighter. When we are all dead, at least Che will still be Che.

Humanizing him: this is the only way we can discuss his thought, his philosophy and his moral values while avoiding clichés, especially that of the guerrilla fighter, which seems too simplistic. Likewise, reducing his literary production to *The Motorcycle Diaries* when he wrote 3,000 pages is terribly simplistic. Guerrilla warfare was for him just a method for attaining liberation, transformation, equality and the end of the exploitation of one human being by another. He came up with solutions to problems that are of pressing importance today more than ever. We tend to forget that, between 1959 and 1965, Ernesto had the status and responsibilities of a head of state. He travelled all over the world on official business and met other state leaders while developing an economic policy in Cuba. He became president of the National Bank and took courses in advanced mathematics with Salvador Vilaseca in order to be able to run it. He was a great reader of Marx, and tried to apply Marx's basic principles to his ministry of industry. These principles had nothing to do with those of the USSR, which had degenerated into materialism and dogmatism. In this regard, he wrote: 'The intransigent dogmatism of Stalin's time was succeeded by an inconsistent pragmatism. And the tragedy is that this phenomenon does not only apply to a specific sector of science; it occurs in all aspects of the life of socialist nations, creating extremely harmful and disturbing effects whose ultimate consequences cannot be estimated.'[5]

Che wanted to build a fair and just society based not on profit but on humanitarian principles and ideals of honour, solidarity and fraternity. He said that 'one needs to be Marxist in the same obvious way that one is a Newtonian in physics or a follower of Pasteur in biology . . . Marx's merit is that he made a qualitative leap in the history of social philosophy. He interprets history, explains its dynamics and predicts the future. Moreover, he goes beyond his scientific duty: he formulates a revolutionary concept. It is not enough to understand the nature of things, it is also necessary to change them. The human being ceases to be a slave and instrument of history and becomes the architect of his own future.'[6]

Unlike Russian apparatchiks, Che refused all privileges. Money didn't interest him. He immediately handed over to his subordinates the gifts he received from other heads of state. Aleida was very disappointed the day he gave a colour television – ultra-rare in Cuba – to a model employee in the ministry of industry.

Ernesto had no need of the Cuban revolution to become anti-dogmatic. He hated ideological barriers. He learned and discovered through practice. If he talked a great deal about dialectics, he did not limit himself to speculation or philosophy. First came action, then thought. He tried to derive theoretical ideas from his actions and to realize his thoughts in action. Right in the middle of the Ñancahuazú campaign, he devoured books. He read the philosophers of ancient Greece to try to understand human beings and their role in history. Then he read them again, in case he had missed anything. His concerns went well beyond guerrilla warfare. He was continually evolving and growing more mature, in political, philosophical and humanistic terms. His thinking was changing constantly. How can the ideal of the new human being be achieved unless we first interpret human existence?

People interested in Ernesto's thought should be able to embark on the process of changing reality and transforming political, ideological, philosophical and cultural thought so as to achieve this *hombre nuevo* that so concerned him. A radically changed society, a society based on justice, should and must involve a complete metamorphosis of human beings: not only the master and the boss need to be changed, but also the slave and the worker. We all need to change our mentality, to improve. The exploitation of human beings does not only happen in the area of work: it extends to all human fields. Economic structures cannot be changed in the absence of a change in human consciousness. The latter can in turn be transformed only with practice. We must first take power, ending the private ownership of the means of production and the avid desire for monopoly.

What is currently happening in Argentina? The same banks, the same Starbucks, McDonald's, Walmart, Carrefour, Farmacity – all foreign companies that have invaded us. Do they leave the money they make with us? Of course not. Indeed, even now they put their names on products manufactured in Argentina. This phenomenon is repeated all over the world. This is standardization. We're losing our differences.

Faced with this remorseless advance, this steamroller, what can I do but sow seeds? Some seeds will be lucky enough to have been planted in a fertile land, others will need fertilizer. I firmly believe in historical coincidences – those, for example, in which a revolutionary situation needs a particular human being to fertilize it and bring it to term. Sometimes we have the circumstances, but not the right person for the job. Sometimes it's the opposite. However, history has shown us that, at times, the stars are miraculously aligned – as on the night Fidel and Ernesto met in Mexico City. Chance had played its role well, but Fidel also had to be able, in the space of a few hours, to recognize Ernesto's qualities.

My mission is not only related to the fact that Che was my

brother. I share his ideas. I am a Marxist-Leninist, a Guevarist. I believe in the transformation of the world and I am confident that the powers that govern us – corporations, cartels, billionaires, armies – are not going to hand back power to us on a plate, without a fight. It is their fault that we are speeding towards catastrophe. We are coming to a turning point. But we lack the impetus to face up to the situation. You have to give people the means to defend themselves. While I do not support armed struggle, I believe in the virtues of a certain violence. We cannot fight the monster with mere words. Violence exists, and is the direct result of capitalism. Someone will and must rise up. Who, what, when, where – these are things we do not know as yet. But we can't go on like this.

The 1960s were bright years filled with hope and vibrancy, thanks to the victory of the Cuban revolution and the defeat of imperialism at the Bay of Pigs. The world seemed divided in two: communism on the one side, capitalism on the other. A decade later, we were in a grey period. Che had been defeated and with him the Bolivian revolution.

This rout cast a widening shadow across Latin America and had an enormous impact on subsequent events, but we had to wait years to gauge the results. In the 1970s, we still hoped to carry out a revolution, to win the battle and impose socialism, at least in Argentina. And then the USSR fell and with it the Iron Curtain. Today we have emerged from the grey years. One has only to watch what is happening in Europe. Are Europeans aware of the seriousness of the problems they are experiencing – unemployment, debt, immigration, etc? The Old Continent is now on a very slippery slope, and the situation is getting worse. What can we do, as we face the enormous concentrations of financial power, the multinationals that seem to govern our lives, the monopolies on armaments, communications, oil, and food-processing? All the fundamental areas of life are concentrated in the hands of a few. Who is able to fight such powers?

For this reason, I am a fervent Guevarist. We may be few in number, but we are gradually awakening to the notion that these ideas are not romantic or quixotic, as they claim. No! Che's philosophy is concrete and practical. Has it been defeated, forced to bend? Without a doubt. Just recently, I attended an academic conference in Buenos Aires. Several speakers argued that Latin America today stands together as a global entity. I do not agree. The United States has a huge influence on our continent and it's not in US interests to see us coming together: we could then escape their dominance.

The United States may also be in crisis, but it's the crisis of a rich and all-powerful country. The US has Wall Street (Goldman Sachs, Morgan Stanley, JP Morgan Chase, etc.), the most powerful army in the world, the largest media groups (Time Warner, Viacom, Comcast, etc.), and the biggest high-tech companies (Google, Facebook, Microsoft). They manage their crisis in such a way as to shift the blame onto others. They keep the best for themselves, and ensure that the worst effects are suffered elsewhere. However, the worst effects are now knocking at their own door. At present, 50 million Americans cannot feed themselves adequately – an explosive situation that could lead straight to the turning point I mentioned. There was a happy time when most of these people belonged to the middle class. They had a car, a house, a surplus of food. They thought they had acquired inalienable rights, but these have evaporated. Can they be satisfied with the explanation that there are poorer countries than the US, peoples who suffer more than they do? Of course not! It's not an earthquake that has taken everything from them, but unfettered capitalism. What, indeed, is the aim of those who hold the most wealth? To ensure that other people don't know how they accumulated this wealth; that those they force to suffer will think that their wretched fates are the will of God and that they will be saved and happy in eternal life; that they will be convinced that their fate is linked to the fact that they are black, brown, stupid or incompetent . . .

Which countries are being forced by rich nations to pay the price of unfettered capitalism? Historically, the so-called third world or developing countries. Today, however, developed countries are beginning to suffer too. Europe is pushing Portugal, among others, to the brink, and the first to go under there are, of course, the poor. The class struggle that Marx spoke of is perhaps defined in other terms these days, but it still exists. It is no longer a question of morality or justice, though there are great injustices, but a practical, concrete, political and economic question. The solution to our problems cannot lie in the anarchy of production that we are now seeing. The only thing that is being proposed is more and more material possessions. Our religion is now one of cannibalistic consumption. So we produce more and more – but why, and what for? To feed the monopolies I mentioned above.

We are told that measures are being taken in favour of the poor. They have state schools, they are taught to read and write. Administrative positions in corporations dominated by the oligarchy are being handed out to the middle classes. Meanwhile, the oligarchy sends its children to private schools and top-ranking universities that produce leaders all trained in the same mould to control us. These future plutocrats are expected to perpetuate the capitalist and imperialist model. From time to time, one of them breaks ranks and demonstrates independence.

The oligarchy is taken aback. It has been provided with all the tools for it to continue to keep those below subjugated. What happened?

Che left Cuba too early for his management of the country and his vision to come to fruition. He tried to go beyond Soviet Marxism and apply a Marxism with a human face to Cuba. He believed his project was on track; because of his death, it was left as unfinished business. Communism ended in failure. Capitalism survives, but at the expense of the planet and its people. Wealth continues to be concentrated in the hands of a few while poverty spreads. Can't people see the relationship of cause and effect?

Human beings have ceased to be important and have been turned into objects of exploitation and abuse. All areas are now affected by immorality and corruption, even football, which has ceased to be a sport and become a filthy trade. We are increasingly losing our humanity, our solidarity, our sociability. Human beings are not born like that, but manufactured to be so.

Do I myself have solutions to these problems? Unfortunately not. If I had, I would be another Che. My brother had solutions. They were unsuccessful. He suffered a strategic defeat, not only in South America but worldwide. He wanted to change people's minds to achieve global transformation. He believed in this.

One of the aims of the association Por Las Huellas del Che is to be present everywhere that Che exists as a thinker, as a social innovator. It must be an enduring association. It isn't going to revolutionize anything and that is not its goal. It must be able to spread the spiritual legacy of Che that has grown up around the world. The Marxist beacon of the twenty-first century will be Che. He identified and signalled the events that have since occurred, the current unresolved calamities. He is a thinker of the future despite the fact that he died in 1967. Looking back, we can see that he had a startling vision of things to come. For example, he predicted the collapse of the USSR. Who else was capable of doing this in 1965? Why was he able to do so? Because he had carried out an in-depth analysis of Soviet society which, according to him, was struggling against capitalism with capitalist weapons, which in fact led to a strengthening of the liberal system. The Soviets had lost their way after their revolution. He blamed the fact that the New Economic Policy (NEP) – launched in 1921 by Lenin to revitalize the country given its economic backwardness[7] – turned into a fait accompli instead of being a temporary measure. Material incentives had assumed a fundamental importance in Soviet society at the expense of human values. The people then became increasingly obsessed with material gain and financial rewards. Che dubbed this phenomenon the law of value and contrasted it with morality, which, for him, was of fundamental importance. Human beings should be stimulated by the desire to do good, to be honest, to keep a clear conscience, to do their duty. The mission of a government should be primarily educational. This does not mean that the material question can be completely eliminated.

Che did not go into an analysis of Soviet repression or the concept of freedom of expression. He came to power in Cuba during the Khrushchev years, so this was the period he analysed. He deplored the dogmatism, totalitarianism and inconsistency of the Soviets. According to him, the USSR had betrayed Marxist principles by transforming them into dogma. What did he write in 1965 in Tanzania, where he was waiting for the right time to organize his departure for Bolivia? 'I have taken advantage of this long holiday to stick my nose into philosophy, something I've wanted to do for a long time. I've come up against the initial problem: in Cuba, there's nothing published apart from the heavy Soviet tomes that have the disadvantage of preventing you thinking: the Party has already done this for you. It just asks you to digest the results. As a method, it's anti-Marxist, but in addition, the content is very poor.'[8]

In the twentieth century, answers to these questions involved armed struggle, revolution, insurrection, riot. Today we can perhaps say that these methods are not the right ones. On the other hand, there is no doubt that capitalism is not going to commit suicide. It's not going to say: 'Okay, that's enough of that, I want a better world. It's over; I'll stop, I surrender.' So the big question is to find the path that leads to fairness and justice.

Che was in favour of armed struggle, for he was convinced it was the only way to end imperialism once and for all. Should we wait for the executioner to cut off our heads, for Dracula to suck all the blood out of us, or must we take up arms to defend ourselves?

In recent years we have witnessed situations of direct aggression against the people, such as the subprime crisis and foreclosures. Yet there have been no large-scale protest movements. Obviously aware of the harm they are doing, the powerful produce the disinformation or distractions needed to keep the masses in a state of brutish ignorance. People are very depoliticized, and not only in the US. The fierce defence of private property, individualism and selfishness is so ingrained in society that it has become extremely difficult to organize ordinary people. They are convinced that there's no solution, this is the way things are and they cannot be otherwise. They've become fatalistic.

So why did I finally decide to talk? Why this book and this association?

The answer to the first question is that I find myself constantly confronted with the obvious: our need to transform society. I have made the ideals of my brother my own. I speak on his behalf. For us to be able to study the great thinkers of history, it was necessary that someone should dedicate himself to reading, publishing and gathering information about them. This is what I am doing with the association.

The answer to the second question is that, if I carried out my mission alone, someone could put a spoke in my wheel – not to mention the fact that I'm seventy-two years old. The enemies of the people can't do anything against a book, especially if it's published in other countries such as France. There was a time when 'subversive' books were censored in Argentina. This is no longer the case. The current approach is to try to prevent us from reading by impelling us to watch TV and surf the net. That is why I am so opposed to these media. I don't like their immediacy. Everything now has to be instantaneous, while we ought to take time to think and reflect. Technology and modern times no longer allow this.

As I'm optimistic and don't think that mankind desires its own death, we must do something, and I feel that the times are conducive to the spread of Ernesto's philosophy. He had such far-reaching ideas but not the time to put his basic principles into practice: so I must at least help to put his thought into circulation.

Che's gift is that he can motivate people. So we must allow his influence to reach far and wide.

16

Che lives on

'Les honneurs, ça m'emmerde!' my brother exclaimed one day in 1960, after the crisis of the Bay of Pigs. 'I can't stand these bloody honours!' He was speaking in French to avoid offending the employees in his ministry of industry, who had come to tell him of their desire to pay him a public tribute 'for the magnificent training he gave to members of the Ejercito Rebelde'.

Ernesto had no use for praise. He looked up at his employees and said: 'I don't think you've understood what I wear myself out repeating in my writings and lectures. Here, what we need are not tributes but work. You consider yourselves to be revolutionaries? So I'll find a battle station for you . . . In a factory.'

My brother was not looking for fame and hated frivolity. What would he have thought of the Mercedes-Benz campaign of 2012? This highly controversial campaign had the nerve to replace the star on Che's cap with the logo of the German car manufacturer . . . When it was unveiled at the International Consumer Electronics Show in Las Vegas, one reporter wanted to know my opinion. There are two things I'd like to say, I told him. The first is that Mercedes-Benz produces fantastic cars. The second is that if Germany became communist tomorrow,

Mercedes-Benz will have been at the forefront of the revolution! Seriously, what is important here is to understand why Mercedes-Benz chose the image of Che rather than any other. The designer who came up with this idea was a genius. He reached two opposite target audiences: the anti-Castroists of Miami (who, incidentally, choked when they saw Mercedes-Benz associate its image with that of a 'sadistic serial killer'), and the others who found it revolting that Mercedes-Benz would use a man of such integrity for vulgar commercial purposes – and above all, for promoting luxury cars! At all events, the campaign caused a seismic shock. The day of its launch in Las Vegas, the CEO of Daimler, Dieter Zetsche, walked up and down onstage under a huge portrait of Che. It was completely surreal. So much so, indeed, that when faced with the public outcry, Zetsche had to stop the campaign and apologize.

Why does Che's image sell things? Why do people choose this image rather than any other to express their opposition, their challenge?

No trader in the world wants to waste money, quite the opposite. For them, Che is primarily big business, as he has become for some residents in La Higuera who have turned into guides. The question is not why people sell this image, but why they find buyers. Diego Maradona and Mike Tyson both have tattoos of Che, the former on his arm, the latter on his belly. What does it mean? It means that Che is present in their lives, that he is such a powerful symbol that they want to have him written into their skin.

I reject the hyper-commercialization of my brother. At the same time, I know that it will make my task easier. Indeed, the seeds are planted, people are already responsive to the image. Without knowing about his ideas, at least they know who he is. I have only to act as a transmitter. I doubt that Mike Tyson or Diego Maradona have studied Che's philosophy, but I know they are receptive. If his philosophy strikes them as consistent with their idea of him, they'll keep their tattoo. Otherwise, they can always have it removed.

The powers that be tried to crush Che by all means, choosing assassination rather than imprisonment, then removing his body and finally trampling over his mind, his struggle, his ideals. They killed him. He has survived in spite of it all. How many times did they depict the Cuban revolution as a foreign invasion, a Soviet bridgehead, instead of recognizing it as a national and patriotic project? Didn't they describe Ernesto as a killer, a savage, a horrible Marxist? Their calumnies didn't work either. Lyricists continued to write songs (at least fifty ballads have been devoted to Che), authors continued to write books and poets poems, street artists still covered the walls with his image, and so on. So Che continued to live, he was more present than ever, it seemed hopeless to try and annihilate him.

The strategy they adopted was to mystify him, to crucify him so that humanity would no longer consider him to be real and tangible. If he's a myth, how can anyone follow his example? He's no longer a man of flesh and blood but a spectral, unattainable figure, impossible to live up to. Gradually, as his legend has been magnified, his ideas have been devalued. He became a shell, beautiful, but empty. Do you think this is any coincidence? Of course not.

A parallel has drawn between Christ and Che. They are alike in death. I said in the first chapter of this book that the famous photograph of Ernesto lying on the cement slab in the laundry room of the Vallegrande hospital is eerily reminiscent of Andrea Mantegna's *Lamentation of Christ*. This analogy, which

I find unnecessary and dangerous, has been used to transform Ernesto into a saint – San Ernesto de la Higuera. His thinking, his determination, his fighting abilities thus disappear behind the legend. Ernesto was anything but a mystic, even if he did define himself as a 'wandering prophet'. This didn't stop him sharing certain qualities with Christ: humanism, a concern at all times for the oppressed, rebelliousness against the powerful, the denunciation of wealth and greed. Jesus sacrificed himself for men, and Che did the same.

In July 1959, on an official visit to India, he wrote to my mother in a way that sheds light on his state of mind:

My old dream of visiting all these countries now occurs in a way that takes away any pleasure. I speak of political and economic problems, I have to attend parties wearing a tuxedo, and set aside one of my purest pleasures: that of dreaming in the shade of a pyramid or over a sarcophagus of Tutankhamen. Moreover, I don't have Aleida here,[1] I haven't brought her with me because of one of those complex mental patterns [sic] which are my secret . . . Egypt was an outstanding diplomatic success; the embassies of every country turned up at the farewell party we organized, and I had the opportunity to see the intricacies of diplomacy when I spotted the Apostolic Nuncio proffering his hand to the Russian attaché with a truly beatific smile. And now India, and new knotty questions of protocol that produce the same infantile panic in me; men who repeat the same polite phrases when greeting one another, etc. One of my colleagues has invented a formula: reply to everything by saying *joinch-joinch*; it works a treat. Furthermore, even if I trotted out dumb remarks in Cuban[2] all day long, my Spanish speaker wouldn't understand a word.

I've developed an awareness of the group in opposition to the individual; I continue to be the same loner seeking his path without assistance, except that I am now aware of my historical duty. I have no home, no wife, no children, no parents, no brothers and sisters, my friends are my friends so long as they share my political opinions and yet, I'm happy, I feel that I'm a somebody. I am not only equipped with this powerful inner strength that I have always felt, but also with a capacity of empathy for others. An absolute fatalistic intuition of my mission takes away all fear.

Che was fighting for the people, and even gave his life for them. That is why, no doubt, his image has spread so quickly, in barely fifty years. In our time, information travels at a phenomenal rate. It goes global, and travels everywhere in just seconds. Nevertheless, we still have much to discover about him. How will he be perceived in two millennia? I hope he won't be a religious figure. People must dwell on his humanism not his religiosity.

The figure of Che endures. He's here, present among us, and we can't get rid of him. He continues to represent a real danger to some people. The young people of the world adopt him as an archetype of rebellion, integrity, struggle, justice, idealism. Here are some current examples. When he met Pope Francis, President Evo Morales of Bolivia was wearing a jacket embroidered with the figure of Che. He also has a portrait of him in his presidential office. In Lebanon, demonstrators protesting against Syria at the grave of Prime Minister Rafiq Hariri wore T-shirts bearing the image of Che. French footballer Thierry Henry turned up at a FIFA party with a red and black T-shirt with Che on it. In Stavropol in Russia, protesters denouncing the cash payment of social benefits paraded with flags of Che. In Dheisheh refugee camp in the Gaza Strip, posters of Che adorned a wall honouring the victims of the intifada. The Chinese rebel and MP for Hong Kong, Kwok-hung, defied Beijing by wearing a Che T-shirt; and in Hollywood, Carlos Santana, who performed a song from the film *The Motorcycle Diaries*, wore a shirt with Che on it while holding a crucifix. Che represents insubordination to central authorities.

17

'A year. Already so long ago.'

A year after Che's death, an Argentinian publication asked Berta Gilda 'Tita' Infante, his best friend, to write about him. It is for me, as I have said, the most beautiful, the most moving thing ever written about Ernesto. That's why I want to finish my book by quoting it.

Tita and Ernesto met at medical school in 1947, three years after I was born. I didn't know Tita personally, or perhaps I did, as she sometimes came to our house, but I was too young for me to remember it now. I learnt what I know about her from others.

Tita arrived in Buenos Aires from Córdoba with her mother and her brother Carlos, a few months before enrolling in college, and three years after the death of her father, a lawyer and politician. When Carlos too became a lawyer, he got to know Ernesto in Cuba, when he took over Radio Rivadavia. Carlos was Ernesto's main supplier in *mate*, which he brought to Buenos Aires in kilos.

Tita was two years older than Ernesto. She was slim, with big eyes and short hair. She was no beauty, and not very talkative, but she was very gentle, cultured and politicized. She was a member of the Young Communists. My sister Ana Maria once said that Tita had a huge importance in the life of my brother; she was a very interesting person, very erudite, with great spiritual resources. Since their first meeting, they had been linked by a mutual respect and affinity. She was the kind of woman that interested Ernesto. The family never really knew what degree of intimacy their relationship reached, but we think that Tita was in love with Ernesto. He wrote to her from all the countries he visited and Tita replied. It was a sustained correspondence.

Tita made a point of visiting the countries that influenced Ernesto: Peru, Venezuela, Guatemala, Mexico and France, where she spent ten years, learning French like him. In his letters, Ernesto confided in her, telling her of his doubts, successes, sorrows, and even his romantic adventures. Someone said he considered her to be 'his companion in intellectual adventures'. Their correspondence often had the air of an ideological debate.

Tita Infante committed suicide on 14 December 1976. It is said that she couldn't survive the death of the man she had loved and admired. Here is her text *Evocación de Tita Infante a un año de la muerte del Che* (*Tita Infante remembers Che one year after his death*), published in 1968:

... Evoking the memory of a great man is always a difficult task. If this man, today, in 1968, is Ernesto Guevara, it strikes me as impossible ... A year. Already so long ago ... Ernesto is dead, but he was born for eternity. He lived all his life blithely following a path that led him towards tragedy. Death blocked this path, but she opened other doors to that life that he loved so much. The memory of his person, his life, his fight will live forever in the hearts of the world's peoples, as Ernesto Guevara was one of those rare men whom, every now and again, destiny sends to mankind.

Over the past year he has been the subject of many writings. Books, articles, studies, essays, biographies. What can I add to these? A close friendship bound us for years: nearly six years of face to face communication, followed by more years of epistolary communication.

This friendship was born in 1947. In an anatomy theatre in medical school ... His accent betrayed the fact that he came from the provinces, while his appearance was that of a handsome, resourceful young man ... The flames that seemed to consume his existence lay concealed under his courtesy; he was a tender log, but his eyes were crackling with flame. A mixture of timidity and self-assurance, maybe audacity, hid a deep intelligence and an insatiable desire to understand, and, deep down, an infinite capacity to love.

We never belonged to the same cultural or political group, nor to a single circle of friends. We were both, for different reasons, a little out of place at medical school, Ernesto probably because he knew he would find little of what he was seeking here. So we only met up away from other people – in the med school, in cafés, at my place, rarely at his ... And at the Museum of Natural Sciences, where we regularly met on Wednesdays to 'study the phylogeny of the nervous system'; these sessions were dedicated to fish, and we alternated between dissections, preparations, paraffin, microtome, cross-sections for slides, microscopes, etc., sometimes guided by an old German professor. Ernesto's affable conversations made the time fly when it might have dragged. He never missed an appointment and was always punctual. He never forgot to call. What a strange *vie de bohême* he led!

Whenever a success surprised us, we repeated the phrases of Gutiérrez that we had both memorized:

Do not sing hymns of victory
On a sunless day of battle.

. . . I often saw him looking preoccupied, serious or thoughtful. Never really sad or bitter. I don't remember any meeting where he failed to show the smile and the warm tenderness that those who knew him appreciated so much. There was no place in his conversation for contempt; with a laconic remark he would make a trenchant criticism that he always followed up with a positive note, looking forward to a productive future. He wasn't against things, but working on their behalf. This is probably why he never had the slightest trace of rancour.

As he was always able to make the most of every minute, even on public transport, he usually had a book in his hand . . . He never had too much money, quite the contrary . . . But his lack of economic resources was never a primary concern, nor did it prevent him from fulfilling what he considered to be an obligation. Neither his apparent casualness nor his negligent dress sense ever managed to conceal the simple distinction of his person.

. . . As a student, he didn't do a great deal of work, but what he did was done well. Within this young man always ready for an 'adventure', who 'often had the itchy feet of the wanderer', there was a deep thirst for knowledge. Not to hoard up treasure in a convoluted mind, but to embark on a tireless search for the truth and, with it, for his destiny.

Everything about him was consistent, and every experience or knowledge, of any type, he absorbed into himself . . . He had a gift for study. He went straight to the heart of the problem and used this as a starting point, branching out from it whenever his many projects would allow. He was able to pause and dig deeper into the matter, examining it from every side when it was a problem that fascinated him: leprosy, allergies, neurophysiology, depth psychology . . . He leapt over practical and theoretical obstacles with the same ease as other obstacles. When he gave his word, he honoured it at any price . . .

He cultivated friendship with dedication and diligence, and poured his profound human feelings into it. For him, friendship imposed sacred duties and equally conferred rights. He paid attention to both. He took as naturally as he gave. And he behaved this way in all aspects of life.

Distance did not mean absence with Ernesto. On each trip, his letters, more or less regular depending on where he was and the state of his finances, prolonged the friendly dialogue . . . He kept the letters his friends sent and never failed to respond.

Returning from his penultimate trip, he spoke of the twenty days he spent in Miami (I will pass over the details, which are in all his biographies) as the hardest and bitterest of his life. And not only because of his economic difficulties! . . . Until the day we said goodbye (at a meeting with him and his closest friends), I only ever saw him leading a life of sobriety: he didn't smoke, didn't drink alcohol or coffee, and followed a very strict diet. His asthma imposed on him a lifestyle to which he submitted with strict discipline.

Each letter from Ernesto was a little work of literature, full of tenderness, grace and irony; he recounted his adventures and misadventures with a comic touch that relieved even the most difficult moments of their seriousness. In each country, he felt most deeply in tune with the native aspects of the culture; his curiosity led him to visit Inca ruins, leper colonies, and copper or tungsten mines. He quickly integrated into village life and rapidly positioned himself within the political and social panorama. His tales were nicely told, in a prose style that was readable, but pure and elegant. He painted his environment and the people around him realistically, without euphemisms, objectively. And when he spoke of his private life, with sadness or joy, he did so soberly, and always asked people not to spread gossip.

I believe that even in the worst moments his love of life was so great that he managed to sustain his optimism with a logic personal to him: 'When things go badly, I console myself by saying that they could be worse and, in addition, they may get better.' In August 1958, when I was preparing to leave, a young journalist I didn't know called me and asked to meet in a café: it was Masetti. He'd just spent two months in the Sierra Maestra . . . Masetti told me at length about the Sierra Maestra: he described everything and everyone, Fidel, Raúl, the camps . . . but nothing, for him, had the same stature as Ernesto, his human characteristics, his courage, his multi-faceted personality. If there was a need to arrange someone's civil status, or organize a school, or make bread, or manufacture and repair weapons, Ernesto was there to take the lead and sort things out. And in battle, he was always in the front line.

There was already talk of his legendary courage and his history was being put together little by little: thanks to the testimonies of these young Guatemalans who had known him and had found a very special refuge in Argentina after the fall of Arbenz . . .

I had the extraordinary privilege of knowing him intimately, enjoying his confidence, sharing a great friendship that was never half-hearted or allowed to fade. I knew him when he was very young, when he was just Ernesto. But he already bore the future Che Guevara within himself. Since these youthful years, I always saw him advancing along his own personal path, always striding ahead; he never stopped, and those who knew him well knew that not only did 'the antipodes have no power to stop him' but that he was marching towards his Destiny . . .

I feel so close to and at the same time so far away from his gigantic figure, worthy of the demigods of Greek legends and the heroes of the Middle Ages.

It is difficult to hold such grandeur together: he was a figure of sensitivity and tenderness, of deep humanity.

Too warmly human to be carved in stone. Too great for us to imagine him as one of us. Ernesto Guevara, however much he was an Argentinian, was perhaps the most authentic citizen of the world.

Appendix I

Excerpts from the Algiers speech, 24 February 1965

Dear brothers,

Cuba is taking part in this conference so that the voice of the peoples of America will be heard, and also, as we have said on other occasions, as an underdeveloped country that, at the same time, is building socialism. It is no accident if our bloc is being allowed to express its opinion among the peoples of Asia and Africa. A common aspiration unites us in our march towards the future: the defeat of imperialism; a common history of struggle against the same enemy has made us allies all along the way.

This conference is a gathering of people engaged in struggle; this struggle is on two equally important fronts and requires all our efforts. The struggle against imperialism, aimed at smashing colonial and neo-colonial chains, whether it be conducted with political weapons, real weapons, or both at once, is not unrelated to the fight against archaic vestiges and poverty; both are stages on the same road leading to the creation of a new society, both rich and fair.

Since the capitalist monopolies seized power throughout the world, they have kept most of humankind in a state of poverty and the most powerful countries have divided the profits among themselves. The standard of living in these countries is based on the wretchedness of our countries. To improve the standard of living of the underdeveloped countries, we must fight against imperialism. And whenever a country becomes detached from the imperialist tree, this is not only a partial battle won over the main enemy, but a contribution to its real weakening and a step closer to the final victory. This death struggle knows no borders. We cannot remain indifferent to what is happening elsewhere in the world, for any victory of one country over imperialism is a victory for us, just as any nation's defeat is a defeat for us. The practice of proletarian internationalism is not only a duty for those peoples struggling for a better future, it is also an inescapable necessity [. . .]

We have to draw one conclusion from all this: the development of countries embarking on the path of liberation must be funded by the socialist countries. We do not state this for the purposes of blackmail or bluff, nor as a way of getting closer to the Afro-Asian peoples; it is simply our deep conviction. Socialism cannot exist unless it brings about in people's minds a transformation that will make it possible to trigger a new fraternal attitude towards humanity, both on the individual level in the society that is building or has built socialism and, globally, vis-à-vis all those peoples suffering from imperialist oppression [. . .]

We believe that it is in this spirit that the responsibility for assisting dependent countries must be assumed; there should no longer be any question of developing trade to our mutual benefit on the basis of price-fixing imposed by market law and international relations, since the underdeveloped countries come off worse.

How can we call it 'mutual benefit' when raw materials are

sold at world market prices, materials that cost the underde-veloped countries untold effort and suffering, while machinery produced in today's big automated factories is also bought at market prices?

If we establish such relationships between groups of nations, then we must admit that the socialist countries are, in one sense, accomplices of imperialist exploitation. One can even argue that the amount of trade with underdeveloped countries is an insignificant proportion of the foreign trade of these countries. This is true, but it does not eliminate the immoral character of the transaction.

Socialist countries have the moral duty to put an end to their tacit complicity with the exploitative countries of the West. The fact that trade is reduced now means nothing. In 1959 Cuba sold sugar occasionally to a socialist bloc country through English brokers or other nationalities [. . .]

There is for us no other valid definition of socialism than the abolition of the exploitation of one human being by another. Until this abolition is achieved, socialism will remain at the stage of construction, and if, instead of this phenomenon occurring, the task of eliminating exploitation is halted and even goes backwards, then we cannot even talk of building socialism.

However, the measures we are proposing cannot be imposed unilaterally. Socialist countries should finance the development of underdeveloped countries. But the forces of the underde-veloped countries should also be strengthened and firmly take the road of building a new society – give it whatever name you want – a society in which the machine, that working tool, is not an instrument for exploiting human beings.

Nor can we lay any claim to the trust of the socialist countries if the challenge is to keep the balance between capitalism and socialism by trying to use the two forces in competition so as to draw definite advantages from them: a new policy of absolute seriousness must govern relations between the two groups of societies.

We must emphasize once again that the means of production should preferably be in the hands of the state so that the effects of exploitation will gradually disappear [. . .]

Neo-colonialism was first developed in South America, across a whole continent. Today, it is starting to be felt in Africa and Asia. Its modes of penetration have distinct characteristics. The brutal face of neo-colonialism has been revealed in the Congo

. . .

Neo-colonialism showed its claws in the Congo; this is not a sign of strength but of weakness; it had to use force, its extreme weapon, as an economic argument, which has led to intense opposition.

This penetration is also exercised in other countries of Africa and Asia in a much more subtle form that is rapidly leading to what has been called the 'South Americanization' of those continents, that is to say, the development of a parasitic bour-geoisie that contributes nothing to the national wealth but accumulates, in capitalist banks outside the country, its huge criminal profits and deals with foreign countries to gain even more profits, with absolute contempt for the welfare of its people [. . .]

Our peoples, for example, suffer from the agonizing pressure produced by the presence of foreign bases on their territories, or else they have to bear the burden of huge external debts. The history of these defects is well known to all. Puppet gov-ernments, governments weakened by a long liberation struggle, and the development of capitalist market laws, have all led to the signing of agreements that threaten our stability and jeopardize our future [. . .]

Liberation by armed struggle from a political power of oppression must be addressed under the rules of proletarian internationalism: it is absurd to think that the director of a company in a socialist country at war might hesitate to send the tanks it has produced to a military front where payment is not guaranteed, but it should seem no less absurd to verify the solvency of a people struggling for liberation or needing arms to defend its freedom. In our worlds, weapons cannot be mere commodities, they must be delivered absolutely free, in the quantities needed – where possible – to the peoples who are requesting them for use against the common enemy. It is in this spirit that the Soviet Union and the People's Republic of China have given us their military aid. We are socialists, we constitute a guarantee of use of these weapons, but we are not the only ones and we must all be treated the same way. [. . .]

I would not like to conclude this intervention, this reminder of principles with which you are all familiar, without drawing the attention of this Assembly to the fact that Cuba is not the only country in Latin America; it is simply that Cuba is the country that has an opportunity to speak before you today; I want to remind you that other peoples are shedding their blood for the rights we enjoy, and here, as in all conferences wherever they take place, we salute the heroic peoples of Vietnam, Laos, so-called Portuguese Guinea, South Africa and Palestine; to all exploited countries fighting for their emancipation we must raise our friendly voices, and must reach out and offer our encouragement to the fraternal peoples of Venezuela, Guatemala and Colombia who today, weapons in hand, are once and for all saying 'no' to the imperialist enemy.

Appendix II

Letter from Archbishop Moure

Comodoro Rivadavia, 27 June 1983
Señor Juan Martin Guevara
Juncal 3786-11-B
1425 Buenos Aires

Dear Juan Martin,
I know you will forgive me for my delay in replying to your letter of 3 June 1983: recent weeks have greatly complicated my schedule, preventing me from fulfilling the duty of attending to my correspondence.

I am overjoyed to know that you are now free. I am sure that the first foot to step out of the U6 [unit 6 of the Rawson prison] was your right foot (no ideological connotations, please!), and that the dramatic lucidity that God has given you will be immediately and honestly placed in the service of the national community.

I have to stop off in Buenos Aires in mid-July on the way to Bogotá for a meeting of CELAM, an organization to which I belong. I will call you: I hope we will have some time to talk, I would like to keep this friendship with you going.

At the request of several prisoners, on 8 August, Monsignor Castagna, of the Episcopal and Social Pastoral Team, will spend the day with the inmates of U6. I forwarded this request to him with great pleasure and he accepted it with the same pleasure, postponing other activities until later. In my view it is very useful for all those who seriously intend to reorganize the country to listen to each other for the common good. When I see you, the meeting with the inmates will already have been held. I'll tell you how it went.

I remain cordially at your disposal, and really look forward to seeing and talking with you. In Buenos Aires, my address is that of the Provincial House of the Salesians: Don Bosco 4002, TE 981-2619.

See you soon. A big hug from your servant and friend.

Notes

Chapter 1

1 In 1998, about the time his Congo diaries were first published. See Ernesto 'Che' Guevara, *The African Dream: The Diaries of the Revolutionary War in the Congo*, trans. Patrick Camiller (London: Harvill, 2001).

2 They spent over a month evading the Bolivian Army and managed to reach a town without being detected. Guido 'Inti' Peredo was hunted down and murdered in 1969.

3 With the waves of terrorism in Argentina, the adjective 'subversive' became a noun, so we will use it in the same way.

Chapter 2

1 The revolutionary army.

2 *Vieja, viejo*, 'old woman', 'old man': in Spanish-speaking countries, these are affectionate ways of addressing your parents.

3 Mauricio Vicent, 'Te podría decir que te extraño', *El País*, 7 October 2007.

4 'Che' is an interjection, a verbal tic, used solely by Argentinians, including Ernesto. This is why the Cubans called him 'Che'.

5 Built to defend Havana from English pirates in the eighteenth century.

6 Little brother.

7 León Felipe Camino Galicia (1884–1968) was a Spanish poet who fought against Franco in the Spanish Civil War and then went into exile in Mexico. When Che Guevara was captured by the CIA, the notebook he was carrying contained seven of León Felipe's poems. (Translator's note.)

8 Julio Llanes, *Che entra la literatura y la vida* (La Habana: Instituto Cubano de Investigación Cultural Juan Marinello, 2010).

9 For Christ's sake!

10 This took its name from a fighter who was killed in battle in the Sierra Maestra. Ciro Redondo had been a companion of Fidel Castro right from the start.

Chapter 3

1 This brigadier general, governor of the province of Buenos Aires between 1833 and 1846, relied on a militia known as La Mazorca to prop up his power.

2 Old fool.

Chapter 4

1 The name given to the inhabitants of Buenos Aires.

2 Furious.

3 The real deal!

Chapter 5

1 We have included a few extracts in the last chapter of this book.

Chapter 6

1 Hugo Gambini, *El Che Guevara* (Buenos Aires: Stockcero, 2002).

Chapter 7

1 A province in the south of the island.

2 The wedding took place on 18 August 1955 in Tepotzotlán.

3 His identity was concealed from the first publication of this letter onwards.

4 Ernesto is surely alluding to the Convent of the Sacred Heart where my mother spent her teens.

5 Lynch Ernesto Guevara, *Aquí va un soldado de América* (Barcelona: Plaza Janés, 2000).

6 A nickname known only to the family.

7 Batista's regime assassinated any journalists covering the guerrilla war.

8 Jorge Ricardo Masetti, *Los que luchan y los que lloran* (Buenos Aires: Nuestra America, 2006).

9 Julia Constenla, *Che Guevara: La vida en juego* (Barcelona: Edhasa, 2006).

10 'Little' – the nickname of Fernando Chaves, who was given it because he was short of stature.

Chapter 8

1 Rogelio García Lupo, 'Un mate en La Habana, y la Argentina en los sueños', *Clarín*, 15 November 2002.

2 Rogelio García Lupo, 'Trece días entre espías y traficantes de armas', *Clarín*, 19 August 2001.

3 This is a typical Argentinian sandwich composed of a steak or sausage served in a baguette, generally sold in the streets.

4 'Deformatorio', a pun in Spanish on 'reformatorio'.

Chapter 9

1 See Appendix I.

2 Ernesto Guevara, *El socialismo y el hombre en Cuba*, an essay sent to Carlos Quijano, editor of the Uruguayan review *Marcha*, 12 March 1965. English translation: *Socialism and Man in Cuba, and other works* (London: Stage 1, 1968).

3 The dates differ.

4 To keep the secret services off their trail, they had travelled via different countries.

5 She was suspected of being an agent in the East German Stasi and the Soviet KGB.

6 Author of the biography *Che Guevara: A Revolutionary Life* (New York: Grove Press, 1997).

7 Ernesto Guevara, *El socialismo y el hombre en Cuba*.

8 Guido Peredo, *Mi campaña junto al Che y otros documentos* (Paraninfo Universitario, 2013). First published in 1970 as a pamphlet.

Chapter 10

1 Her real name was María Estela Martínez Cartas de Perón. The first wife of Juan Perón, Aurelia Gabriela Tizón, died of cancer of the uterus on 10 September 1938, nine years after their wedding. His second wife, the famous Eva, also died of cancer of the uterus, in 1952, at the age of thirty-three.

2 This was unrelated to the French Confédération générale du travail.

3 A decree of the dictator Alejandro Agustín Lanusse had prevented Perón himself from standing for president.

4 Both men apparently belonged to the P2 Masonic Lodge.

5 Province of Chubut.

6 See Appendix II.

Chapter 11

1 Reynaldo Bignone was the last president of the military junta. He was replaced by Raúl Alfonsin. Since Rafael Videla's resignation, four presidents had succeeded him in two years.

2 Jean Daniel, 'Une affaire de famille, où en est Cuba? Che Guevara a répondu à Jean Daniel', *L'Express*, 25 July 1963.

Chapter 12

1 Argentina experienced seventeen military dictatorships from 1854 onwards.

2 The son of Teodoro Roca, a famous lawyer, journalist, university administrator and activist.

Chapter 13

1 Aleida was born in 1960, Camilo in 1962, Celia in 1963 and Ernesto in 1965.

2 Ernesto Guevara, *Obras*, 2 vols, vol. 2 (Paris: Casa de las Americas and Maspero, 1970).

3 La Poderosa is these days exhibited at the Che Museum in Alta Gracia.

Chapter 14

1 All Spaniards are called 'Pepe' by the Cubans.
2 Female inhabitants of Buenos Aires.

Chapter 15

1 Argentinian intelligence service.
2 Fernando de la Rúa (10 December 1999 to 21 December 2001), Ramón Puerta (21 to 23 December 2001), Adolfo Rodriguez Saá (23 to 30 December 2001), Éduardo Camaño (30 December 2001 to 2 January 2002), Éduardo Duhalde (from 2 January 2002 to 25 May 2003).
3 I acted as a consultant for this film.
4 From Santa Clara.
5 Ernesto Che Guevara, *Apuntes críticos a la economia política* (Havana: Centro de Estudios Che Guevara, 1966).
6 Ernesto Guevara, *Notas para el studio de la ideología de la Revolución Cuba*, in *Obras completas* (Buenos Aires: Legasa, 1960).
7 This was a 'strategic retreat' in the building of socialism. Lenin justified it in these terms: 'We are not civilized enough to pass directly to socialism, although we have the political base for it.'
8 Letter to the Cuban minister of education, Amando Hart.

Chapter 16

1 Ernesto refused to let Aleida accompany him, even though she was his private secretary in addition to being his young wife; his colleagues came without their wives, so he refused to be the only one to enjoy such a privilege.
2 Just as Québécois French is different from the French spoken in France, Cuban Spanish is different from Mexican, Argentinian Spanish, etc.

Bibliography

Borrego, Orlando, *Che: El camino del fuego* (Hombre Nuevo, 2001)

Constenla, Julia, *Che Guevara: La vida en juego* (Edhasa, 2006)

Gambini, Hugo, *El Che Guevara* (Stockcero, 2002)

Gonzalez, Froilán and Adys Capull, *Amor Revolucionario* (Txalaparta, 2004)

Guevara, Che, *Che desde la memoria* (Ocean Sur, 2004)

Diarios de Motocicleta (Planeta, 2004)

La Guerra de Guerrillas (Ocean Sur, 2006)

Guevara Lynch, Ernesto, *Mi hijo El Che* (Sudamericana-Planeta, 1984)

Aquí va un soldado de América (Plaza Janés, 2000)

Larraquy, Marcelo, *Los 70, una historia violenta* (Aguilar, 2013)

March, Aleida, *Evocación, Mi vida al lado del Che* (Ocean Sur, 2011)

Masetti, Jorge Ricardo, *Los que luchan y los que lloran* (Nuestra America, 2006)

Peredo, Guido, *Mi campaña junto al Che y otros documentos* (Paraninfo Universitario, 2013)